Professional Practice for Architects and Project Managers

Professional Practice for Architects and Project Managers

David Chappell

WILEY Blackwell

This edition first published 2020

Registered Offices
John Wiley & Sons, Inc., 111 River Street, Hoboken, NJ 07030, USA
John Wiley & Sons Ltd, The Atrium, Southern Gate, Chichester, West Sussex, PO19 8SQ, UK

Editorial Office
9600 Garsington Road, Oxford, OX4 2DQ, UK

For details of our global editorial offices, customer services, and more information about Wiley products visit us at www.wiley.com.

Wiley also publishes its books in a variety of electronic formats and by print-on-demand. Some content that appears in standard print versions of this book may not be available in other formats.

Library of Congress Cataloging-in-Publication Data

Names: Chappell, David (David M.), author.
Title: Professional practice for architects and project managers / David Chappell.
Description: First edition. | Hoboken : Wiley, 2020. | Includes index.
Identifiers: LCCN 2019034995 (print) | LCCN 2019034996 (ebook) | ISBN 9781119540076 (paperback) | ISBN 9781119540090 (adobe pdf) | ISBN 9781119540113 (epub)
Subjects: LCSH: Architectural practice.
Classification: LCC NA1995 .C445 2020 (print) | LCC NA1995 (ebook) | DDC 720.1–dc23
LC record available at https://lccn.loc.gov/2019034995
LC ebook record available at https://lccn.loc.gov/2019034996

Cover Design: Wiley
Cover Image: © Topp_Yimgrimm/Getty Images

Set in 10/12pt WarnockPro by SPi Global, Chennai, India
Printed and bound in Singapore by Markono Print Media Pte Ltd

10 9 8 7 6 5 4 3 2 1

Contents

Preface

The idea for this book came from several people who had been unfortunate enough to hear me speak at one of the lectures I used to give up and down England, Scotland, Wales, and Northern Ireland.

I have written a great many books on construction industry topics (70 at the last count): books about the popular forms of contract, about the kinds of letters architects and contractors might write, about architectural, practical, and legal matters. My aim was to make most of the books as simple as possible and some people have been kind enough to say that my books are relatively easy and helpful, if not actually enjoyable, to read. It is easy to make a complex subject even more complicated and we all see this every day. The trick is to make a complex subject simple. This takes time but it is rewarding.

The construction industry and its associated disciplines are afflicted by what seems to be a modern disease: the inability to use one word if three words can be found to say the same thing. Even worse is the desire to invent new terminology, so that many of us no longer understand what we used to understand perfectly before new phraseology was used to explain it to us. Phrases like 'strategic outcomes', 'soft landings', and the like are not helpful, neither is the current obsession with delving into activities so as to break them down into many sub-activities and then explaining how each of these sub-activities should be accomplished. This kind of thing has been going on since I was a young architect. We used to joke and say that we would all be soon following the mandatory six steps in sharpening a pencil. I hope none of my books have ever ventured into this territory and I am not very good at it anyway. However, my previous books do quote contract clause numbers, legal cases, and Acts of Parliament in considerable quantities.

What this book tries to do is to concentrate on the principles underlying what construction professionals, principally architects, do. There are no references to legal cases, no clause numbers, and minimal reference to Acts of Parliament. I try to avoid legal jargon and explain the principles as simply as possible with the help of any anecdotes which spring to mind. Hopefully, long after my other books are out of date, this book will still be relevant to professional practice in the construction context.

It is wholly reasonable to question why I think I am qualified to give this kind of advice. That is an awkward question. The main reason is because enough architects have told me so when I have given what seemed like straightforward advice. All I can do is to set out a brief career history.

I spent the first 20 years practising as an architect with four local authorities and two private practices. In the last of these, I was briefly a partner until the practice fell on hard times and my partner did an overnight disappearing act with the cheque book and a company car, leaving me to sort out the mess. I then spent time as contract administrator for a building contractor following by a few years lecturing in a college of building. Since 1989, I have practised as a contracts consultant and adjudicator, beginning by working for a company and then for the last 26 years as director of my own companies. During this time, I frequently lectured to constructional professionals, contractors, sub-contractors, and Part III architecture students and acted as an adjudicator. I have been a specialist advisor to the Royal Institute of British Architects since 1995, answering questions from thousands of architects on the Information Line service and perform the same service for the Royal Society of Ulster Architects. I was Senior Research Fellow and Professor of Architectural Practice and Management Research at the Queens University Belfast on a part-time basis and Visiting Professor of Practice Management and Law at the University of Central England in Birmingham. Those are the facts. It is not for me to say whether they qualify me to give advice, but that is what I have been doing for the last 30 years.

The book is divided into short pieces which reflect some general issues then moves on to specifics in regard to the progress of projects.

Contractors and sub-contractors are treated as corporate bodies (i.e. limited companies) and referred to as 'it'.

I must express my thanks to my long-standing friend Michael R Jones Dip Arch RIBA, who kindly reviewed parts of the book in draft and gave me the benefit of his long experience.

Particular thanks are due to my one-time client and subsequently friend Richard Dunkley RIBA, who has read and commented (often at length) upon each of the topics covered by this book. He has generously given me the benefit of his extensive knowledge and experience and I could not have written this book without him. His comments have been invaluable, but more valuable than his comments have been his constant encouragement and fund of anecdotes.

Wakefield, September 2019 *David Chappell*

Abbreviations

ARB	Architects Registration Board
BIM	Building Information Modelling
CIC	Construction Industry Council
ICE	Institution of Civil Engineers
JCT	Joint Contracts Tribunal
NEC	New Engineering Contract
RIBA	Royal Institute of British Architects
RICS	Royal Institution of Chartered Surveyors

Section I

This and That

1

Professional Standards

Codes of Conduct

Every construction professional will have undergone an intense period of training in his or her chosen profession. After academic or theoretic qualification come professional practice and final qualification, with most professionals joining the appropriate professional institutes. These institutes lay down codes of conduct and if it is shown that the professional in question has failed to comply with the code there will often be some kind of sanction.

Architects are Unusual

Architects are unusual because unless they are registered with the statutory body (Architects Registration Board, ARB) they cannot call themselves architects. Anyone calling him- or herself an architect in the course of business (except naval or golf course architects) and not registered is liable to be fined by the courts. It is not the function which is protected by statute but the name. Anyone, qualified or not, can carry out work usually associated with an architect just so long as they do not call themselves an architect. Many people, including me, think that is a ludicrous situation.

An unqualified person can adopt the rather grand title of 'architectural consultant' without a problem. Many clients seeing that title would assume that the person in question was at least an architect and possibly rather better than that. The sorry fact is that such people are not governed by any professional code as their clients sometimes discover to their cost. A client receiving a poor quality of service from an unqualified so-called professional will have no professional institute interested in listening to their complaints. Spare a thought then for architects, who have two such bodies: one set up by statute where membership is compulsory and one set up by the profession (RIBA) where membership is not compulsory but generally expected.

What You Say You Are

In case I have been guilty of putting ideas into certain heads, it is worth pointing out that the courts will treat you in accordance with the profession that you profess. Some years

Professional Practice for Architects and Project Managers, First Edition. David Chappell.

ago, a man appeared in court accused of negligence. He had worked as a draftsman in a ball-bearing factory, but told his clients that he was an architect. The house he designed for them suffered severe defects and started moving down the hill. I used to try to enliven my lectures by musing on whether the problem was that he had incorporated ball bearings into the design. Anyhow, his defence in court was that he was not an architect so could not be expected to properly design the house in every respect (unbelievable). The court made clear that having put himself forward as an architect, that was the standard by which he would be judged. It may not have been a ball-bearing factory, but the rest is probably accurate, the liability position certainly is correct.

This is relevant for all those architects who put themselves down as quantity surveyors in the building contract if no actual quantity surveyor is appointed. 'Quantity surveyor' is not a protected title under statute, but if an architect holds him or herself out as capable of acting as a quantity surveyor, or structural engineer or electrical consultant etc. that is how they will be judged. In case they are feeling smug, it also applies to quantity surveyors, structural engineers etc. who hold themselves out, not as architects because that would be a statutory offence, but as being able to do an architect's job and receive a claim alleging negligence.

Professionals who claim they are able to carry out the duties of another profession must be sure that (i) they can do it and (ii) their professional indemnity insurers are happy with the situation.

2

How to Appear Confident

Basic

'How do you appear confident?'

I was asked this question by a recently qualified architect. It is a simple question but it has several layers and just one real answer. Presumably the architect wants to appear confident to colleagues, to partners in the firm, and when meeting the client or making presentations. Oh yes, and when dealing with the contractor on site, of course. The one real answer is that an architect will appear confident when he or she is confident as a result of thoroughly understanding what it is that they are doing or talking about. Knowledge and experience give confidence and when someone is knowledgeable, it usually shows in their speech and actions as confidence.

Misplaced Confidence

Of course, an architect can be, and often is, assailed by severe doubts about the matter in hand but still can appear confident. That is a dangerous path to tread. Then again, we have all experienced someone talking what we know to be sheer nonsense with great confidence, like the city architect many years ago who interrupted my lecture to his architectural staff on building contracts by standing up and telling them gravely that 'the thing to remember is that an architect issuing a certificate is in the position of an arbitrator and immune from actions for negligence'. No one, of course, should remember that because it is quite wrong (see 87: The Architect's Conundrum). His undoubted confidence was misplaced in that instance, but his confidence was the result of years of experience and the fact that others had at some time thought so highly of his abilities that they had made him city architect.

Even if an architect knows everything there is to know about a topic, that same architect may not appear confident. We have all met those extremely knowledgeable people who are yet very diffident and shy about saying anything. In that case, those architects should seek some assertiveness training.

Professional Practice for Architects and Project Managers, First Edition. David Chappell.

Don't Pretend

But what about the newly qualified architect with some knowledge but little experience, like the architect who asked this question? This brings us to the unspoken nub of the question: 'How do I appear confident when I am not confident, because I do not have all the necessary knowledge and experience required'? The answer of course is that the young architect should not try to have a confidence that is not actually there. The architect should go on site and listen respectfully to the site agent and the clerk of works, but should not confirm anything until back in the office with the opportunity to seek the advice of a more experienced architect. The ability to listen to another's point of view is usually seen as demonstrating confidence in one's own ability. It is the inexperienced architect, anxious to appear confident, who can be recognised by a desire to press their point of view without reference to others. A newly qualified architect should not be sent out on site alone until that architect has had several trips to different sites in the company of, and with the opportunity of watching and receiving tips from, experienced architects.

A young architect must have been with a thoroughly competent architect many times to see clients and observe the ways in which different architects approach a client before being able and confident to do the same. I stress 'thoroughly competent' because it is unfortunate that there are some thoroughly or partially incompetent architects who may radiate supreme confidence while striding purposefully in the wrong direction.

Forget those films where the new recruit solves a problem that all the experienced people have failed to resolve. It does not happen in real life. It is pointless to try for a false confidence to colleagues and partners; they will soon realise the truth.

3

Perks

Employers probably call these 'benefits'. Essentially, a perk is something an employee gets as a result of being employed at that particular firm. As a rule of thumb, larger companies probably offer most perks. But perks aren't everything and there can be disadvantages. Let's look at some of the most common perks.

Cars

Some organisations offer pool cars. Put simply, if you have to visit a site, you can collect a key and use one of the pool cars. Because they are used by all staff, they do not get the loving care which an individual may bestow on his or her own car. They are simply utility models; there to do a job. If you are the kind of person who likes to roll up at site or at an office in an envy-inducing vehicle, forget pool cars. Murphy's law says that there won't be a car available when you want one and it becomes not a help but another irritant. The pool car idea seems to be on the wane in any event.

What most employees want is a company car. That is the case even though you will get taxed on it. Usually firms allow the employee to choose a car within a particular price band. In the worst case, you may inherit a car bought for a previous employee whose shoes you have been taken on to fill. Some firms allow you to put more money to the purchase to get something which is more like your idea of the kind of car you deserve. That can be complicated and it is not a good idea because it is better if your firm rewards you with a better car because they are keen to keep you. Rewarding yourself is pointless unless you are a sad person. I once knew a man who had a very inflated opinion of himself and a very clear idea of what his status within the organisation should be. Deciding that his office not sufficiently prestigious, he bought a new deep pile carpet, new large desk, vast leather chair, two smaller visitors' chairs, and a couple of arty standard lamps out of his own pocket. He had a better office than the directors, but because of his actual lowly status he just looked silly.

If you don't like the car you are offered, you may be offered the option of a car allowance provided that you always have your car available for business use. The allowance is commonly a lump sum per month plus petrol allowance. The great advantage of this is that, if you leave the firm, you still have your car. If you don't have a car allowance, firms usually offer to pay for petrol used in carrying out your duties. The payment may be based on the mileage you do or on petrol receipts, the latter provided that you only reclaim petrol used on firm's business. That can be a tricky business to

Professional Practice for Architects and Project Managers, First Edition. David Chappell.

assess. Some employees may take advantage of the system to fill up just before taking a motoring holiday and rarely if ever pay for any petrol themselves while the firm's directors or the practice manager may work on the basis that every employee is trying to cheat the firm. Whatever the situation any kind of rough and ready system is apt to leave both parties feeling aggrieved. A checkable mileage payment system is far better.

Provision of car parking is a valuable perk, particularly in town centres. Where parking is not available next to the office, the firm may pay parking costs instead to some employees. More often, only the directors, partners or associates get this perk.

Medical Insurance

This is becoming much more common. Going private means that consultants may call you 'Sir' or 'Madam'. Levity aside, and more importantly, you will be able to arrange consultations and non-urgent operations to suit you. There are some drawbacks.

- Medical insurance will usually exclude all existing conditions and anything remotely connected to previous conditions. Therefore, if you have had any chest investigations, treatment or surgery, you might find that all future chest conditions are excluded.
- Normally, you will require a referral from your GP.
- Although getting an appointment with a consultant will usually be much quicker than if you went through the NHS, your appointment may be in the evening.
- If you are admitted for an operation, there may not be the numbers of consultants, registrars, and doctors available at night that you would find in an NHS hospital.
- In the case of some small private hospitals, there may be nurses but only one doctor on duty at night time.
- Serious operations are thought to be best done in an NHS hospital or one of the larger private hospitals because of the availability of trained staff and up-to-date equipment.
- If you are admitted to an NHS hospital for some reason, it may not be possible for them to access information about procedures carried out privately. All private treatments will be notified to your GP and put on the surgery computer system. Because this is linked to the NHS system any NHS hospital can access it, but there is unlikely to be the same detailed reports as with the NHS.

Loans

Many firms will provide loans to employees for various purposes, usually on an interest-free or low-interest basis. Commonly a loan will be to assist with the purchase of a car, but loans for other reasons have been known. Complications may occur when the employee leaves the firm. It pays to read the small print in detail. Sometimes the employee is faced with paying back all the loan prior to departure. At best, the employee will move to a loan with a commercial interest rate.

4

Nosebags

Prologue

The paint representative had secured a meeting with a very senior architect in a local authority. This was a breakthrough and the rep was nervous as he entered the architect's first-floor office. He wasted no time in asking if the architect would be prepared to include the name of his firm in the council's specifications as one of the approved paint suppliers. The architect smiled and led the rep to the window. He pointed to a nice shiny bright car in the car park. 'XXX gave me that', he said. 'Can you do any better'?

It is rare that one encounters from architects or others such upfront demands for gifts. That kind of thing is commonly referred to as 'nosebags' for obvious reasons. Sadly, there are many individuals happy to take bribes (to give the real name) for favours. The episode I recount above was given to me by the rep involved. It happened many years ago and I cannot vouch for its truth, but you can see why it stuck in my mind, especially since some years later I met the architect involved, who bragged to me that all the furniture at his home had been 'donated' by grateful reps after he had specified their products.

This kind of thing is plainly and simply corruption and no architect or other professional should get involved in it. Even if a person is not worried, on ethical grounds, about the occasional nosebag, I should make clear that it is a criminal offence.

Secrecy

An element of corruption is secrecy. Therefore, if the contractor delivers an expensive piece of the latest electronic equipment quietly to your home and you accept it, you are both guilty of corruption. The fact that you have not repaid the favour is of no consequence. The implication is present that you will be likely to favour the contractor in the future.

It used to be the custom for contractors and suppliers to give presents to architects at Christmas. One used to come across two cars side by side in the office car park with a crate of something alcoholic being hastily transferred from one boot to the other. Certain quantity surveyors were entertained to long expensive lunches by the contractor when they went out all day doing a valuation. In the offices of some construction professionals a list was kept indicating the quality and 'length' of nosebag on offer from respective reps.

Professional Practice for Architects and Project Managers, First Edition. David Chappell.

What to Do

The signs are that this kind of thing has dropped off, but not entirely disappeared, in recent years. The basic rule is that all gifts should be returned to the sender with a brief note of appreciation for the thought. If you wish to acquire a reputation for complete integrity, and you should, refuse all gifts in whatever form they take. There is probably very little chance that you will be corrupted by accepting a diary or calendar, but be careful. In particular, do not accept invitations to have lunch with the contractor or suppliers. It may be difficult to refuse if you are at a site meeting and the contractor suddenly produces a tray of drinks and sandwiches, but there is probably safety in numbers on this occasion. Avoid those cosy little lunches in which you are on a one-to-one basis with a supplier. It may be perfectly innocent on your part, but the fact that you have accepted hospitality may influence you in the future when you are considering what product to specify. That, of course, is just what the supplier intends. It is blind to pretend that the supplier is wining and dining you purely out of good nature. There is nothing wrong with having contractors or suppliers as friends, but in such circumstances you must take extra care that your conduct is above reproach. It is not so much what you do as what you are perceived to do which is important. Do not get involved in anything, even something that may be entirely innocent, if it can be perceived as a nosebag.

Travel

Occasionally a contractor or supplier may offer you an 'all expenses paid' trip to the other end of the country or overseas to see a new development. There may, indeed, be a legitimate advantage to be gained on behalf of the client if you accept. However, you accept at your peril. In such a case the correct procedure is to declare the offer immediately to your client. Let him decide. If he agrees that you should go and, better still, decides to go with you, there is little chance that you could be accused of corruption because everything is out in the open. It must be emphasised, however, that it is not a good policy to accept even in these circumstances and you should point this out to your client.

Do Not Bribe

It may be accepted that you will occasionally take the client out to lunch. Your motives are, of course, exactly the same as those of the contractor and supplier: you are hoping for further work. Even here, you must take care. If the client is a large public body, for example a local authority, it is not acceptable that you give any favours to the officers of that authority. Indeed, you ought to find that they will not accept them. In the case of a small private client, the situation is different and, provided that you direct your lunch invitation to the client himself and not to his agents or employees, there should be no suggestion of corruption.

The golden rule is not to give or receive gifts of any kind. If you must break this rule, give sparingly to your client, not to his employees. If you need some tarmac on your drive, ask a contractor who is not engaged on one of your firm's contracts to do it and pay in full. Remember that many a good career has been blighted by accepting or giving gifts. There is no such thing as a free lunch.

5

Design

Although entitled 'Design', relax, this section is not a treatise on design theory, but about one or two points which relate to design management. There are numerous theories of design. Every architect has his or her own and you are entitled to have yours, but do not inflict it upon your client, who will be unlikely to understand. In other words, you should obviously design the building in the way which you consider is best, but do not make the mistake of thinking that you can convince your client of the worth of your design by trying to explain some of the more abstruse aspects of design theory, particularly if you are fond of using the kind of descriptive words beloved of some architects but incomprehensible to most clients – you know what I mean. In 99 cases out of a 100, your client is simply interested in the basics, i.e. Will it keep out the rain? Will it be warm enough? Will it function well overall? Will it look good? etc. Provided that you cater (as you should) for all these points, your client should be satisfied.

Usually, you will produce several embryonic schemes before you eventually produce one which satisfies you. It may be that you finish with two schemes which answer the problems in different ways, but each adequately. Only in rare instances should you present both schemes to your client. The client will often find it difficult enough to understand and discuss one scheme. If you present two, it will be far more than doubly difficult. It is your job to present the best possible scheme to your client, one on which you can advise acceptance. Any differences in schemes should be a matter of detail at this stage; the kind of detail which you should have resolved yourself before showing the client your proposals.

The correct point at which to resolve the kind of major decisions which could give rise to totally different schemes is at feasibility stage, when you are justified, indeed you are required, to present the principal options to the client for decision. But at that early stage, you will be directing the client's attention to a straight choice of options with clearly defined consequences. Clients should be completely involved at every stage of design. Their participation generates understanding and acceptance of responsibility for decisions as the design evolves in logical stages.

If you present your client with two totally different schemes after feasibility stage, it can mean that you have not put all the important options before your client at the right time.

Professional Practice for Architects and Project Managers, First Edition. David Chappell.

When you present your design to your client, you should present a report with it. By all means make an oral presentation at the same time, but a written report enables your client to study what you have to say at leisure. It may not be necessary to include a report with each successive stage of the design, only you can decide that, but if you are dealing with a large scheme, a formal report at each stage may be advisable, if only to keep a record of the progress of the design as it becomes ever more detailed (see 45: Design Development).

6

Copyright

What is Copyright?

Most people have a vague idea about copyright and, for most people, a vague idea is probably good enough, but for anyone involved in the creation or the reproduction of information, whether drawings, 3D or text, it is important to have a better than vague idea.

Let me say at the beginning that copyright or intellectual property is a complicated matter about which there are statutory provisions and quite a lot of decisions from the courts. What follows, as promised in the Preface, is not a detailed legalistic analysis of the position, but hopefully enough information so that the average architect, engineer, or surveyor will be able to understand the main principles of copyright.

People create all kinds of things: music, song lyrics, a performance, articles, books, paintings, photographs, films, architecture, a lecture presentation etc. Whenever a person creates something, that person owns the copyright to what has been created. The lawyers would say that copyright 'vests' in that person. That means that no one else may produce, copy or use that music, song lyric etc. without the permission of the creator. There are a few conditions. Whatever is created must be recorded in some concrete form before it acquires protection (I use concrete in its general sense of course), but it does not have to be registered or published. In general terms, copyright usually last for the creator's lifetime plus 50 years after that. The period for architectural design work is the creator's lifetime plus 70 years.

Someone who wrongly uses or copies something for which another person owns copyright is said to 'infringe' the copyright.

Who Owns Copyright?

Copyright in drawings, reports, specifications, and other documents produced by an architect working for a firm belong to the firm, not to the architect who created them. That is the case even if the firm consists of one architect who employers another. If the employee does work outside the office (usually known as 'moonlighting'), the employee would usually own the copyright unless the employer could show that the contract of employment said that the employer owned the copyright in all architectural work carried out by the employee, even outside normal office hours. A problem may be to decide

Professional Practice for Architects and Project Managers, First Edition. David Chappell.

the meaning of 'normal office hours' because most architects appear to work many evenings and sometimes through the night!

Licences

So, if no one else may copy or use an architect's drawings and specification, how can the contractor on site use the drawings and specification to construct a building and isn't the finished building a copy of the drawings? The answer is that the architect gives the client permission to use the drawings and pass them on as necessary to the contractor in return for the fees paid by the client to the architect. This permission is called a licence. The client does not get the copyright, but only a licence to use the information to construct the building shown on the drawings and described in the specification.

Obviously, ownership of the copyright may be transferred from the creator, but this is not usual and not advisable. If done, it must be done in writing. An architect who actually sold the copyright in the drawings to the client for a fee could not then make use of the drawings in connection with another commission because the client would own the copyright. It is commonly, but wrongly, thought that it is necessary to indicate copyright ownership like this: © Emma Crow (2019). The copyright symbol is useful to warn people and it is good evidence of the existence of copyright, but it is not essential so far as this country is concerned.

Moral Rights

In the UK, the author of the copyright work in general has the right to be identified as the author, but the right must be claimed. It is called a 'moral right'. One often sees that kind of claim printed in the front of books. An architect can claim or assert moral rights simply by notifying the client. This is best done when the original appointment is made. The creator has the right to be identified whenever any kind of copy of the work is issued to the public and the right to be identified on the building. The right not to have the work subjected to derogatory treatment is also recognised. Treatment is derogatory if it is a distortion or mutilation of the work or is otherwise prejudicial to the author's honour or reputation. In the case of a building, the author has the right to require the identification on the building to be removed.

If a moral right is infringed or if anyone is about to use the architect's material without consent, the architect can ask a court to order the infringement to cease. If the court agrees, this is known as an injunction. However, the courts will not grant an injunction if the work has been commenced because they consider that damages in the form of a suitable fee for reproduction will amply recompense the architect and stopping expensive building work is not generally justified. It can sometimes be difficult to decide if and when exactly work has commenced.

Infringement

It can be difficult to prove infringement of copyright. It is easy to show that a design has been copied if every detail is exactly the same as the original, but the position is not so straightforward if only some parts of the design have been copied. Architectural plans are subject to copyright, but if there is effectively only one answer to a design problem, an architect will not be liable for infringement of copyright by arriving at the same solution as another architect previously engaged on the same project. In addition, there cannot be copyright in something that is not original. For example, an architect cannot prevent another architect from using a pitched roof or using chimneys, windows, and doors, but if the pitched roof, chimneys, windows, or doors had some unique distinctive features, they may be subject to copyright.

Small alterations to a design will not overcome the rights of the original designer. If a substantial and recognisable feature of the original design is copied, the original designer is likely to have a good case. The issue is a matter of degree and is very uncertain in many instances. It is usually better for the two parties to seek a reasonable settlement.

When I was in architectural practice, we once had a very distressed chap come to see us. He had bought an off-the-peg house design from a draughtsman and started to self-build only to discover that the design had actually been done in the office of a contractor who was busy building homes two streets away and would surely recognise his house type when completed. The problem was that all the foundations had been laid and the substructure brickwork commenced. Moreover, the unfortunate chap had ordered all the external doors and windows and they were on site. So, we could not design him a new house without having to discard all the work and materials on site already. The upshot was that we designed a house in the same footprint and using the same windows and doors but arranged in a completely different way so that, when finished, the only thing that was the same was the overall dimensions on the ground. Even the internal planning was amended. There was no chance of it infringing the contractor's copyright. The easy way out, and one which the chap had contemplated before good sense prevailed, was to slightly adjust the window positions: one 30 mm to the left, another 60 mm higher and so on. It is very doubtful that it would have been sufficient to overcome the copyright because the general appearance and all the internal arrangement would have been the same.

In an action for infringement of copyright, a court may have regard to the flagrancy of the infringement and any benefit gained by the person doing the infringement when considering whether to award additional damages (money to compensate for the infringement) taking everything into account.

7

Flowcharts: Physical and Mental

I must admit to being a fan of flowcharts. They are helpful to explain the way in which things must be done. What is even more helpful is to prepare a flowchart oneself. For example, when trying to understand what a contract means, it is useful to apply the same technique as would be used if preparing a flowchart. Essentially this simply involves asking a question about each activity in such a way that the answer is either Yes or No. For example, suppose the contract says that 'if the contractor spots a discrepancy between the contract documents it should notify the architect, who should issue an instruction'. This can be broken down as follows:

Does the contractor spot a discrepancy between the contract documents?
  If Yes, the contractor should notify the architect
  If No, the contractor should do nothing.
Does the contractor notify the architect?
  If Yes, the architect must issue an instruction.
  If No, the architect should do nothing.
Does the architect issue an instruction?

and so on. Figure 7.1 shows how this can be expressed as a flowchart.

That is a simple example, but it demonstrates the principles. The Yes/No principle is very useful for testing the most complex of processes. Anyone who has to spend time looking at contracts or method statements and seeing if they work gets into the habit of the mental flowchart. That simply means that in considering any activity one has to ask oneself the Yes/No question for each stage of the process. It is common for planned processes to fail the test. In the example above it is the final question which is likely to show a problem because someone writing the process will often just assume that the architect will issue the instruction. But what if the answer to that question is 'No', what happens then?

If there is no clear answer to either the Yes or the No (usually it is the No that is left out) there is something wrong with the process and that portion needs to be rewritten. The system can be applied to any process and it is essential when trying to get to grips with a procedure which involves the interaction of several people, all of whom have specific tasks to perform. A well thought out method statement, contract, or any other process will have been subjected to the flowchart test to find and fill any gaps. It is related to the production of a programme, but it clearly shows the consequences if the process does not go through all the Yes boxes.

Professional Practice for Architects and Project Managers, First Edition. David Chappell.

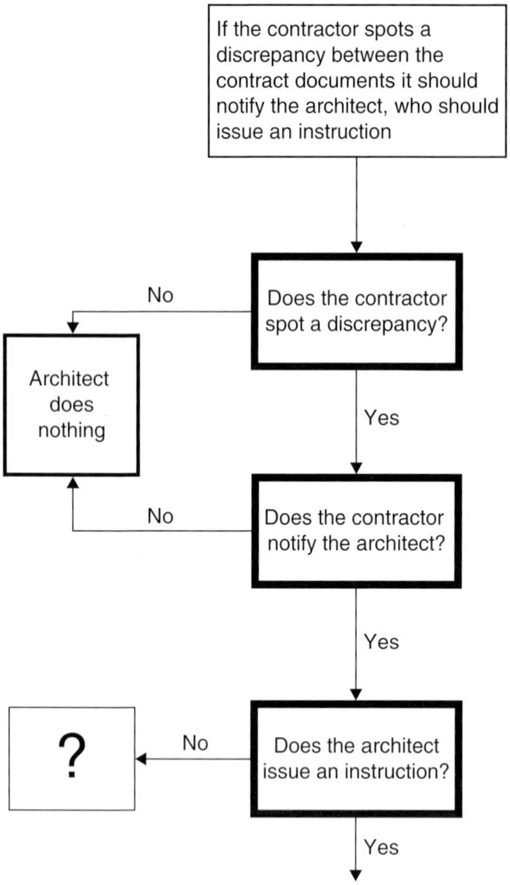

Figure 7.1 Flowchart.

8

Making a Decision

General Things

There are thousands of decisions to be made on even the smallest project, from deciding what the brief is and whether to go ahead, to choosing the shape and material of the smallest handle on an insignificant piece of furniture. Many of these decisions are urgent and they all must be made in the correct order so that the right result is achieved. A colleague of mine used to say, only partly in jest, 'If the worst comes to the worst, we can always make a decision.' That is the problem about decisions. They tend to be put off as long as possible. Until the decision is made, the need for a decision is always there in the background. We can never relax because eventually we know that the decision must be made. Never defer urgent decisions.

Simple Decisions

We all tend to make decisions without thinking them through properly. If the decision is not very important, this does not matter very much. What I want to consider here are those really important decisions which need time taken to decide. Most of us have experienced trying to make an important decision, setting aside time to consider the problem and then spending that time mentally going over the same old things and, not surprisingly, getting the same results (I am told that is a symptom of insanity). Some people advocate the simple expedient, for each available option, of writing all the plusses down one side of a sheet of paper and all the minuses down the other side. That system can work very well for simple decisions.

The Really Big Decisions

The making of any really big decision should be carried out in a logical and methodical way. Construction professionals are often called upon to make big decisions. This is the system which I have used very effectively for major decisions. Before you laugh out loud at what appears to be its complexity, try it and you may be surprised. It is not suggested that you should laboriously go through the method outlined step by step for every problem you encounter; as noted above, simple decisions require a simple approach. But if

Professional Practice for Architects and Project Managers, First Edition. David Chappell.

you study the principles thoroughly, following the procedure should become so much a part of your professional life that you will not consciously think about it.

When you have to make a decision, it will be because there is a problem. Many of the decisions you make in order to answer the problems you face will be minor ones, but are interwoven with other decisions so that the whole may appear impossibly complicated. These are the steps to take:

1. Isolate the various decisions you have to make so that you can consider them one by one. Some decisions will affect other decisions, others will simply affect an isolated part of your work. The decision to be made first is the one which affects most other decisions.
2. Decide whether a particular decision is of major or minor importance. This will determine the amount of time you should spend on it. There is absolutely no point whatever in agonising over a decision that has very little implication, even if it is wrong. This is probably the most important stage in the decision-making process and you must give it enough thought.
3. Make sure you know the problem. Do not act like students in an examination who often answer the question that is not asked. One thing you should ask yourself is 'Is it my problem'? Very often architects, being generally helpful souls, put themselves to endless trouble solving other peoples' problems without really understanding that they should stand back and let the client, client's solicitor, client's insurance broker, contractor, consultant (delete as appropriate) answer it.
4. Assuming that you identify the problem as one which you must deal with, write it down in as few words as possible. The act of writing it down will help to clarify the matter you are to consider.
5. Examine every aspect of the problem. Write down as a series of notes all the implications: time scale, financial, physical, special conditions, side effects on other actions, etc. Often, the real reason for being unable to make a decision is because we do not know all the facts. So, find the facts.
6. Do some research among documents (drawings, bills of quantities, etc.), colleagues, publications, and on site if appropriate. Go through your list combining items which are linked and crossing out duplications.
7. Then prepare another list by going through your notes and identifying the most important consideration and putting it at the top.
8. Carry on until you have rewritten all the points in order of importance. You now have the criteria for your decision in order.
9. Take another sheet of paper and using the points from your first sheet, note down as many possible solutions as you can. Do not worry at this stage if some of the solutions seem impracticable.
10. Examine each solution in turn against your list of criteria and note the results as a schedule. The schedule should show the good and bad results of each possible solution in each area. It should be possible to eliminate some possible solutions immediately.
11. Armed with a sheet of paper listing the problem and its consequences, side effects, and implications in every way and another sheet listing possible solutions analysed against the first sheet, you are in a position to come to a decision. Since you can only arrive at one decision, you should strike out any solution that clearly does not satisfy the criteria.

12. You should be left with two or three solutions which appear equally well suited to the problem. Sometimes, you will simply be left with one solution which, after this analysis, shines out clearly above all the rest.
13. If you find that two solutions appear to be equally good, examine them carefully to see if one is slightly better in some respect not hitherto considered. If that fails to produce a best solution, you can choose either one.
14. Save all the notes you made. At some time in the future, someone may ask you (perhaps in an adjudication or arbitration) why you made that decision and you will be able to explain it very thoroughly.

At the end of the process you may find that there is nothing you can do to solve the problem adequately. That is rare. There is a solution to most problems. Consider all the options again. More common is that no solution solves the problem as adequately as you would wish. If you cannot find an ideal solution, you must use the best solution you have. Never rush a decision. You will save no time by doing so because your decision under pressure is unlikely to be as good as it could be and will probably have to be revised. There are two questions which you can ask yourself when trying to decide between two courses of action:

- What should I *not* do?
- If my decision is wrong, what is the worst thing that could happen?

9

Approvals

Must the Architect Approve?

Architects are pathologically opposed to approving anything, including programmes. Very occasionally, a quantity surveyor preparing bills of quantities will include an item stating that the contractor must produce a programme for the architect's approval. This is calculated, perhaps on purpose, to bring the architect out in a cold sweat. Architects much prefer to comment on a programme, but not to 'approve', which is sometimes thought to have the sense of agreeing to it and, indeed architects think, taking some responsibility for it. Even if there is nothing in the preliminaries to suggest that the architect must 'approve' the programme, it is very common for a contractor to send its programme to the architect with a request for approval.

Does it matter if the architect does approve a programme which turns out to be hopelessly optimistic? The answer is: not usually, no. Unless it is an unusual contract, the contractor is entitled to set about construction in any way it wishes. It can, if it feels so inclined, start with the roof, raise it on stanchions, and proceed to fill in underneath.

Is the architect entitled to say that the programme is not approved and that the contractor should build it in another way? Again, the answer is: not usually, no. So, is the approval of the architect meaningless? Pretty well, yes, unless the contract expressly states otherwise.

Meaning of Approval

So, when architects say that the contractor's programme is approved, all they are really saying is that the contractor can construct the building like that if it wishes to do so. Since the architect usually has no power to control the way in which the contractor proceeds, the fact that the architect sanctions it is meaningless. The architect is not taking responsibility for what the contractor proposes to do. In the end, it is the contractor's own programme. The architect has not imposed it. It is difficult for the contractor to credibly argue that because the architect approved its programme and the programme wrongly showed the floor tiles being laid before the floor screed, that the architect is responsible for the cost of taking up the prematurely laid tiles. That contractor would be a laughing stock.

Professional Practice for Architects and Project Managers, First Edition. David Chappell.

What to Do

However, in order to avoid any confusion and possible fruitless arguments, the sensible course is for an architect, presented with a contractor's programme, to avoid expressing approval. Instead, it is better to ask various sensible questions about it. Questions such as: 'Are you sure you have allowed enough time to construct the foundations?' or 'Will there be access for your crane when block Y is finished?' Likely as not, the contractor's manager will respond in a huffy kind of way that he or she has been in the industry for countless years and what he or she does not know about building is not worth knowing etc. The architect need then only say that if the contractor is happy, it should proceed. It is not normally the architect's job, still less skill, to pontificate about a contractor's programme. The only thing the architect really need check is that the programme starts on the day for possession of the site and finishes no later than the contract date for completion.

If the Contractor has Design Responsibility

While on the subject of architect's approvals, what is the position if the architect approves a contractor's drawing if the contractor has design responsibility? Much will depend upon what it says in the contract concerned. However, if the contract gives the contractor the responsibility to design something, the contractor cannot easily shrug it off by saying that the architect saw it or approved it. Generally, the fact that the architect has approved the contractor's drawing will not move the design responsibility from the contractor to the architect. The architect will want to see the contractor's design drawings before they become a reality, but the architect will only be checking to see that the contractor appears to be complying with the performance specification. Thus, if the performance specification calls for a piling solution to the foundations, the architect will be expecting to see piled foundations not trench fill or a raft. The architect will not be expected to check that the piles will, in fact, hold up the building.

Sub-contractor's Drawings

What if, under a traditional contract, the contractor sends a sub-contractor's drawings (sometimes referred to as 'shop drawings') for the architect's approval before they are manufactured? This is a common occurrence. For example, the contractor will send off the architect's drawings to the window supplier and the window supplier will produce its own set of drawings of all the windows showing sections and elevations with dimensions. Instead of the contractor checking the shop drawings, it is easier to send them to the architect and ask the architect to check them.

I used to work with a very brave architect who would simply send back the drawings to the contractor with a note which said: 'If you have produced these drawings in accordance with my drawings, they are correct. If not, they are wrong'. He had supreme confidence in his own ability to produce 100% correct drawings. Naturally, most rather less confident architects welcome the chance to check through shop drawings to see that neither they nor the supplier has missed anything, but that should not be confused with the architect assuming responsibility for the drawings. The architect should make clear in the reply that the drawings have been examined ('checked' is not a good word in these circumstances) and there are a few comments. However, the accuracy and performance of the windows is entirely a matter for the contractor. Not, you will note, a matter for the supplier. So far as the architect is concerned, it is the contractor who is responsible for supplying and fixing everything in the contract, unless the architect is unwise enough to try to name a supplier or sub-contractor. Whether the supplier or sub-contractor has got it right is a matter between the supplier or sub-contractor and the contractor. By trying to deal directly with a sub-contractor in this situation, the architect will only make matters worse (see 88: Sub-contractors and Suppliers).

10

Replacement Architect

The Building Contract

Different building contracts say different things about replacing an architect. Some contracts say nothing at all. Therefore, if you are asked to replace an architect in a building contract, you must carefully read the relative part of the contract to see what is required. Some contracts refer not to an architect but to a contract administrator or a project manager or PM.

If the building contract refers to an architect, that post can only be filled by someone who is on the register of the ARB because the title is protected under statute. If it simply says 'contract administrator' or 'project manager', the post may be filled by anyone, although arguably restricted to a person with relevant qualifications.

Different Disciplines

Sometimes, if the contract simply refers to a contract administrator, an architect may resign and the employer may appoint a building surveyor as a replacement. Or the contract administrator may be a quantity surveyor whom the employer replaces by an architect. Occasionally, the employer may appoint a person who is not qualified to be a contract administrator or might even appoint him- or herself. The contract may not specifically say that an architect must be replaced by another architect or a surveyor by another surveyor or even by a suitably qualified person. Obviously, the contractor cannot object to the appointment of a replacement architect if the original architect resigns, because there must be someone to issue certificates and instructions in accordance with what the particular building contract says. Can the contractor object to the appointment of a contract administrator of a different discipline? Yes, it can, unless the contract specifically allows it.

The reason why the contractor can object is quite simple. The contract administrator or PM is the key figure in the administration of the contract. When pricing the project, the contractor will have taken the identity and discipline of the contract administrator into account. The director of a contracting firm once revealed to me that he always added 2.5% onto his price if he knew that an architect was to be the contract administrator because architects were notoriously 'picky' and difficult to please. By this I assumed he meant that architects actually insist on the contractor providing what it agreed to provide. On that basis, it could be argued that appointing a different discipline would

Professional Practice for Architects and Project Managers, First Edition. David Chappell.

favour the contractor, but I have also known contractors who prefer architects because they see them as rather unworldly creatures with heads in the clouds, allegedly easy to influence. Although, when replacing the architect, the employer cannot preserve the identity of the original contract administrator, there is no real difficulty in ensuring that the discipline and experience of the replacement is similar to the original. Therefore, if the original appointment was an architect, the replacement should also be an architect. If the original was a building surveyor, the replacement should be the same.

Unqualified Replacements

Unless the building contract says otherwise, the employer can appoint a completely unqualified person to be contract administrator provided the name is included in the tender documents so that the contractor can check out that person's credentials. So, the employer could state that his or her mother-in-law was the contract administrator even if she had spent her working life at HMRC. It might be an extremely foolish thing for the employer to do, but sometimes people do foolish things. I was once consulted by an employer who had appointed his brother-in-law (a retired baker) as contract administrator and he wondered why the contract was in chaos.

Employer as Contract Administrator

An employer who replaces a contract administrator with him or herself is behaving unlawfully. The contract administrator provides the contractor with a layer of protection. He or she has a duty to act in a manner which is independent, impartial, fair, and honest when carrying out certain duties such as certification. The employer cannot instruct the contract administrator to issue or withhold a certificate. If the employer suddenly takes over that role it is entirely wrong. The situation is different if the employer has indicated in the tender documents that he or she will act as contract administrator so that the contractor can tender with that in mind. It all boils down to the contractor's knowledge. In that case the contractor has entered into the contract with its eyes open. Having said that, the employer acting as contract administrator from the beginning is still in a difficult position. The employer's actions would be closely scrutinised by a court or arbitrator and certificates issued will not have the same status as if issued by an independent contract administrator.

The Code of Professional Conduct

The RIBA has a Code of Professional Conduct which sets out how architects should conduct their professional lives. In line with this book's intention to avoid specific references to clauses and to concentrate on principles, I am not going to enter into a detailed examination of the requirements of the Code. In any event, the Code is revised from time to time in its detail. However, it is important to know the approach of the Code to the replacement of one architect by another. The first and most important point is that no architect should actively try to replace another. It does happen, although not commonly so far as I am aware. But bluntly, if you approach prospective clients to try to persuade them to get rid of their current architects and use you instead, you will incur the wrath of the RIBA and the profession as a whole.

If a prospective client approaches you with a view to replacing the current or former architect, you should proceed carefully. Ideally, you should immediately inform the current or former architect of the approach. Realistically, that may not be possible because the client may approach you in confidence and you must respect the client's confidence. There may be legal proceedings in view. Nevertheless, if you agree to take on the commission, you must then immediately notify the architect you are replacing and inform him or her of the situation.

In those circumstances it is common for the previous architect to write to you and perhaps complain that the proper termination procedures under the contract have not been used and that the client still owes fees. It is plain common sense that you make sure that the termination of the previous architect's engagement has been properly carried out before you proceed to take on the commission. For all you know, the client may simply be using you to persuade the architect to do something and using replacement by you as a threat. The only time you would be justified in taking on the commission without seeing proper evidence of termination would be if you have seen what appears to be a termination letter from the client and the termination itself may be the subject of legal proceedings.

I have heard a number of mature architects express the view that if the former architect is owed fees by the client, another architect may not take on that commission until the former architect has been paid. That may sound like a really good idea, but it is quite wrong. It is wrong because it requires the replacement architect to make a judgement about whether the former architect or the client is telling the truth about whether the fees have been paid or, indeed, whether they are payable. That is a matter for a judge, arbitrator or adjudicator. The project may be on site and the contractor may be waiting for details. It is just not practicable to wait for a judicial decision on the matter because the client loss would be greatly increased and, of course, the client would have a duty to mitigate loss. Therefore, if the client assures the replacement architect that the fees have been paid, the replacement architect should proceed.

There is another point that any replacement architect should bear in mind. That is that copyright in the drawings and other documents produced by the former architect is owned by that architect and a replacement architect must be sure that the client has a licence to use the drawings and to allow the replacement architect to use the drawings or, at any rate, the information contained on them. If the former architect indicates that the licence has been suspended or withdrawn, it would be unwise for the replacement architect to continue unless the client is prepared to provide a letter of indemnity. In simple terms, that is a letter confirming to the replacement architect that the client has the legal right to use the drawings and that if the architect faces any claims or legal proceedings as a result of infringing the former architect's copyright, the client will pay all the expense and costs that the replacement architect incurs as a result (see 6: Copyright).

11

Agency

Getting It Clear

It is a surprising thing, but I find that many architects do not really understand what is meant when we say that the architect is agent for the client. Of course, that statement itself is not strictly accurate because it needs qualifying. The architect is not an agent for the client for everything, only in certain limited respects. If it was true to say that the architect was the client's agent, it would suggest that the architect could act on behalf of the client in everything that the client might want to do: book a holiday, buy a new car and so on. Put like that, most architects would say that of course it is understood that the architect is only the agent in certain areas. How does the architect know when he or she is acting as the client's agent? The simple answer is that it should be clear in the terms of engagement.

What Does it mean to be an Agent?

Architects and clients really do need to be sure about agency or expensive mistakes can occur. We must get the principles clear. The relationship between architect and client is in some degree, but not in everything, that of agent and principal. The architect is the agent and the client is the principal. The agent can do things on behalf of the principal, and in doing so the principal is bound by what the agent does so long as the agent was authorised by the principal (in this case the client) to do it. For example, the client may authorise the architect to order special equipment to be provided for the contractor to install in a house. That is actually not a good idea at all, but more of that elsewhere (see 88: Sub-Contractors and Suppliers). In that example, the architect is authorised to choose and order the items on behalf of the client. Provided that the architect makes clear to the supplier that the items are being ordered on behalf of the client, the client will be responsible for paying the supplier.

However, if the architect forgets to make clear that it is actually the client ordering the items, the supplier is entitled to charge the architect for them. One of the greatest dangers for an architect is that of exceeding the authority which the client has agreed. The possible consequences have already been touched upon: the architect may become liable for something instead of the client. Although it would be very unusual, an architect could be authorised to enter into a contract on behalf of the client. Therefore, although

Professional Practice for Architects and Project Managers, First Edition. David Chappell.

the architect would execute the agreement, it would be the client who was a party to the contract and not the architect.

Solicitors often act as agents for their clients for specific purposes, for example to receive a notice of adjudication. Architects do not act as agent to receive notices intended for clients. I once had to reassure an architect who had received a notice of adjudication from a contractor under the building contract. I pointed out that the architect was not a party to the building contract and, therefore, neither contractor not client could adjudicate against him under the building contract, although the client could adjudicate against the architect under the architect's appointment because they were both parties to that agreement. The client's written authority should be obtained if there is any doubt about whether the architect is authorised to act as agent in any particular instance. Alternatively, the architect could confirm instructions back to the client in writing.

How can the Contractor know if the Architect is Acting as Agent for the Client in any Particular Instance?

The architect and the client may get into an agency relationship in any of four ways:

- *Expressly*: when the client specifically appoints the architect either in writing or orally. This is the most satisfactory, particularly when done in writing, because there is little scope for misunderstandings or mistakes. The contractor must be made aware of this.
- *By implication*: when it is clear to others that the architect must be acting as agent. Such an instance may occur because the client behaves as if the architect was acting in an agency capacity, or simply because the architect is doing the kind of things normally done by an agent in such instances.
- *By necessity*: when the architect acts for the client in an emergency even though the architect has no authority to do so. Obviously, it would have to be a real emergency and not just something that ought to be done quickly. It is unlikely that this kind of agency will figure prominently in most architects' experience. There will be few instances where an agency comes into being in this way for an architect. One might just visualise a situation where the architect must give an instruction on the client's behalf in order to save the destruction of property. Otherwise the architect may not be empowered to give that particular instruction.
- *By ratification*: when the architect performs an act which the client subsequently ratifies. Two conditions must be satisfied: (i) the architect must carry out the action on behalf of the client and (ii) the client must have been capable of carrying out the act at the time it was performed by the architect.

The agent's authority is important. It may be actual or apparent. An architect's actual authority is set out in the conditions of engagement. Apparent authority is the authority the architect seems to possess so far as anyone, other than the architect and client, are concerned. An architect is liable to the client for acting beyond his or her authority, but provided the architect is behaving in the way in which others expect the architect to act, the client will usually be responsible for such actions to third parties. For example, suppose that an architect issues instructions to the contractor. Provided the contract states that the architect may issue instructions of the kind that the architect has issued, the contractor is entitled to carry out the work and be paid. The fact that the architect's terms of engagement may require the architect to obtain the client's authorisation before issuing any instructions does not concern the contractor even if the contractor knows that the architect has not asked the client first.

An Agent's Duties

The law sets out the duties of an agent, which are quite stringent:

- *To act*: If the agent fails to act when action is needed, the client may sue.
- *To obey instructions*: Provided that the client's instructions are lawful and reasonable.
- *To exercise skill and care*: The kind of skill and care normally to be expected from a member of that particular profession, in this case, the architect.
- *Not to take any secret bribe or profit*: The client may recover damages including the amount of the bribe (see 4: Nosebags).
- *To declare any conflict of interest*: Every architect should know what this means (see 37: Conflict of Interest).
- *Not to delegate without authority*: If the architect is appointed agent for something, the architect cannot pass the task to another person.
- *To keep proper accounts*: So that the amount and movement of money can be accurately traced.

These duties may be amended by the architect's terms of engagement.

Agency may be terminated by the death of the agent or client, by the completion of performance of the agent's contract, by mutual consent, by breach on the part of either the agent or client, and by bankruptcy of the client, but not necessarily bankruptcy of the agent.

12

Presentation

Purpose

The purpose of the presentation is not just to 'sell' your design, but more importantly to ensure that the client knows exactly what the finished building will be like. Some architects try to blind their clients with virtuoso renderings and intricate drawings. This is a bad policy. If the client does not properly understand your drawing, you may get an agreement to something the client does not really want. The client will realise the mistake later when the building is in course of erection, or even completed, and nothing can be done about it. It is in your own best interests that the client thoroughly understands and approves. If there is anything which you feel unhappy about, explain it to the client and take the client with you in the decision to proceed or attempt a revision.

Method

The most important point is that you must involve the client at every stage of the design process so that the finished appearance of the project does not come as a surprise and, hopefully, not as a shock! So, as the design evolves in logical stages, you discuss it with the client. The client's participation generates understanding and acceptance of responsibility for decision. In this way, your presentation is not one particular event when the design is settled, but a series of mini-presentations at each stage.

The way in which you present the scheme to the client is very important. Every architect has his or her own ideas about presentation, but the most important thing is to present the scheme so that the client can understand it. Never overestimate the client's capabilities in this direction. Many, otherwise highly intelligent, business men and women find great difficulty in understanding plans, sections, and elevations, and yet architects continue to insist on making those plans, sections, and elevations the basis of their presentation. Clients love models. Let's face it, we all love models. We squat down to get an eye-level view and we imagine ourselves inhabiting the model. Computers can provide simulated three-dimensional views and 'walk throughs' of the building. They can be very useful tools, but nothing attracts attention more than a good model. Consider making your presentation around a model of the proposal.

This is not a new idea, of course, but the production of a model tends to be restricted to very large schemes or is postponed until the scheme has been accepted, when its primary function is to sit on a boardroom table to impress visitors. I strongly suggest

Professional Practice for Architects and Project Managers, First Edition. David Chappell.

that you get into the habit of producing working models. That is to say, models which clearly explain the scheme at the stage you are at. This will help you and your client. The model need not be elaborate. Use it to supplement plans and perspectives. When making a presentation, let the client get the idea of the scheme from the model, then elaborate on it by using plans. Indicate what it would actually look like by quickly drawn perspectives. If you are a talented and quick freehand draughtsman, you could do some perspective views for your client on the spot. We all love to watch a talented artist draw. It is not appropriate in all circumstances, but if you can do it, it will impress more than all the elaborately drawn perspectives, carefully rendered and mounted. It is not a good idea to take sections and elevations to show the client. A building never looks like its elevations, and sections are only useful if the levels are exceedingly complicated. Even then a model that can be disassembled can explain levels far better.

Plans should be clearly drawn in black and white with room names printed clearly in each room. Do not use a key at the side and number the rooms. If the client is anything like me it will be infuriating having to check the room names with the key. State the scale and include a drawn scale, but do put a few dimensions on the drawing so that the client will get the overall impression you want. If there is some particular aspect of the building, the reception area in a hotel, for example, about which the client is concerned, do a separate drawing showing this to a larger scale with an indication of furnishings and finishes on it.

13

Abortive Work

Architects

'Abortive work' is a phrase that architects often use to refer to work that they have carried out but which is of no use. For example, a client may ask you to design a two-storey house of a certain floor area. After the design is finished, the client may decide that a single-storey house would be more appropriate. At that point, you might well refer to the two-storey house design as being 'abortive work'.

Strictly speaking that would be a wrong use of the phrase because what abortive work actually means is work that has come to an end prematurely. Nevertheless, we all would know what you meant and I suspect that 'abortive work' has already gained the alternative meaning through usage.

In the example above, you ought to be able to charge a fee for the abortive work because it was carried out correctly on the instruction of your client. I say 'ought to be able' because in order to claim you would have to have something in your terms of engagement which allowed you to claim for incurring extra costs due to things outside your control. Every architect ought to have a clause like that of course.

There are other reasons for abortive work which would not allow you to claim extra fees, such as an error in measurement which results in a design that would not fit on the site or a failure to design in compliance with the Building Regulations. So abortive work caused by the client should entitle you to additional fees whereas if you are the cause of the abortive work, no additional fees woould be chargeable.

Contractors

Contractors also carry out abortive work from time to time. For example, after constructing part of the project, the client may have second thoughts and tell the architect to instruct various changes to the work already constructed, which would then be abortive work. On the other hand, it could be the contractor who makes an error in construction and continues to build on top. The error would be defective work but the work built on top, if correct in itself, would be simply abortive work because it would have to be taken down and rebuilt at the contractor's cost in order to correct the defect in the work below.

Thus, referring to 'abortive work' is meaningless unless the context is stated or already known.

Professional Practice for Architects and Project Managers, First Edition. David Chappell.

14

Telephone

Calls Out

Telephones are an essential feature of life. This is not the place to go through all the types of sophisticated equipment available today but it is the place for a few comments.

Telephone calls should be as brief as possible. Unless there is a particularly good reason not to do so, you should always place calls yourself. That tends to be the situation if construction professionals conduct all their business by mobile phone. Calls placed from the office on a landline are a different matter and some people routinely get their secretaries or the switchboard to place their calls. This might be excused if you are having great difficulty in finding someone or you are in the position of trying to make dozens of short calls in a very limited time. Otherwise, it is simply discourteous. It sends a signal that you are much busier and your time is much more valuable than the person being called. Unless you are returning a call, you are telephoning because you are wanting to speak to the other person. It is you who has the particular reason for calling. Good business practice, not to mention courtesy, dictates that you must do the waiting, not the person called.

Calls In

What do you do if you receive calls made by a secretary or switchboard? In my first office, I used to receive many of those kinds of calls. Having ascertained that I was in fact present and waiting on the end of the phone, the secretary would sometimes come back on the line to say that the person who initiated the call seemed to be out of his or her office and would I hold the line while a search was made. I soon got into the habit of hanging up as soon as I was asked to 'hold the line'. This inevitably provoked another call and inevitably the secretary would say that we appeared to have been cut off. That was my cue to say that we were not cut off, but that I hung up because I was just as busy as the caller and perhaps he or she would like to call me directly in future. That strategy worked very well, it still does, and I recommend it.

It is worth remembering that the person who takes the initial calls in any practice is the practice so far as callers are concerned. Therefore, a competent telephone operator with a good voice and manner is essential. This is a fact that is widely understood in theory, but frequently ignored in practice.

Professional Practice for Architects and Project Managers, First Edition. David Chappell.

Records

All construction professionals should keep a written record of all phone calls. You never know when a particular call may be important in the future. It may be the fact that a topic was discussed or that someone agreed something or simply the fact that the call was made. How much you choose to write down or type into your computer diary is a matter of judgement, but at least record the date, who called, the topic discussed and the times the call started and concluded. For example, the record of a simple call may just be '08/05/19, 14 : 00 X called, cancel tdy's mtg. 14 : 10'. There are times, perhaps most times, when taking the time to jot down notes of a call may seem to be an unnecessary waste of time and energy but, if done routinely as the call progresses, all that needs to be done at the end of the call is to record the time. Get into the habit of recording all calls in some way and if it is obvious that a call is important, copy those details to the appropriate file.

Mobiles

Mobile phones are now essential. The great advantage is that you can be reached wherever you are. The disadvantage is that you can be reached wherever you are. You must know when to turn off your phone. Many people have two mobiles, business and personal. Unless there is an extremely good reason, explained to all present, you must never leave a mobile phone switched on during a meeting. It shows the most complete disregard for others. It signals to everyone that the offender believes that he or she is the busiest and most important person present. Some companies arrange important meetings away from the office precisely because they do not want the participants interrupted by telephone calls or urgent consultations. To take a mobile phone into that environment defeats the object.

15

Writing Letters (or Emails)

Basic Principles

Most architects who are interested in architecture are uninterested in writing letters. I don't know any schools of architecture that teach letter writing, although some may do so. Most architects of my acquaintance simply picked up (or failed to pick up) the art of letter writing as part of their experience. Just as important is email writing. In business matters, it is best to treat emails like letters and compose them accordingly. There is no place for sloppy informality in business emails. No matter how your correspondent writes emails, yours should be models of clarity. Although below I refer only to letters, the same principles apply to emails. You will have your own style of writing and that is good, but it is important to observe certain principles. These are the principles which I have picked up, analysed and which have served me well over a long career, only part of which was as a practising architect:

- Know why you want to write the letter. That may sound obvious, but many people have only the vaguest idea why they are writing a particular letter.
- Always write letters to confirm what is agreed.
- Always write letters to answer questions or to confirm your oral answers.
- Always conclude a long letter with a reminder of the purpose of the letter. For example, 'Therefore, if I do not receive your response to the above by the 8 May 2019, I will be obliged to …'
- If writing a long letter, prepare notes first so that everything is in the correct order. That makes the letter easy to write and to understand. Many people start writing a letter with an imprecise idea of what they want to say, much less how they want to say it. The finished letter will often demonstrate the same imprecision.
- One occasionally still encounters business shorthand such as 'thank you for your letter of even date'. At best this is sterile. Say 'Thank you for your letter of the 8 May 2019'.
- Do not dictate letters. Although it takes longer to draft either by hand or by computer, the results are much better than dictation and save time in the long run. Good dictation usually requires notes prepared beforehand and a great deal of experience in dictation. Since one can only gain that experience at the expense of dictating a lot of very poor letters, it is not acceptable. Dictated letters can often be recognised by their rambling nature, repetition of the same things, and obscurities of meaning (see below).

Professional Practice for Architects and Project Managers, First Edition. David Chappell.

- When dealing with contract administration, always try to use the words of the contract.
- When being harassed by receiving long and complicated letters or several letters from the same person on the same day, try and write a one-line reply such as: 'Thank you for your six letters dated 8 May 2019. I will respond in due course.' Or 'Thank you for your exceptionally long and complicated letter dated 8 May 2019. I have difficulty understanding what you are trying to convey. I should be grateful if you could rephrase your letter to make it comprehensible.'
- Always try to sound reasonable. On no account give vent to anger in writing.
- Write clear letters.
- If your letter is going to be very long, consider whether it might be better written as a report sent with a brief covering letter.
- Remember that your letters may be read out in court one day and you may be asked to explain them.
- Do not fill your letters with abbreviations and acronyms. Much better to write the word in full. If you are going to have to refer to a complicated name several times in letter, write it in full once and put the abbreviation or acronym in brackets which you can then use throughout the rest of the letter.
- Never simply acknowledge receipt of a letter: it may be taken as agreement. Either respond fully or in one of the ways above or simply say that you are considering the contents and will reply in due course.
- Never say that you expect to hear from the other person 'in a week's time' or 'a fortnight' or even '7 days'. Always state the actual date, e.g. 'I expect to hear from you by 8 May 2019'. That leaves no room for dispute over the actual date.
- Never accept letters containing ambiguities. Press for a clear, comprehensible answer.
- Neither you nor your correspondent can assume anything from silence unless the contract states that you can. If someone sends you a letter containing a proposal and says 'If you do not reply by 8 May 2019, you will be deemed to have agreed with my proposal' it is meaningless.
- Never answer what you assume the other person intended to write. If you are not sure what they are trying to say, tell them and ask for clarity.
- Sometimes a correspondent (solicitors are often guilty of this) will say that they require you to respond by a certain date. They may even refer to it as a 'deadline date'. Generally, it is just another bullying ruse to obtain a reply quickly. Unless there is some good reason, for example to comply with a legal requirement, it is a good idea to wait until a few days later before sending a reply. That will send a message that you will not be bullied. Of course, if it is an offer of payment which says that if it is not accepted in X days it will be withdrawn, that will suggest a prompt reply if you or your client wishes to accept.
- Never make a threat that you are not prepared to carry through or you will look silly at best when your correspondent ignores it and you have to write again.
- Always give yourself manoeuvring space.
- Read through your letter as though you were the person who will receive it.
- When trying to get someone to do something which they are resisting, try giving them an honourable way out of the difficulty.

Is Dictation a Good Idea?

Although nowadays most business is carried out by email and letters tend to be the exception, there are certain communications that should be by letter and post. Many people now type their own letters but there are people in all walks of business life who always dictate letters because they say it is much easier and better than drafting by hand. I have witnessed and experienced two kinds of dictation: dictation to a secretary or to a machine. If it is a very simple letter, dictation is certainly a quick way to achieve it, especially by machine. But most letters are complicated and anecdotal evidence is that, when faced with having to dictate a complicated letter, there are various approaches which do not vary even when a secretary is employed:

- The whole letter is virtually written out before being dictated thus largely or wholly nullifying the use of dictation.
- The letter is set out in rough notes so that the structure is clear. This is the best way.
- A few random notes are scribbled so that they are not forgotten. This ensures that all the points are included but not necessarily in the right order, which is at best confusing and at worst misleading to the reader.
- There are no notes and the dictator indulges in a stream of consciousness, mentioning things as they come to mind; if indeed they do. This can be a fun way to write letters; fun that is for the dictator but not for the recipient because it gives rise to those incomprehensible letters one often receives and about which one has to seek clarification, thus wasting time for everyone. This kind of letter often takes longer to dictate than it would to write out because the dictator often has to stop and either get the machine to replay what has been said or get the secretary to read it out.

Whichever approach is adopted, dictation to a machine has the disadvantage for the typist that, unless the dictation is given with the utmost precision and clarity, there are bound to be words that are difficult to understand – thus wasting more time. So, the moral (or at least my moral) is that letters should normally be drafted and only dictated if they are very short.

Facsimile (Fax)

Sending something by fax is now the exception and many, perhaps most, offices no longer have a fax machine. Even if they have a fax machine, it may not have seen a fax in years and the few sheets of paper in the stack are probably curling with age. Faxing has now almost vanished and it has been replaced by the sending of documents by email. Faxed documents are poor in quality and do not compare to scanned documents by email. However, solicitors still seem to maintain a love affair with faxes and often draft agreements which permit faxing but not emailing.

Emails

Most communication is carried out by email, which in certain circumstances is now accepted as a good way to send a notice intended to have legal effect. Emails are often used as a means to form a contract, although I do not recommend forming a contract by email. As noted above, care must always be taken to make sure that the contract in use allows emails.

There are several problems with emails, which stem from the ease with which they can be sent. Here are some of them:

- They encourage the sending of trivial messages.
- It is as essential to retain print-outs of all emails, which are other than trivial, as of other correspondence. The paperless office is a myth. We all know that a computer or a server will let us down at important times.
- Emails are often treated by the writer as though they were the equivalent of the spoken word. They are not. If printed they are communications in writing. If not printed, the electronic version can be printed and submitted as evidence in adjudication, arbitration or litigation.
- It is too easy to get into the habit of sending an email with a click of the mouse as soon as it is composed. It essential to take a few moments at the end of every email in order to decide whether it should be sent at all and, if so, whether there is anything in it which you might regret. Some email systems do have a way of cancelling an email a few minutes after sending, but that is not always the case.
- It is important to write emails with the same restraint as if writing a letter to be sent in the post.

If some form of legal proceedings is commenced, possibly two or three years after the project is complete, it is vital that all your emails are easy to find and download. I have experienced architects, called to give evidence in adjudications, having to spend many hours trawling through ancient and discarded laptops to find emails. A system of constantly saving emails to a central backup is easy to set up.

The great thing about emails is the ability to send large quantities of information across long distances. There are size limits to what can be sent, but the transference of large numbers of documents can easily be achieved by the use of information transfer systems like WeTransfer or drop boxes. Drop boxes are useful on projects which require access by the project team to large quantities of documents.

An architect should remember that an email sent is essentially the same as a letter. When printed out, it is documentary evidence of something. The sender of an email should take as much care as if composing a letter to be sent through the post. There is a growing practice of sending letters by email and by post. If urgent, there is good reason to send a letter by email. If not urgent, the letter should be sent by post. There must be a good reason to do both. Do not do it routinely.

A Final Thought

I once worked in an office where all letters had to be dictated through a special, but rather temperamental, system incorporated into the internal telephones. The turnaround of finished letters was notoriously slow. One day, I dictated (from very full notes of course) several letters, then foolishly threw away my notes. Two weeks later, the typing pool manager rang to say that apart from my name, there was nothing on the tape. I was very busy at the time, sending many letters and could not remember the content of any of the letters I had dictated. The odd thing was that there were never any repercussions arising from the missing letters. I never remembered what they contained or to whom they should have been sent. I learned a valuable lesson: think carefully before writing any letter. If in doubt, don't write, because many letters are unnecessary.

16

Information Technology

Say 'information technology' and everyone immediately thinks of computers. This is a term most commonly used to refer to the electronic storage, retrieval, processing, and dissemination of information, but of course it can apply in general to all formal systems developed for the same purposes. Nowadays, if you refer to an IT person, I immediately know that you are referring to someone who is, hopefully, an expert in dealing with computers and software, and especially their problems.

The amount of information which may be required by an architect is finite, but not known. The amount of information available increases far more quickly than any one person can assimilate it. This is true of any profession and particularly so of architecture.

An important part of an architect's task is to use information. Architects are not expected to remember masses of information. The important thing is to remember basic principles and most other necessary information can be readily obtained from computers and online.

Coping with the information has become a science in itself. In theory, all necessary information can be put onto a computer and programmed so as to be readily accessible as required. In practice, things are not so easy and information is constantly changing and being changed, not to mention the programs that are supposed to deliver the information.

It always seems to me that computers, their operating systems, and most software are not produced to assist people who want to use computers as a working tool. Computers are apparently produced for people who just love computers for their own sakes. How one's heart sinks when informed on the screen that the computer system is going to be upgraded and reconfigured. All the millions of people who love to fiddle with computers are no doubt overcome with joy at the prospect of a different set of rules to be learned and played with. Anyone with my approach to computers swears, not always silently, at the thought of hours wasted trying to work out how to do all the things which they did without difficulty before the update.

Despite their problems, computers are now essential. Always back up work and essential information on a constant back-up going on as work continues.

Professional Practice for Architects and Project Managers, First Edition. David Chappell.

17

The RIBA Plan of Work 2013

Before 2013

Most architects know exactly what they are required to do in carrying out full architectural services. In performing those services, they carry out the right activities but, as Eric Morecombe famously said, 'not necessarily in the right order'. The idea of the Plan of Work is to list the many activities and set them out in the right order. When I first started practice, there was no RIBA Plan of Work, so most architects produced their own plans so that they could tick off the jobs as they were done. Of course, the problem with trying to reduce a series of activities to a sequential list and divide that list into comprehensible sections is not easy. That is partly because the activities interlock with each other and in some circumstances the right order changes.

It was in 1964 that the RIBA first published its Plan of Work in the *RIBA Handbook of Architectural Practice and Management*. It was based on certain assumptions which are no longer important. It was revised in 1999 and 2007, and the last revision was in 2013. The 2007 Plan was considered by most architects to be very helpful. It was simple and easily understandable. There are many instances when two or more stages may be combined and that was not a problem. The Plan showed the principal tasks for the various disciplines located at the stage when they were usually carried out. Usefully, the architect's tasks were shown in two sections: design function and management function. The beauty of the Plan was that it was fairly comprehensive yet simple. It enabled the architect to assess each project and adjust the Plan to suit. Because the Plan was so simple, the adjustments required were minimal. Yes, it was based on the assumption that it was traditional procurement, but it served well. The stages of the RIBA Plan of Work 2007 are set out in Table 17.1.

2013

Despite the popularity of the 2007 Plan of Work, the RIBA decided to revise it quite significantly and a new Plan was published in 2013. The 2013 Plan matches the Construction Industry Council (CIC) Schedule of Services. Before proceeding, it should be stated that my view from the outset, when the RIBA invited comments, was that the 2013 Plan was too complex in its philosophy and execution to be useful to the average small to medium-sized practice. It is worth noting that there is a sizable section of the

Professional Practice for Architects and Project Managers, First Edition. David Chappell.

Table 17.1 The 2007 RIBA Plan of Work showing stage titles.

Stages	
A	Appraisal
B	Design brief
C	Concept
D	Design development
E	Technical design
F	Production information
G	Tender documentation
H	Tender action
J	Mobilisation
K	Construction to practical completion
L	Post practical completion

Table 17.2 The 2013 RIBA Plan of Work showing stage titles.

0	Strategic definition
1	Preparation and brief
2	Concept design
3	Developed design
4	Technical design
5	Construction
6	Handover and close out
7	In use

architectural profession who still work to the 2007 Plan because they find it more sensible and easier to understand than the 2013 version and so do their clients.

The stages of the 2013 Plan are set out in Table 17.2.

Some General Observations

The idea of the 2013 Plan is that the architect, using the facilities provided by the RIBA, will be able to tailor the 2013 Plan to suit each project. More than that, the plan can be varied in accordance with changes in circumstances as the work progresses. The idea of this book is to address principles, not to delve into details which rapidly become out of date. Therefore, you will be relieved to hear that I do not intend to carry out a thorough examination of the 2013 Plan of Work. Here are some brief points.

There are a number of changes which do not seem to make a great deal of sense unless it is to emphasise that the 2013 version is different to the 2007 version. It seems deliberately obtuse that the first stage is labelled '0' and the eighth stage labelled '7'. It would seem more logical to label the first stage '1' and the last stage '8'. The current bizarre labelling means that the user has to remember that the third stage is actually stage 2.

The 2007 Plan had the stages listed from top to bottom of the page and the tasks in each stage were described horizontally alongside the stages. The 2013 Plan lists the stages from left to right on the page and the tasks are separated into categories from top to bottom of the page. Unsurprisingly, in a phrase borrowed from computers, the list of categories is called the 'task bar'. Following computer practice in this way does seem to put the cart in charge of the horse.

Needless to say, the 2013 Plan of Work and its supporting website and publications assumes that the user will be prepared to devote a significant amount of time to producing the tailored Plan of Work before starting work on the project.

The use of any plan of work will not get rid of errors, but it should at least ensure that important things are done in a logical order. In this complicated world, it has always been my view that one should strive to make things simple. The danger of a highly complicated plan of work is that almost becomes an end in itself; the object being to get the plan of work right rather than to produce a splendid building.

Of course, a plan of work is important but it is not the most important thing. Many architects still refer to 2007 Plan of Work stages in their fee proposals and in planning their work because it is simple. My long experience dealing with architects' problems is that architects generally dislike that kind of paperwork and they are not good at it. Having said that, there is obviously a chunk of the architectural profession which loves paperwork, otherwise we would not have the 2013 Plan of Work. The question one ought to ask oneself when using something like the RIBA Plan of Work is quite simply whether the project actually needs a highly complex set of pieces of paper in order to take it from start to finish or whether something simply signposting the crucial stages is going to be better.

18

Building Information Modelling

What is Building Information Modelling?

You can read all about the intricacies of building information modelling (BIM) in other books. It is a good idea in its place. Like many other good ideas, BIM can be extremely time consuming and you must think carefully whether or not to use it for any particular project. Let's be clear: there is no point whatsoever in using BIM for a small house. It is only worth the effort if the project is going to be a substantial one. The National Building Information Model Standard Project Committee defines BIM as follows:

> Building Information Modelling (BIM) is a digital representation of physical and functional characteristics of a facility. A BIM is a shared knowledge resource for information about a facility forming a reliable basis for decisions during its life cycle; defined as existing from earliest conception to demolition.

That is the kind of definition that I find intensely irritating. It tells you nothing unless you understand what it is all about without the definition and it is presented as though the writer does not particularly care whether you understand it or not.

Put simply, BIM is a system which is capable of receiving all the information about a project and then converting that into three dimensions. If computer-aided design (CAD) is 2D then BIM is 3D. A lot of information can be put into a CAD system. BIM can include all the relevant information about specification, manufacturer's details, geography, topography, geology, green issues, and virtually everything else. The advantage is that the user has together in one place all the relevant information about a project. This information can be easily turned into quantities, ordering information, and a realistic programme to achieve the work. Indeed, the building can be virtually constructed in stages, enabling all concerned to see how everything fits together and any potential problems. Already you can see that it is probably a waste of effort using this system to produce a village hall.

An important but potentially problematic aspect is that other professionals having an input into the project can access the model and input their own information directly. Clashes between pipe runs, structural steel, and the building fabric should be able to be identified and eliminated. Degrees of access of various people can be controlled. Various parts of a building can be related to other parts so that if a part is being given special consideration, it will retain its relationship and, if changed, the dependent parts will

Professional Practice for Architects and Project Managers, First Edition. David Chappell.

also change. In theory, the system should almost eliminate errors and remove discrepancies. However, and this is the big 'HOWEVER' which bedevilled all those people who thought, and still think, that the computer is the answer to all problems, the computer is just a glorified calculating machine. The old adage 'rubbish in: rubbish out' still applies. There is still a need to input data of all kinds accurately; wrong specification will not automatically be detected, although the chances of detection should be much greater.

Good and Bad

BIM is intended to support project management, cost control, and the entire life cycle of the project. In theory, the model can grow and develop over time as repairs are carried out and changes made. The model can be used for maintenance issues. A decision to cut into part of the fabric can be taken with precise knowledge of what lies beneath the surface provided, of course, that the information is correct and up to date.

All this sounds absolutely wonderful and I realise that I am an old spoil sport, but experience shows that if one puts all one's eggs into one basket, a slight misadventure can become a disaster. There is another aspect which does not seem to have attracted much attention for obvious reasons. That is the rapid development of computer technology. Although the production of a computer model containing everything there is to know about a project and imputing all changes as they occur (and if someone remembers) to get an ongoing record of the building throughout its, possibly, 60-year life is a very enticing scenario, realistically in 20 years' time or less the way in which this information can be stored and displayed will have changed beyond recognition. One only has to look at the record industry to see the way in which the technology changes. People now smile at my cherished collection of cassette recordings, and CDs are going out of fashion as people store or simply pluck recordings out of the ether. Just saying.

Levels of BIM

The various 'levels' of BIM, sometimes called 'levels of maturity', may be summarised as follows.

- Level 0 is the use of CAD files.
- Level 1 is a combination of 2D and 3D information used by the architect as an aid to visualising the project.
- Level 2 is entirely 3D with all team members inputting information into the model. This will include the contractor and designing sub-contractors.
- Level 3 requires the complete integration of all parties to the model and the use of the model for costings, management, briefing, life cycle, and facilities management and its use as a resource for other projects.

Sounds good, but be careful.

19

Computer-aided Design

The First Question

The first question we should be asking is: does the computer aid design? If not, this title, which is in general use, is a misnomer. The computer certainly aids the preparation of production drawings and, without it, building information modelling (BIM) would not get off the ground of course. BIM is changing how buildings, infrastructure, and utilities are built and managed, and all except the smallest practices have a BIM system; or so I am led to believe. Computers are absolutely great and wonderful in enabling architects and others to see the design in three dimensions or sections through any part of it, views upwards, downwards, and from any angle, but do they help to design the building in the first place?

Most people I know who allegedly use computer-aided design (CAD) for design actually spend most time designing by use of a pencil and tracing or detail paper before putting the results into the computer to test it. Some architects say that they design straight into the computer, but I have difficulty understanding how that can be done if the building is complex. I suppose those architects have a very developed spatial awareness.

In conclusion, it seems that the computer does aid design but mainly by the ability to test the design once prepared. Only the whole, I prefer to think of it as computer-aided drafting.

CAD in Practice

Most offices now use computers to prepare production drawings but most offices use other methods at the initial design stage. Working in CAD is slower in the first stages of producing the drawings, but it is far easier to make amendments to the drawings and the computer ensures that amendments to one drawing are reflected throughout all related information. Keeping to design, the use of the computer is most exciting when it is programmed to allow a walk-through of the building in the early stages. As a tool for explaining a project to a client it is unsurpassed by the most artistic perspective renderings. Without it BIM would be impossible.

There is no doubt that CAD is complicated. In the early days, offices using CAD had just one or two people who were the CAD operatives and it was their job to transfer

Professional Practice for Architects and Project Managers, First Edition. David Chappell.

the drawings produced by others into the CD system. Now virtually all architects can use CAD. Many people find working with CAD difficult but there is only one way to find out how to use CAD and that is to use it. Of course, there are a lot of basic things to learn but exploring and experimenting are the best ways to learn how to really use the system. Remember that the computer will only do what you tell it to do. Computer systems very often, and often irritatingly, try to predict what we are trying to do, but they cannot actually think for themselves – yet.

20

Technical Information

Then and Now

At one time, architects had a very limited number of materials to specify in the construction of buildings. Brick, stone, timber, slate, plaster, and roof, wall, and floor tiles were the principal materials and every architect was able to absorb the fundamental properties and recognise different kinds of wood, stone, bricks etc. But for many years now, architects have been faced with an almost endless array of possible materials, products, and processes for use in and on buildings. It is impossible to understand and evaluate every new process and material. In short, the architect is now reliant to a great extent on information provided by the manufacturer and the main skills are in choosing something that will do the job required and knowing how to choose correctly.

Literature

A great deal of reliance is placed on manufacturers' technical literature. That is often the starting point of course, but it should never be the ending point. There are two kinds of literature put out by manufacturers. The first and fairly useless type has glossy pictures and describes the product in glowing terms. The second is intended for the construction industry and contains technical specifications and information about test results and approvals. Sometimes, the two kinds are issued together but it is only the second kind that is really useful. Having said that, do not place all your faith in what it says about the product in the literature. Many architects do that, believing that if the manufacturer has said, for example, that the product is ideal for use in all weathers, that constitutes a statement that is legally binding on the manufacture and, if the product is not ideal in all weathers, the employer will have grounds for a claim.

The reality is not quite so straightforward. The courts have a distressing tendency to categorise that sort of statement as a 'puff'. In other words, everyone should understand that the statement is not literally true but said simply to bolster or puff up the product and is not to be relied on. So, do not place reliance on what the literature says regarding use. The way a product is written up may often allow the manufacturer to escape liability. Of course, the test results and other strictly factual information should be correct. Unfortunately, architects and others in the industry are not usually equipped to decide whether all the technical jargon means that the product will perform satisfactorily.

Professional Practice for Architects and Project Managers, First Edition. David Chappell.

Reps

I am sorry to say so, but I have always found the trade representatives less useful than the literature. There are some good ones of course and, if you find one, he or she should be treasured. Usually, they are simply sales reps although sometimes they are knowledgeable about the product, especially if sent by the manufacturer in response to your direct request. I once met a rep who represented several different companies. He arrived with a large suitcase and, when he could not interest me in one product, he dived into the suitcase and produced another. The problem is that, because they are engaged in an oral conversation either face to face or, worse, on the telephone, they can promise all even if they deliver nothing. How do you know if the rep is simply spinning you a line? Answer: you don't know. The reps are there to give you reassurance, they never, or very rarely, say that their product is not what you should be using.

Years ago, I learned a very salutary lesson when trying to devise a way of dealing with water penetration through the roofs of a set of garages built into a sloping site, the concrete roofs acting as a path above. The council concerned said that ordinary tanking was too costly and I was persuaded by an apparently knowledgeable rep that his firm's product was just the thing and when brushed onto the ceilings, it would resist the downward pressure from the water ingress and all would be well. He even inspected the garages and pronounced them perfect for the product. He provided references and I contacted them all and they all said that the product seemed to work for them. I questioned and cross-questioned the rep because the basis of the application of the product went against everything I understood. Eventually, I specified the product only to find that, within days, it was hanging from the ceilings like a set of huge balloons. The balloons, if pricked, emitted streams of water. Telephoning the referees, I heard that they were now experiencing much the same problem. The moral is the good old one: if it seems too good to be true, it probably is. Trust your own judgement.

Things to Do

The most important thing that you must try to establish is that the product actually does what you want it to do. That is the key thing. The secondary thing which you must establish is that, if there is a problem, the manufacturer will be obliged and able to correct it, by providing a different product if necessary. These are the ways of doing this:

- Get references from other users of the product and go to see it in use to establish:
  - where it is used,
  - when it was installed and
  - what it was there to achieve.
- Get references from appropriate technical organisations.
- Find out how long the product has been on the market.
- Check that the manufacturer is financially secure.
- Check for product certification marks.
- Check whether the manufacturer gives a guarantee, but beware of silly conditions.
- Get the manufacturer to provide a standard warranty.

Importantly, write to the manufacturer setting out precisely how you intend to use the material, product or process with drawings if possible and ask for written confirmation that it will be suitable. Once you have that, the manufacturer will find it difficult to avoid liability.

21

Bonds and Parent Company Guarantees

Bonds

I dimly recall my early years as an architect, but I do remember hearing the word 'bond' several times and it always had a rather legal connotation, like 'indemnity' or 'covenant', quite scary in fact. So, let it be said at the outset that bonds are usually good things so far as architects and employers are concerned. They are also good for contractors, although they may not always be considered so. Having said that, they may be quite complicated. There are standard forms for different kinds of bonds and where there is no standard form, one can be drafted by a solicitor or anyone who is skilled in that particular field.

A bond is a special kind of agreement usually in the form of a deed. It is in the form of a deed because, if you turn to 23: Contracts you will see that although a simple contract requires both sides to give or forego something, a deed does not. Therefore, a deed can be given by one party even if it appears to get nothing in return. It is also the most serious kind of contract. The principle is that one party (called a 'surety') agrees to be responsible to another party (in this case the employer) for the proper carrying out of obligations by yet another party (in this case the contractor). A bond is a guarantee and, therefore, it must be in writing. I know, I know, I said that I would not use legal phrases, but there is no alternative here. You need to know the proper names of these things, otherwise you will be calling bonds 'important bits of paper' and the surety will be 'someone who gives important bits of paper'. Most people would agree that it is worth learning 'bond', 'guarantee', and 'surety' to avoid referring to important bits of paper and sounding silly.

Now that is out of the way, what is the purpose of a bond? So far as construction is concerned the following are the usual kinds of bonds:

- performance bond
- payment for off-site materials bond
- advance payment bond
- retention bond.

Performance Bond

A performance bond is a written undertaking given by a surety to the employer which states that the surety promises to pay the employer up to a stated sum if the contractor fails to carry out the contract. It provides money to enable the Works to be completed.

Professional Practice for Architects and Project Managers, First Edition. David Chappell.

The bond comes to an end either when the surety pays the stated sum or on a stipulated date. The stipulated date is usually stated to be the date of practical completion but sometimes it is the date when all defects have been rectified at the end of the defect liability period in the contract. It is dangerous to state a fixed date such as the date for completion in the contract because it is common for the contract period to suffer delay. Stating 'the date of practical completion of the Works' is far safer because that is a moveable date.

The stated sum in the bond can theoretically be anything, but in practice it is usually 10% of the contract sum. On a very large project it might be less and on a small project it might be more. Details of the bond will be included in the tender documentation and the contractor will include the cost of obtaining a bond in its tender price.

The surety is usually the contractor's bank or an insurance company. There may be disadvantages for the contractor associated with the contractor using its bank because the bank will normally simply reduce the overdraft available to the contractor by the amount of the bond. This then gives the contractor less money to use during the construction. An insurance company will take steps to ensure that it has security also, but that should not directly affect the contractor's bank overdraft. Therefore, the contractor will want the expiry date of the bond to be as early as possible.

There are two kind of bonds:

- 'on default' bonds
- 'on demand' bonds.

If the employer wishes to claim some or all of the money in the bond, this is referred to as 'calling in' the bond. If the employer wishes to call in an 'on default' bond, the employer has to demonstrate that the contractor is in default of the contract duties which are the subject of the bond. That can be a lengthy process. The employer can call in an 'on demand' bond by simply demanding it whether or not the contractor is in default. It is sometimes referred to as a 'cash in hand' bond for that reason. At one time, most bonds in the United Kingdom were 'on default', but 'on demand' bonds are becoming the norm.

'On demand' bonds are favoured by banks and insurers because when they receive a demand, all they have to do is to check that the demand conforms with the requirements for the demand stated in the bond. They can pay without having to decide whether the contractor actually is in default or not. If an 'on default' bond is involved, the surety has to satisfy itself that the contractor is in default in a way that is covered by the bond. That may require a long and expensive investigation by the surety and there is always the danger of making the wrong decision, which might lead to litigation and more expense. The employer need not call in the full amount of the bond. For example, if the bond is stated to be for £20 000 but the employer only needs £5000, the employer should only call in £5000. If the actual cost of completing the Works is £30 000, the employer can still only call in the bond for the sum of £20 000.

Payment for Off-site Materials Bond

A payment for an off-site materials bond is provided when the architect agrees to certify the value of materials or goods held by the contractor but not on the site itself. Obviously, if the architect certifies the value and subsequently the contractor becomes insolvent before bringing the items to site, the employer may find it difficult to prove that the items in question have been paid for and are, therefore, owned by the employer. Some contracts allow certification of materials off-site and some do not. The bond is for the full value of the items until they have been delivered to site (see 94: Materials Off Site).

Advance Payment Bond

An advance payment bond is provided by the contractor if the contract or some other agreement stipulates that the employer will pay a sum of money up front to the contractor. It does not expire until all the money advanced has been repaid by the contractor.

Retention Bond

A retention bond is provided by the contractor if the employer and the contractor have agreed, and it is recorded in the contract, that the traditional retention will not be deducted from interim payment certificates, but instead the contractor will provide a bond equal to the retention which would have been deducted (see 70: Retention). This kind of bond, which is becoming popular, normally expires on the date by which a traditional retention would have been completely released to the contractor.

Parent Company Guarantee

Parent company guarantees are sometimes confused with performance bonds. The idea of a parent company guarantee is that the guarantee is offered by the parent or holding company of the contractor. In most instances, a parent company guarantee guarantees the performance of the contact. That means that if the contractor defaults whether by insolvency or otherwise, the parent company will itself complete or pay for the additional costs of completion by another company. A disadvantage is that careful checks must be carried out to ensure as far as practicable that there is little chance of the parent company becoming insolvent at the same time as, or even before, the contractor. This kind of guarantee is usually drafted by or on behalf of the parent company. It is often offered where the contract calls for a performance bond. It should not be accepted in lieu of a performance bond unless it has been thoroughly checked by the employer's solicitor.

22

Assignment

This word is bandied about frequently but rarely understood by the person using it or the listener. It is found in building contracts and terms of engagement, usually on the basis that neither party can assign something without consent.

When two people agree a contract, they each agree that they have certain rights and certain duties. For example, in a building contract, the employer has a right to receive the finished building but has a duty to pay the contractor for it. The contractor has the right to receive payment but has a duty to construct the building.

The person having rights in a contract can transfer those rights to another person. That is assignment. So, a contractor can assign its right to receive payment to another party, for example a bank. The assignment must be in writing and the other party to the contract (in this example the employer) must be notified. Once done, the contactor no longer has the right to receive payment, the bank now has that right and the employer would then comply with its obligations under the contract if it paid the bank instead of the contractor.

Duties cannot be assigned except by novation (see 59: Novation), but they can usually be sub-contracted. The contractor's duty to provide the building for the employer can be sub-contracted to one or more other persons. However, sub-contracting does not remove the duty from the contractor, which is still responsible for providing the building.

There is normally a clause in construction-related contracts which forbids assignment without the permission of the other party.

Professional Practice for Architects and Project Managers, First Edition. David Chappell.

23

Contracts

General

Every person involved in the construction industry must understand what is meant by a 'contract'. Ideally, everyone whether in the construction industry or not should understand contracts because they affect much of our lives. Like anything else, it is easy to make contracts a complicated topic, but the essentials are pretty straightforward.

We all have duties to one another under the general law. For example, the law says that I may not walk up to you and punch you in the face. Even if the law did not say anything about that, it would be something that hopefully we would all understand. There are complicated laws dealing with road users and purchase of property which apply to all.

But sometimes two people or two companies may want to agree rights and duties to each other which are additional to what the general law would imply. For example, I may want you to design a house for me and you may stipulate £1000 as the fee for creating it. I have a right to receive a design from you, but I have a duty to pay you £1000 for it. You a right to the £1000, but a duty to supply me with the design. That would be a contract.

Of course, there would be all kinds of other things which also would have to be agreed, such as the date by which I wanted the design and what exactly I wanted from the house. You would also want the timing of payments of the fee to be agreed. That is why even the simplest contracts can become quite complicated. It is sometimes said that for a contract to exist, there must be an offer and an acceptance. That is true so far as it goes, but I think it is simpler to understand to say that there must be an agreement.

A contract may be in writing, such as one of the RIBA Professional Service Contracts, or an exchange of letters or emails. A contract may be oral, i.e. by word of mouth, or it may be partly in writing and partly oral. The problem with oral contracts is proving that they exist and what the terms are. It can be confusing. The late film producer Louis B. Mayer is alleged to have said: 'An oral contract is not worth the paper it's written on'. Although the sentence is meaningless we all know what he meant.

What is Essential in a Contract?

People get confused between a promise by one person to do something for another person and a contract. For example, if I agree to meet you for a meal at a nearby restaurant and later I think better of it and simply do something else instead, can you sue me for not

Professional Practice for Architects and Project Managers, First Edition. David Chappell.

doing what we agreed? First of all, the law does not treat social agreements as binding legal contracts. So, a broken promise to attend dinner in a restaurant would usually not be a broken contract. If the meal had been arranged in connection with some business deal and was an essential part of the deal, it may be a different story.

Without getting into huge complications, the basic essentials for a contract are:

- an agreement
- an intention to create a legal relationship
- something given by both persons.

Agreement

An agreement is usually demonstrated by showing that one person made an offer and another person accepted it. In the earlier example you offered to design my house for £1000 and I accepted it. Sometimes, of course, it is not nearly as clear as that and whether there is an agreement only becomes clear by looking at dozens of email exchanges or a mixture of email exchanges and telephone calls or texts. What it really comes down to is this: would a reasonable person looking at all the information conclude that there was an agreement?

Another question follows on from whether there was an agreement: agreement about what? In other words, what must be agreed in order for there to be a contract? In general, the following must be agreed:

- the identities of the persons involved (seems obvious but believe me it can get complicated, like a project I know where two limited companies effectively swopped names)
- what each is to do (e.g. design, construct, pay etc.)
- any time constraints.

Acts of Parliament may stipulate things which must be in certain kinds of contract.

Intention to Create a Legal Relationship

An intention to create a legal relationship is usually assumed where any kind of commercial transaction is involved and, if there is a disagreement with that assumption, the person disagreeing must prove it.

Something Given by Both Persons

Something given by both persons sounds simple and it usually is simple, but it can become complicated. In my example you give the design and all the skill and experience required to create it and I give the £1000. In a construction contract, the contractor constructs the building and the employer pays the price. Lawyers call this 'consideration', but I promised not to mention overtly legalities (such as consideration) and I hope that is the last time.

An example of a not quite so simple giving of something is if Lucy agrees not to do something that she was going to do if Joe agrees to do something. Both situations count as 'giving' something although Lucy could be said to be giving up something. Obviously, what each person does has to have some benefit for the other, but the benefit does not necessarily have to be equal. Very often a third person seeing what has been agreed may be surprised at what seems to be an unequal bargain. The only criterion is that what each does must have some value to the other.

When talking about contracts, it is customary to refer to the 'parties' to the contract. That is convenient when reference to 'persons' would not be appropriate, for example where one or both parties are local authorities, universities, or limited companies.

Breaking the Contract

It is usual to talk about a contract being signed or 'executed' (the legal term I'm afraid). The kind of contracts we are thinking about are legally binding. What that means is that once the contract is agreed, neither person can simply decide to ignore it without serious consequences. If one person does something which the contract does not allow or fails to do something which the contract requires to be done, this is called a 'breach' of contract.

In my example, if I refuse to pay the full £1000 or if your design is late or if you do not design the house I asked for, these are all breaches of contract. It is said that the unconventional American architect Frank Lloyd Wright could get away with telling his clients what he was going to give them (despite what they asked for), but that is not for ordinary mortals to try. It is not always appreciated that a contractor who provides a better-quality item than specified is also in breach of contract, although most clients would happily accept the breach in that instance.

The person who is not in breach is usually entitled to receive payment from the person who commits the breach to make up for the breach. That is called 'damages'. The amount of money to be paid is normally calculated so as to put the injured party back in the same position as if the breach had not occurred. Sometimes that is easy, for example I could be ordered by a court to pay the balance of the £1000. Or you might be ordered to pay the fees of another architect to finish the design you failed to complete. Often it is more complicated than that.

Repudiation

A really serious breach of contract may be what is called 'repudiation'. That is a breach which is so serious that it shows that one of the persons is not prepared to comply with the contract in an important way. For example, if I refused to pay anything for your design or you pocketed my £1000 but refused to provide a design. A contractor would repudiate the building contract by simply walking off site before the job was finished. An employer could do it by telling the contractor to whistle for his money.

If you are faced with a repudiation by a client, you can either accept it and seek damages or say that you are going to carry on with it (this is called 'affirming the contract'). You would still be entitled to seek damages even after affirmation. Obviously, there are many instances where it is just impossible to carry on as if nothing had happened, for example if the client sends an email telling you that you are sacked.

Two Types of Contract

There are two types of contract:

- simple contracts
- deeds (or specialty) contracts.

Most contracts are simple contracts. If you wish to make a contract in the form of a deed, it has to be done in a particular way. Before 1989, all deeds had to be made by fixing a seal to the document. That could be in wax, but more often it was simply a circular piece of red paper or even a rubber stamp. Nowadays, Acts of Parliament set out the process. In brief, the document must clearly state that it is a deed and both parties must sign in one of a number of ways. The alternative ways are usefully set out in JCT contracts in the attestation section (the pages where both parties sign).

A deed is a very serious type of contract. The main characteristics of a deed are:

- There is no need for both parties to 'give' something. A promise that one party will do something for the other is legally binding.
- The limitation period is 12 years (see 24: Limitation Period).
- Statements in a deed are conclusive as to their truth so far as the parties to the deed are concerned.

Therefore, do not rush into signing a deed.

24

Limitation Period

Some General Thoughts

It is recognised by the law that there must be limits on the length of time after an event that another person can take legal proceedings about that event. It is generally agreed that a civilised society cannot accept that you should be able to sue me 20 years after you say that I did something that cost you a lot of money. I would certainly not remember (that is particularly true nowadays) and I would be surprised that you remembered. The limitation period is mostly something which has been decided by Act of Parliament. It is important for architects in various ways. Actually, there are several different limitation periods. They are called 'limitation' because they limit the periods during which a person may start successful legal proceedings in various circumstances.

Most people have a general idea about what the limitation period is. People sometimes say that 'time is barred' meaning the same thing. We have limitation clauses in contracts and we hear about limitation of actions. Unfortunately, most of the general ideas are not wrong but only partly correct. That is worse than being totally wrong of course – a little knowledge and all that.

What follows concentrates on the periods most likely to affect people in the construction industry. For example, the periods relating to crimes or accidental injury are not considered.

In the Case of a Contract

Where simple contracts (see 23: Contracts) are concerned, the period is 6 years from the date of the breach of contract. Put another way, the injured party must start legal proceedings within 6 years from the date of the breach.

A breach of contract is when someone does not do something which the contract says they must do or does something which the contract says they must not do. This is probably the most common situation in construction where the limitation period is involved. For example, if the contractor omits a damp proof course which is specified on the drawings and in the bills of quantities or in the specification, that is a breach of contract. The breach probably occurs when the contractor should have inserted the damp proof course but failed to do so.

Reading this, you are perhaps thinking, 'Why has he written "probably," what we are looking for here is a bit of certainty'. I do sympathise with that view, but the fact is that,

Professional Practice for Architects and Project Managers, First Edition. David Chappell.

although the Acts of Parliament may state the basic position, it is left to the courts to interpret individual cases. If there is a great deal of money at stake and the limitation period is on the brink of expiring or not quite expired, there may be a big argument about when exactly the breach occurred. In the example of the damp proof course, the argument might be whether the breach occurred when the first part of the damp proof course should have been inserted or whether it did not occur until the last part should part been inserted or whether there was a succession of separate breaches when each part of the damp proof course was omitted.

In the case of a construction contract, there may be dozens of breaches of contract by the contractor, each one of which has its own 6-year limitation period. Very importantly, the 6-year limitation period for all of those breaches starts again on the date of practical completion. That is because the contractor has two sets of obligations. The first is to do the work in accordance with the contract as the work progresses. The second obligation is to complete the work in accordance with the contract. Therefore, in the case of a very lengthy contract, the employer may take action for a breach of contract which occurred near the beginning of the work and for which the limitation period may have expired or the employer can simply wait until practical completion has been certified and then there is a further 6-year period available.

If the contract is a deed, sometimes known as a specialty contract, the limitation period is 12 years from the date of the breach. Otherwise, the comments for simple contracts with a 6-year period apply to deeds with the alteration of the period of time.

Of course, it is not only contractors who might be sued by employers. Architects may be sued by clients for breaches of the conditions of engagement (or clients sued by architects of course). If the limitation period is about to run out, there may be serious arguments about whether the architect's alleged breach occurred when the drawings were issued or when the contractor built from them. In general terms it is likely that the 6- or 12-year limitation period so far as claims by the client against the architect are concerned probably starts from the issue of the final certificate for a particular project.

In the Case of Negligence, Trespass, and Nuisance

Negligence, trespass, nuisance, and several other less common situations are all called by the collective name of 'torts'. In the case of negligence, the limitation period commences when the damage occurs and the period is 6 years. Problems arose in the past because damage can occur even if no one is aware of it. There was a famous example where a chimney suffered cracks long before anyone was aware. That kind of unknown damage is called 'latent damage' and Parliament decided that statute should be changed to allow for that. Therefore, the position is that in the case of latent damage to buildings, the period is either 6 years from the date on which the damage occurred or if the potential claimant did not know about the damage at the end of 6 years, 3 years from when the claimant became aware of the damage and any other relevant facts. There is a cut-off date of 15 years after the date that the damage occurred even if the potential claimant still does not know about it.

For various reasons, proceedings in negligence are not as easy and, therefore, not as common as they used to be.

Legal Proceedings

Just because the limitation period has expired does not mean (except in Scotland) that the claimant has no right to sue. What it means is that if proceedings are started after the end of the period, the person being sued simply has to refer to the limitation period and the case will be thrown out even if it is clear to everyone that the person should be liable. Invoices can be affected if not paid within 6 years of the invoice date. However, the period is re-started if the debtor admits the debt. Sometimes a court will say that the limited period does not apply at all. This is usually in a case where some fault has been deliberately concealed on site. In that kind of case, a court will probable allow the case to proceed even if well outside the normal period. Architects may be caught if called in by a client within the limitation period to comment on a presumed defect and if the architect gives the client reassurance which turns out to be misjudged, causing the client to do nothing until the limitation period has expired. The period will often be treated as unexpired in that situation.

If the limitation period is almost expired and the potential claimant has not decided whether to sue or not decided who should be sued, the claimant's solicitor may cause a claim form (used to be called a writ) to be issued to safeguard the claimant's position. The potential target of the claim form may be totally unaware that it has been issued and it may be some months later that the claim form is actually served on (i.e. given to) the target person. There is a limit to the length of time after the claim form is issued before it must be served or expire.

Amended by the Contract

It is not always realised that a clause can be put into a contract changing the limitation period. Although the change is usually to extend the period, it is open to the parties to a contract to stipulate that legal actions under the contract must be commenced earlier than the 6 or 12 years. Even if the contract is executed as a deed, the limitation period may be reduced from 12 to 6 years or even less by a contract clause. It is very common in professional terms of engagement to find that an attempt has been made to increase the limitation period. So beware.

25

Confidentiality

Different Kinds of Confidentiality

Confidentiality is a much-misunderstood concept. It is also quite complex. Leaving aside situations where information is protected by statute, such as the Data Protection Act 1998 etc., the basic principle is that someone who has been given information in confidence is not entitled to take unfair advantage of it. That is pretty straightforward and easy to understand. There are four classes of information for this purpose:

- trade secrets
- personal confidences
- government information
- artistic and literary confidences.

The law recognises that certain relationships give rise to a duty to maintain confidentiality, but the obligation to respect confidence is not limited to cases where the parties are in a contractual relationship. Nevertheless, the instances where architects, quantity surveyors, and other professionals in the construction industry become involved in confidential matters usually concern employment and relationships between professional and client.

Employment

Every person in employment has a duty to safeguard confidential information. In an employment scenario, the information is mainly, although not exclusively, things that are categorised as 'trade secrets'. This is the information which an employee may obtain during the course of employment, but which is specific to the particular employer. Such things as fee rates, profits, and financial information generally fall into this category, but also discussions about such things as the future direction of the practice, ways of obtaining commissions, and long-term plans. It is unlawful for an employee to reveal such matters to others even after leaving the practice. The kind of information that an architect or surveyor gains while carrying out various projects is not usually confidential, it is simply part of professional experience. 'Artistic' but probably not 'literary' confidences may be involved where artists and architects are employed by architects in connection with projects. This is similar to trade secrets but specifically related to artistic work.

Professional Practice for Architects and Project Managers, First Edition. David Chappell.

Relationship Between Professional and Client

In any architect/client relationship there must be confidence and trust if it is to work properly. This falls generally under the 'personal confidences' category. Each must be aware that discussions about the project are mostly confidential information and not to be shared with third parties except with the permission of the other party. Most terms of engagement make this clear by including confidentiality clauses between architect and client. Even if there are no specific confidentiality clauses in the terms of engagement, there is still likely to be a similar duty of confidentiality implied. Photographs of the interiors of houses taken by the architect may offend against privacy and thus breach confidentiality unless permission from the client is given. Photographs of the exterior are less likely to breach confidentiality, but photographs of gardens may do so.

What if there is a Breach of Confidentiality?

The injured person may ask the court to award an amount of money (damages) to compensate the injured person or to make an injunction (see 6: Copyright) against the infringer. Damages will often be appropriate but in some instances the court may also make an injunction to stop the infringer revealing more confidential information or to prevent a threatened revelation.

Some General Things

A thing cannot be confidential if everyone knows about it, but it may be confidential even if a few people already know. Many building contracts have a clause preventing the contractor from revealing information about the project to third parties. It is usually obvious and a matter of common sense whether information is intended to be confidential.

In deciding whether to allow publication of what would normally be considered confidential, the courts can take into account whether or not it is in the public interest.

Discussions with local authority planning officers would be treated as confidential by the courts. If you discuss a development idea with the officer, it would be a breach of confidentiality for the officer to reveal it to a third party.

'Government information' may arise where professionals, contractors, and subcontractors are involved in projects for government purposes and those involved may be required to sign various undertakings.

26

Reasonable Time

This is a phrase that is often seen and heard. Contracts are fond of stating that something should be done in a reasonable time. We have all heard it, but what does it actually mean? If you are expecting a simple answer, you might as well stop reading here and move on to another topic. Every professional person has heard the phrase ‘reasonable skill and care’, but what does ‘reasonable’ mean in that context? The reasonable in ‘reasonable skill and care’ ought to be well known to all architects. It has been defined as the standard of the ordinary skilled person exercising and professing to have that special skill.

What is a reasonable time will depend upon the circumstances of each particular case. It is used when it is impossible to set down exactly how much time is intended, but it is not desired to allow as much time as the person performing the action decides to give it. It could be described as an ‘appropriate time’ in some cases. A contract may say that a contractor must rectify defects within a reasonable time. We all know roughly what that means. It means that the contractor does not have to treat the defects as extremely urgent. But, on the other hand, the contractor is not entitled to leave the defects for several months unattended. One person may say that the contractor should do the rectification within a month, another might say within 6 weeks and another, 2 weeks. But then, the contractor may say that it has to organise the several different sub-contractors to do the work and some of the defects are quite substantial and require careful preparation. That, of course is one of the circumstances that has to be taken into account.

If a contract does not fix a time for doing something, it will usually, but not always, be implied that it should be done within a reasonable time. Because we all have our own ideas about what is a reasonable time or a reasonable anything else and because each idea will probably be different and because only a judge, arbitrator or adjudicator can say with any authority what a reasonable time is in any particular situation, we must be flexible when confronted with this phrase and, in practice, use a broad-brush approach.

It is much, much better to be specific if at all possible.

Professional Practice for Architects and Project Managers, First Edition. David Chappell.

27

The Build

I know this is a digression, but I do hate the way that in the last year or two, people have started talking about 'the build' when they mean 'the construction'. 'How are they getting on with the build?' people ask. What they mean is 'How are they getting on with the construction?' 'Build' is a verb, not a noun. Some architects are guilty of this misuse. I have even seen court judgments containing the expression. It all seems to stem from a certain TV programme during which members of the public with a yen to construct their own houses, seemingly with little or no assistance from architects or surveyors and with occasional assistance from various tradespeople, are depicted lurching from one near disaster to another until everything turns out well in the end. The construction process is always referred to as 'the build' as though to emphasise the sheer amateurishness of the whole thing. I am surprised that JCBs are not called 'big shovellery things' and bricks 'wall bits'. Enough of that.

Professional Practice for Architects and Project Managers, First Edition. David Chappell.

Section II

Dealing with Clients

28

Extent of Services

Full Architectural Services

Let me describe a common situation. Mr and Mrs Smith want you to design a house. You are engaged for full architectural services. You survey the site, take the clients' brief, secure planning permission and building control approval. You then prepare full construction drawings and a specification and invite tenderers on behalf of your clients, possibly advising your clients about the best tender. Around about this stage, your clients drop their bombshell. They tell you that they have decided that, now they have all the approvals and a set of drawings and specification, they do not need you because they feel sure that the contractor will be able to carry on without your assistance. Another key factor in their decision, but rarely actually mentioned, is that they will also save quite a lot of money on your fees.

A surprising number of architects take the news as just their bad luck and nothing to be done about it. Actually, there is quite a lot that can be done about it. The first thing to understand is that, if the appointment document states that you will carry out full services and the clients will pay you for that, there is a legally binding contract. Therefore, if the clients decide that they do not want you to continue after a certain stage and refuse to pay you after that, they are in serious breach of contract. The breach is often referred to as a 'fundamental breach'. It is a repudiation of the contract (see 100: Termination). If you accept it, and you really have little option, you are entitled to damages from your clients to compensate you for the breach. That kind of damages usually consists of the profit you would have made if you had been allowed to continue. So, the good news is that you can ask Mr and Mrs Smith nicely for the lost profit and if they do not pay, you can ask your solicitor to get the money for you.

Unacceptable Partial Services

However, what Mr and Mrs Smith may have said when informing you that they did not want you to carry out the remaining services was that they or the contractor may well seek your advice about various things as they go along, for which they would be happy to pay you on a time charge basis. Many architects will seize the opportunity to see the project to conclusion, be able to earn at least some fees from the new situation, and will agree to provide ongoing telephone advice and even visit the site if requested to do so. Hopefully, now aware that you are entitled to all the lost profit, you will not succumb to the temptation to earn additional fees this way because they would only be deducted from your damages in any event and, as we shall see, possibly give you liabilities you can do without.

There is a danger if you agree to be available on a casual basis. Many architects are engaged on the basis that they will perform a complete service up to the point of a contractor being selected and then revert to a casual basis after that.

Let us be clear. If you are to provide a full service, your clients will be relying on you from the initial survey and brief right to the final certificate you issue. If you completely stop providing the service after the contractor has been selected, the clients will no longer be relying upon you, they will be relying on the contractor. If you are providing a full service, you will be responsible for the design and, if there is an error on your drawing, it will be up to you to put it right. If the contractor does not construct in accordance with your drawings and specification, the clients will expect you to discover any important failures on the contractor's part and the clients may be able to sue you for damages if they can show that you did not carry out your inspection duties properly. If you completely stop providing the service, not only will the contractor be responsible for constructing the project in accordance with your drawings and specification, the contractor will also be responsible for checking that your drawings and specification work. It is no use the contractor saying that it built to your drawings and there was a mistake in them. The contractor should have checked them. It is all a question of whom the clients rely on.

Dangers

If you have allowed yourself to be used on a casual basis, the position is not at all clear. You will certainly be liable if you give the contractor or your clients the wrong answer to any questions. The clients would no longer be simply relying on the contractor; they would be relying, at least partly and probably to a substantial degree, upon you. If you visited the site in response to a message from the contractor to sort out a problem with two drawings which do not quite correspond and you did not carry out a full site inspection on that occasion, you might well become liable for a defect which was present somewhere on the site at the time you visited. But your clients will not be happy to pay for a full site inspection. Once you are removed from the project, you have no idea what the client and contractor may have decided to do. There is a strong possibility that the contractor will have done various things which do not correspond with your drawings or specification. That might include, as in one notable case I recall, adding another metre or so on to the end of the building. How can you possibly give limited advice about a building in those circumstances?

I once had to defend an architect who was not employed after tender stage, but who was asked to visit site by an urgent call from the contractor. Unfortunately, she did what many architects would do: she went to site, although she had no duty to do so. Whilst there, she assisted in what she believed was the solution to the problem. Only later, when the client decided to report her to the Architects Registration Board did she realise that the contractor had not revealed important information that day on site. Nevertheless, she was subject to serious allegations of unprofessional conduct and incompetence. Fortunately, it was decided that there was no case for her to answer but you may not be so fortunate.

What to Do

The golden rule in this kind of situation (my golden rule anyway) is that you can give a client a partial service, if that is what they want, but the partial service must start at the beginning (RIBA Stage 0) and may stop at any convenient point. For example, you can just proceed as far as making a planning application or producing drawings sufficient for building control. Obviously, once you commit to acting as contract administrator, there is no sensible place to stop until you have issued the final certificate. Once you have stopped, by agreement or at the request of the client, you must make clear to the client that you cannot, under any circumstances, be involved again.

Some architects cannot understand and a common objection is that the client will think it very strange if they make that kind of stipulation. Frankly, one of the problems with the architectural profession is that, for one reason or another, they sometimes fail to act like professionals. It can be very instructive in these situations to compare what an architect would do to what a solicitor or hospital consultant or any other professional person would do in a comparable situation. For example, can you imagine the reaction you would get if you engaged a solicitor to act for you in a case going to the high court and after counsel had been engaged and drafted the initial pleadings you said to the solicitor: 'Well, thank you for what you have done so far, I think I can do it myself from now on. If there are any problems, I will get some more advice from you.' I am pretty sure the answer would be that either the solicitor would be retained to manage the rest of the court process or the client could forget about getting further advice.

A hospital consultant will order you various tests and diagnose your ailment then prescribe a course of treatment under his supervision, perhaps as a patient in hospital. If you tell him that, having heard the proposed treatment, you feel that you can deal with it at home because your brother used to be a nurse and he can help you and will the consultant just write out a prescription for the drugs involved, the consultant will doubtless impress upon you that you do need his professional help in a hospital environment. That might be the moment at which you tell him that, if you have any problems, you can always give him a ring. Obviously, the consultant would have nothing to do with your silly plans.

It may be thought that these examples are rather far-fetched, and so they are, because that kind of situation must rarely occur with solicitors or hospital consultants or, indeed, other professionals. Yet it occurs with astounding regularity where architects are concerned. Clients frequently tell architects that they do not want them after tender stage, but they will get in touch again if there are any problems – and architects agree.

Acceptable Partial Services

Of course, there are other kinds of partial services which are perfectly fine, for example if a client needs to appoint a replacement architect for one who is no longer acting in that capacity. The project may be at a stage half way through the production drawings or it may actually be on site and the building partly constructed. You should be able to take on this kind of role, but you must be aware that you are not entitled to assume that anything done before is done correctly. You must allow time, and the appropriate fees, to carefully check everything before you start your input. You will be liable just as if you had been the architect from the beginning unless you identify any errors and notify your client.

You may be engaged to report on defects or act as an expert witness or provide a specific piece of advice. These are all straightforward matters, although they do require different skills. But what if you are appointed to provide architectural services on a project where you will not be the contract administrator, but where there will be a project manager or construction manager organising all the disciplines involved and carrying out all the certification and instruction duties which would normally be done by an architect?

The essential point is that you must have terms of engagement which set out exactly what you will be doing and how that fits in with the powers and duties of the other members of the team. You must not enter into any appointment which leaves your duties vague. Requirements that you will attend on site or meetings etc. 'as and when required by the project manager' are unacceptable and should be rejected. If anything cannot be specified, it must be made clear that it will be subject to a separate time charge. If you are to be liable for advising the project manager of the presence of defects or whether practical completion has been achieved, you must be entitled to visit the site as and when you see fit and not simply when the project manager feels ready to issue a certificate. Job titles such as 'Lead Designer' or 'Lead Consultant' or even 'Architect' are not sufficient in themselves to accurately specify your duties in that kind of contract environment.

29

Difficult Clients

What do I mean by 'Difficult'?

Many architects complain about difficult clients. We must differentiate between difficult clients and clients with difficult problems. The first are not to be tolerated, but the second is the architect's bread and butter with occasional jam. There are lots of awkward clients but the trick is not to have a problem with them. They tend to be senior professional people or business executives who are used to getting their own way and who are used to making important decisions. This kind of client should be avoided, but it is difficult to spot them at a first meeting because they will be unfailing charming. As a project progresses, difficult clients start to show their true temperament.

They are usually bullies. They will expect you to read their minds, finish your initial sketch designs almost before the first meeting has finished. They will tell you that your suggested feasibility study is just another way to charge more fees, and think you are not giving a good service unless you present at least four options for the scheme and are prepared to produce scheme after scheme until they are entirely satisfied. At this point they may decide that they want to build on another site with a fresh design. Any complaints and they tell you that it is just design development (see 45: Design Development). They refuse to pay any additional fees no matter how much extra work they want you to do. They insist that construction work must start two or three weeks after the final design is chosen and they continue to change the brief as you are producing drawings for construction. These clients insist on having good old Bill Smith who once built them a garden shed included on the list to tender for a new office block. When tenders come in, they interfere with the process and demand that the cheapest, but half a day late, tender is accepted. When the project eventually comes to site, they visit site and give direct instructions without telling you and when the contractor submits valuations, they insist you certify less and so on and so on.

Some Thoughts

I was told by one client that I was the first architect to attempt to charge for additional work caused by factors outside my control. Another large client informed me that I was the first architect to suggest the use of consultants. Those clients who kindly imparted this information stared me straight in the eyes with frank honest expressions on their faces – always something to distrust in my experience. There is something very

Professional Practice for Architects and Project Managers, First Edition. David Chappell.

crushing about being told that I am the first person to raise a particularly distasteful topic, especially if accompanied by a disbelieving stare suggesting that I have taken leave of my senses. It is a ploy, of course, and one which is being used with increasing frequency.

If your client tries to intimidate you by saying that you are the first architect who has ever suggested that he or she should give detailed answers to your briefing questions rather than simply drawing up the ink smeared sketch you have received, say, 'Obviously the others were not doing their jobs properly'.

People respect doctors and surgeons because they rummage about inside people and prescribe medicines with unpronounceable names. Solicitors are respected on account of the arcane legal cases they can quote. The sad fact is that what architects do appears to be easy. Someone sees a finished building and probably thinks, 'I could have done that'.

The Answer

The question is: what can you do about these people? The answer is straightforward but not easy for many architects. In general, although with notable exceptions, architects are gentle souls, nice people who want nothing more than to see their designs built. They love solving design problems and they dislike confrontation. Well, we all do, but most architects will do a lot to avoid it, and there is the problem.

You cannot avoid getting the occasional difficult client. But you must always behave in a thoroughly professional manner. The client must understand, right from the outset, that you will be friendly but not over-friendly and that you will provide an excellent service, but that you are not prepared to cut corners; in short, that there is only one way you practise and that is the right way. Do not accept invitations to have dinner with your clients or accept anything which might make you indebted to them even to a small extent. Do not smile in a knowing conspiratorial way when your client tells you that he has a plan to get around the VAT rules. Do not even think about agreeing to produce construction drawings depicting the scheme that the planners turned down when your client tells you that no one will know. Always be able to say, 'No, I am not going to do that'.

Once your client has accepted that you are going to act in a very straightforward professional manner and do your job, not inordinately quickly but properly, you will be ready for the first difficulty which crops up. As things progress, you must never agree to something which is unprofessional or bad practice. If you give in to bullying once, it will be more difficult to resist the next time. If your client wants you to say that you can get tenders in and a start on site in an unfeasibly short time, you must say that it is not practicable to do that while still delivering a good project. Always get client's instructions in writing, email is fine, and always, always confirm in writing what you say to your client. If, in one or two early situations you stand your ground, it is likely that your client will get the message and a reasonable relationship should develop. If not, if your client persists in being difficult, make sure that your terms of engagement allow you to terminate your engagement at will, then simply terminate. It is not worth the aggravation and hassle of going on.

I have had my architect clients say to me that it is very difficult to say 'No' to a client. But that is because the architect concerned has never said 'No' before. Of course, there are other considerations. Clients know that some architects are desperate for work and they take advantage of that desperation to become really unpleasant. There is no real answer to that except to say that working for no one is better than working for bullying clients because bullying clients will cost you money and you may finish by facing a large claim. Architects often ask me how they can walk away from a difficult client. It is a real problem for them.

Sometimes clients will become abusive. There is only one way to deal with this and that is to plainly state and confirm in writing that any further abuse will result in your immediately terminating (make sure that your terms include the right to terminate at will). I have only once had an abusive client. Well, he was not strictly abusive, but he was shouting and screaming down the telephone. It might well have contained some abuse, but I did not hear properly because I hung up and terminated my engagement and submitted fees to date which were paid. The man's wife was surprised when she heard that I had terminated and asked me why. I said that her husband had been shouting and screaming down the telephone at me. 'Oh', she said, 'He does that sometimes'. 'Not to me', I said. I have never put up with difficult clients for long.

30

Getting Appointed

The Problems

Some architects cannot wait to have their own practices. As soon as they have done their obligatory professional practice time working in offices, passed the final examination, and registered as architects, they leave to set up in business alone or with some other like-minded person. If they have any business sense at all, they will have made sure that they have one or two projects to do. The days when an architect could simply put up a brass plate, sit back, and wait for a string of commissions are long gone, if they ever existed. When the initial project is drawing to a close, the worry will inevitably be where the next job is coming from. Many such young practices survive and go on to become prosperous, but many more soon collapse as shortage of jobs and, therefore, income makes it necessary to abandon self-employment and seek a position in an established office. Even established architectural practices suffer from lack of work at various times. This may be due to changes in the general economic climate or something more particular to the office location and experience.

At some point in the history of every practice, large or small, the question of how to get appointed to the next job becomes very important. Human nature being what it is, the question sometimes does not get consideration until it is suddenly realised that there will be nothing to do in six months' time and partners' meetings suddenly become more frequent. To be realistic, that question should always be in the forefront of the minds of sole principals, partners or directors. Although I can remember when the idea of a professional person openly marketing services was frowned upon or even prohibited, that is no longer the case.

The very best way of getting appointed to a commission is to build up a large number of clients who keep returning every time they require some construction work and recommend you to others. In that way, you will be automatically appointed. Of course, in order to get to that situation, you have to make sure that the service you give to every client is the very best. In order to give that service, you must attract clients in the first place.

Below is a list of things you can do to attract clients and other thoughts in no particular order with a few comments on each.

Professional Practice for Architects and Project Managers, First Edition. David Chappell.

Market when You are Busy

This sounds silly. Why market if you are busy? The answer is that a busy bustling practice attracts clients provided that an effort is made to do so. For a client to walk into an architect's office where there seems to be nothing going on is discouraging. I once worked in a practice where, due to a countrywide depression, the work had fallen off to the extent that 30 architects became 10 and there were lots of empty drawing boards (those were the days). An important potential client was expected and the three studio rooms were transformed. We did not go to the extent of hiring people to come in and sit at the boards for the day, but we did make sure that every drawing board had a drawing pinned on it, coats were hung on the back of most of the stools where we sat and, during the visit, everyone stayed in the office and half busily went from one room to another carrying rolls of drawings or other papers while the other five sat at their boards working earnestly on mostly fictitious work. We had got a friend outside to keep telephoning the office so that the phones were always ringing. They were desperate measures, but we secured the commission. I am not suggesting that you should emulate that but it does show the effect of a busy office on a potential, but possibly undecided, client.

Keep in the Public Eye

If you send out mailshots, make sure that the letter gives information, perhaps about an interesting new building that you have completed or an exciting new construction technique or material, but do not give more than a significant fact and invite the reader to contact you for more information.

Try writing articles, not for the professional press but for local newspapers or journals. Choose a topical subject and whatever you do, do not indulge in that dreadful 'architectspeak' so beloved of a certain kind of architect. If you are explaining a building, do it simply and clearly. Do not expect to get paid for the article.

Make sure your local TV and radio stations and local press know that you are always available to give comments from an architect's point of view on any news item that may arise. Then make sure that you are always up to date on local affairs. When being interviewed by journalists, be careful what you say and on radio or TV speak clearly and to the point, '… hms' and '… ers' are to be avoided.

Offer your services as a lecturer on architectural topics to local societies. Amenity societies and the like are always looking for a good speaker. History societies are another good contact if you have a good grasp of, and interest in, architectural history, particularly of any local building.

Advertise in local newspapers or journals, including making sure that the local press is in attendance, including photographers when any of your buildings are completed.

There is nothing wrong with having a practice brochure, but it is more important to have a frequently updated website and note it on your letters and emails. If you must have photographs of 'the team', forsake all those casual, lounging about the office or laughing group photographs. Potential clients are not really interested in whether you all get on really well together or had a spiffing time when you visited the brewery. Photographs of staff are fine, but they should be separate portraits with something about the expertise of each person.

Do not forget social media, which can be very effective provided it is used with discretion.

Competitions

If you win an architectural competition, it will generate lots of publicity for you as well as for the project for which you compete. Be careful that you do not invest too much time and effort in this because it is obvious that more people are unsuccessful than those who succeed. However, if the building is very prestigious, there may be exhibitions featuring all the shortlisted competitors.

Contacts

Contacts may be a good method of securing appointments if they are the right contacts. The old joke about people joining golf clubs to get work but only meeting other people seeking work has more than a grain of truth. In my experience, most successful contacts are those one makes accidentally. Although you cannot plan that, by making sure you have as high a local profile as possible, you increase the chances of making useful contacts.

Direct Approaches

It is always worthwhile taking the initiative by directly contacting a company if you hear that it may be thinking of expanding or even just refurbishing its factory or offices. Unless you have a contact in a fairly senior position, it is best to simply write to the chief executive, offering to call and discuss possibilities.

A Few Don'ts

- Don't waste your time doing freebies for friends you never knew you had.
- Don't accept a commission at a poor fee because the project is fantastic. It will not seem fantastic when you are not earning enough to pay your mortgage.
- Don't accept lots of commissions to do very small projects (garages and kitchen extensions) on the assumption that some of them will lead to much bigger projects; they will only lead to more small projects. Accept them of course if you want to make a career of small projects.
- Don't accept a commission if the client is not going to allow you sufficient time to do the project properly – it will end in tears.
- Don't accept a commission if you do not have the necessary skills.

Conclusion

The best form of marketing is relatively low key. Build up a client base by providing an excellent service and cherish them. The worst thing you can do is to appear desperate for a commission. That really puts people off.

31

Fees

The Importance of Proper Terms of Engagement

The most important question for all construction professionals really is fees. I have been asked 'How much should I charge?' ('as much as you can get'), 'Can I charge extra for dealing with claims?' (usually yes), 'How can I make my client pay?' (excellent question).

Before trying to answer any question about fees, it is necessary to establish the terms of engagement. If it is a professional who has been commissioned on one of the professional bodies' own appointment documents or on the professional's own terms and if the documents have been properly filled out to reflect the particular project, the terms should be clear. It should simply be a matter of seeing whether the fee question falls within one of the terms.

It is my experience that it is common for architects to enter into commissions on the basis of only an exchange of emails or that the contract is entirely oral with no, or the very briefest of, scribbled notes despite the RIBA and ARB Codes of Conduct. I once had to advise an architect who said he was owed a considerable sum in fees. He had carried out several projects for the same client, but on no occasion had he mentioned fees or terms either in a letter or orally. Therefore, recovering fees was by no means easy. When I asked why he had not quoted his fee rate at the beginning of each commission, he said that if he had done that, his client would have turned him down as being too expensive!

What if there are no Terms?

It is a common belief that even if architects and others do not enter into any kind of formal agreement with their clients, they will still be entitled to be paid for the work they do. That is broadly correct but, like most broadly held assumptions, there is more to it than that. It is uncertain whether there would be a legally binding contract, but the law would say that the client, in instructing the architect to perform services while knowing that architects charge fees for their services, had impliedly promised to pay the architect a reasonable sum for the services. This is what is commonly referred to as a *quantum meruit* and this is where the difficulties start. How much is a 'reasonable sum'?

'Haha', I hear you say, the courts must have already decided what a 'reasonable sum' is. The answer is 'Yes' and 'No'. The courts have certainly decided what a reasonable sum is in particular cases but they have not laid down any generally applicable rule to cover all cases and, of course, they cannot lay down one rule for every case. They would

Professional Practice for Architects and Project Managers, First Edition. David Chappell.

say that a 'reasonable sum' is one that is reasonable in all the circumstances. In other words, every situation will be different and must be judged on its own merits (see 26: Reasonable Time). It is sometimes said to amount to 'a fair commercial rate', but that gets you only a step further. At this point you are bitterly regretting your failure to enter into a proper contract with properly stated fees. The problem is that, whatever names we give to the payment, the difficulty is in translating that into what it actually means in money terms. Unfortunately, casual oral commissions do not include the method of calculating the actual fees due and you will either agree a payment which is much less than you would like or take your chances in court.

What are some Terms?

Sometimes the architect will have written to the client setting out the architectural service to be carried out and noting that terms are to be as 'RIBA terms'. Bear in mind that if you have not included a copy of the RIBA terms in question, the client may not be bound by them. One problem is that unless the client is used to dealing with RIBA terms, the client will not understand to what you are referring and, therefore, they will not be binding. Another problem, even if the client is aware of RIBA terms is that the RIBA issues appointment documents in several versions and each one is heavily dependent on the architect filling in the blanks with what has been agreed. To make matters worse, the client will often respond agreeing some things and disputing others, the architect in turn responds and at some stage during this procedure the architect starts work on the project. The question then is: 'At what stage did the parties agree on terms, if indeed they did, and what were those terms?' Unless agreement can be reached, the next stop will be the court and it will be expensive to find out what, if any, terms governed your appointment.

Claiming Extra Fees

Frequently, the architect will ask the client for extra fees as a result of extra work. Clients dislike the idea of extra fees intensely. They think that for a standard fee the architect should be prepared to do everything that becomes necessary whether at the whim of the client or otherwise. That is obviously unreasonable, but sometimes architects bind themselves to do just that. Some professional appointment contracts have clauses which deal with this kind of problem. You must ensure that clients give written agreement to budget costs for a project when the commission is received. I have dealt with instances where initial tenders were in excess of what the clients considered to be the limit of their budget and refused to pay the architects' fees in reducing the specification to save costs. In every case, the architect was clear that the actual lowest tender price was very near the budget figure. Where these architects made their mistake was in not at least confirming the budget figure to their clients at an early stage. Mistakes can be made and misunderstandings arise in every human endeavour. Confirming instructions in writing is not a sinister action but it is simply prudent, good business practice, and concentrates the recipient's mind wonderfully.

Architects sometimes wonder if they can charge extra fees for dealing with a contractor who is being particularly difficult in the matter of a claim for loss and expense, sending letters excessive in number and in length, demanding meeting after meeting and requiring the architect to be specific in giving reasons for rejecting the claim. It seems to me that there are two things to consider in dealing with this question. First: What does the architect's terms of engagement say? Second: is the contractor in breach of its contract?

Obviously, the architect's duties under the building contract include dealing with claims. However, most professional services contracts refer to dealing with contractor's claims for extensions of time or loss and expense as additional services. That is obviously because the architect cannot make any kind of estimate of how long it will take to deal with a contractor's, as yet unknown, claims.

The contractor must comply with the building contract in submitting claims, unless the claim is made outside the contract at common law in which case the architect could not deal with it. Therefore, the client probably has a claim against the contractor for that amount of these additional fees incurred as a result of the architect having to deal with contractor's claims which are wrongly made. In that case the contractor would be liable to the client for damages resulting from the contractor's breach of contract.

So far as the contractor's unreasonable demands through letters or meetings are concerned, the architect ought to be able to deal with those in the normal course of administering a contract (see 15: Writing Letters). It is difficult to say when an architect may be able to claim extra fees for dealing with an excessive number of defects or defects of great complexity. Dealing with defects is part of the architect's contract administration duties. It is a matter of judgement when the defects warrant so much work by the architect that it is greater than the architect ought reasonably to be expecting.

Getting Paid

How an architect can get the client to pay is a difficult question, the answer to which is like finding the Holy Grail. All that can be said is that you will have no chance of getting paid unless the conditions of engagement clearly state the amount you are to be paid, or some method of working out the sum, and when it is to be paid. If you are owed money by a client, you should be able to say something like: 'We agreed that I should be paid a total of £X in Y number equal instalments beginning on the Zth of each month and at monthly intervals thereafter'. If you can say that or something equally precise, you will have an excellent chance of being paid because the client will have no room to manoeuvre.

Of course, you can ask for money up front and payments on account thereafter. That is a good system if you can make it work. Do not make the mistake of getting money up front but then not invoicing until that up-front payment has been used. Aim to always have a balance in hand. Solicitors seem able to do it with impunity.

How much can be quoted is a matter for each architect. There will always be a price below which the architect will lose money. That is the bottom line. Timesheets kept for other projects should indicate an appropriate rate on which the architect can get the return required. The moral of all this is not just 'get terms in writing', but rather 'get terms clearly in writing'. Then you should have no substantial fee recovery problems.

If the sum owed is under £10 000, a claim through the small claims court is useful. This is relatively cheap and even if the architect loses, the judge will not award huge sums in costs. If claiming through that court, remember that the judge will not be an expert in construction matters and the claim will simply be for money owed but not paid. Your claim will stand the best chance of success if it is presented simply and clearly with numbered paragraphs giving details of the relevant part of the appointment dealing with payment, the invoice amount, and any letters requesting payment. If it is lack of payment for drawing work, it will assist the judge and your case if you produce copies of the drawings in question, time sheets etc.

Adjudication is not usually appropriate for claiming smallish sums of money because of the costs of paying someone to present the case. Although adjudication started out as something that anyone might do (see 107: Adjudication), there have been so many legal decisions that it needs a real expert to represent you. For example, if it costs £5000 to get representation to refer the dispute to adjudication and the amount claimed is £5000, at best you will waste time and resources to, financially, stand still. However, it could be worthwhile if you are chasing £25 000 because, If paying £5000 for representation, you could clear £20 000.

'Without prejudice' is a phrase used in a letter or email if you, or some other person, is making an offer of settlement of a dispute. A statement headed 'without prejudice' cannot be produced in court, adjudication or arbitration by the other person because it is privileged. Therefore, if your client owes you £5000 and offers to pay £2000 without prejudice, you cannot draw the judge's attention to that letter or email if the other person later says he owes you nothing. However, putting 'without prejudice' on the top of a letter does not allow you to write whatever you wish with impunity. Remember that it only protects an offer made to settle a dispute.

How a Court Calculates Fees

To some extent, this is the easy part. If the terms of appointment can be established and if, hopefully, payment terms are included, they are simply applied to the situation and that is that. Assuming the parties cannot agree on the amount of fees and the dispute goes in front of the court, how will the court decide? What standing has a standard fee scale and will it be applied if there are no other payment terms? The answer to that question is no, not quite, although it may be taken into account. In arriving at the appropriate fee for a project the court will consider the following:

- *Qualifications:* A highly qualified architect would generally be expected to command a higher fee than an architect who is less qualified.
- *Experience:* The more experienced the architect in the field in question, the higher the fee.
- *Time taken:* The length of time taken to do the work has a bearing on the total fee charged, but it is not conclusive because an experienced and highly qualified architect may be able to work much faster than architects who are less experienced and qualified.
- *Degree to which the desired result is achieved:* The extent to which the architect has satisfied the brief (or failed to do so) is important.
- *Degree of architectural merit:* Presumably the views of other experienced architects would be sought on this point.

- *Whether inspiration played a part:* A sudden burst of inspiration whereby the architect solved a problem in minutes which might otherwise have taken hours or days is worthy of appropriate reward.
- *Scale fees are a yardstick:* When all criteria have been considered, it is useful to test the result against any standard fee scale. Ideally, there should be little difference.

Comparison with fees charged by other architects is not necessarily relevant. When I was representing an architect and trying to explain to the architect's client why he should pay the architect's fees, he said that he could have engaged another architect nearby for half the fees. 'Then why didn't you?' I asked. There were several possible answers to that question ('I thought I could screw this architect on fees' or 'Because this architect was much better than the architect nearby' or 'Fees weren't an issue at that time') but none of them excused his failure to pay the current architect. Sophisticated clients will sometimes say that the architect's fees are fixed by 'a course of dealing'. Usually, such clients are labouring under a misapprehension. The principle of 'a course of dealing' is that where two people contract for the same kind of work on the same terms in a large number of instances and if on one occasion they neglect to specify any terms, a court may decide that they obviously intended to contract on that occasion on the same terms as before. A court will not reach that conclusion lightly and certainly not unless the pattern has been well established.

32

Consultants

Definition

Strictly speaking, a consultant is anyone who is consulted about something. In the medical profession there are GPs in private practice and junior doctors in hospitals who are supposed to know about all aspects of medicine but not necessarily in great depth. They are supported by hospital departments staffed by doctors, registrars, and consultants who specialise in particular branches of medicine such as cardiology or urology. Once the GP has referred a patient to a consultant, the GP is not usually involved again until the patient is discharged by the hospital.

Consultants in the construction industry have a broadly similar function but the analogy cannot be taken too far because, in the construction industry, consultants are engaged usually by the client to provide expert advice about a specific aspect of the project on which they have expertise beyond that of the architect. They do not take over from the architect as a consultant takes over from the GP. Instead they compliment the architect's own knowledge and experience in their own specialist field while the architect normally acts as the team leader because of the broad scope of the architects' training. The most common types of consultant are probably:

- quantity surveyors or cost consultants
- structural engineers
- electrical services engineers
- mechanical services engineers.

Of course, there are many other possible consultants, such as landscape architects, interior designers, and acoustic consultants, the possible list is almost endless depending upon the project. A consultant, of course, can be anyone the client or the architect considers necessary to assist in the development of the project.

On small projects, there may be no consultants because the architect feels able to deal with the whole of the design, production information, and administration, including inspection on site. In some projects the architect may be a consultant on the same basis as other consultants if another professional is the lead consultant or perhaps where a project manager has been engaged by the client (see 33: Project Managers).

Professional Practice for Architects and Project Managers, First Edition. David Chappell.

Engaging Consultants

Consultants must never be employed by the architect because they are essentially consultants to the client. Then the client is responsible for paying their fees directly and the consultants are responsible to the client for the proper performance of their services. This also allows the client to seek advice directly from any consultant without having to go through the architect to do so. Having said that, it is obviously desirable that the client does not discuss anything concerning the project with a consultant unless the architect is also present.

The practice, particularly by some corporate clients, of engaging the architect and insisting that the architect engages all the consultants makes no sense besides putting the architect in the position of having to pay consultants' fees, even if the client defaults. It also means that if a consultant is negligent, the client has to sue the architect and then the architect sues the consultant (usually in a procedure referred to as 'joining' the consultant in the action) which makes the process overall costlier and involves the architect in legal proceedings even though the architect is acknowledged as not being liable. Moreover, if the client simply refers the dispute to adjudication, the architect cannot 'join' the consultant into the adjudication, unless the consultant agrees (fat chance) and the architect is then faced with having to start another separate adjudication against the consultant, but the likelihood is that the architect will be in the position of having to pay the client before receiving anything from the consultant (and that is assuming that the architect is successful). The architect must also take care when engaging the consultant to ensure it has professional indemnity insurance and checks that it is being maintained. Even then, insolvency of the consultant can be a disaster.

Importance of Early Appointment

It is essential that consultants are appointed as soon as possible. That will usually be when the brief is known. It used to be the practice of architects to get to the stage of producing sketch designs or even preliminary working drawings, then sending them to each consultant asking for them to apply their particular expertise to the virtually concluded designs. Architects were fond of telling the consultants to 'make it work'. Ah, those were the days. Chaos usually ensued. The biggest problems were mechanical, electrical, and structural consultants. Well, they were not the problem, actually we architects were most of the problem.

I remember being shocked when the electrical consultant informed me that he would need a dedicated electrical control room and a high-level duct requiring a suspended ceiling along each corridor of my modest block of flats. The fault was entirely mine. When I was working later on a very large and complex local authority office block, the project architect told me airily that when producing the sketch design, he had simply allowed for what he considered to be a huge vertical duct in the middle of the building and suspended ceilings through to deal with all services. Needless to say, services proved to be a difficult problem on that project.

It can never be too early to involve consultants.

General Points

Clients are often surprised to hear that consultants are required as well as the architect. The client may have to be taught how the whole design and construction process works and how the involvement of consultants at the start of the project can save fees on needless redesign later. Indeed, the client must understand that whether or not consultants are involved at an early stage is not a matter for discussion, it is the way design is carried out: no one would contemplate designing a concert hall without substantial early input from an acoustic engineer, but less obvious consultants are often required.

At the first meeting with all concerned with the project, it will be important to agree the way in which the team will work. Teams work in different ways and it is not for me to dictate any particular best way of working. The important point is that your team must agree the way it is going to work, exchange information, and determine the precise responsibilities of each. Part of the consultant's duties will be to inspect the particular specialist work as appropriate during its progress and to make inspections before practical completion and at the end of any defects period in the contract. In my experience, many disputes arise because the interface between professionals is not clearly defined.

Consultants are rarely mentioned in building contracts. Generally, the only people mentioned are the architect or contract administrator (sometimes referred to as project manager), sometimes the quantity surveyor, the contractor, and the employer.

Instructions

It is very important that every consultant understands that, under a traditional contract, only the architect may give instructions to the contractor. Consultants should not visit site unless authorised to do so by the architect, presumably for the purpose of inspecting work. If the consultant does visit site, it should be preferably in the company of the architect. If unaccompanied, the consultant must be careful not to answer any questions from the contractor, from any operative or from the clerk of works. This is difficult to achieve in practice, but if the consultant does not rigorously stick to that discipline, it will lead to difficulties later. It must be made clear to the contractor at the pre-start meeting that the consultant is not authorised to issue instructions and that if the contractor carries out any instructions directly from a consultant, they will not attract any payment, being a breach of contract, and the work may well have to be replaced at the contractor's cost. Consultants wishing to issue instructions should issue them to the architect first so that the architect can issue them as architect's instructions.

33

Project Managers

Definition

I was once asked, in the middle of a lecture about something else entirely, how I would define a project manager. On the spur of the moment I said that 'he is someone who is large, red-faced and shouts a lot'. It got a good laugh, but there was more than a grain of truth in that description. Many project managers have no contractual status and, therefore, the contractor need not comply with their instructions. Hence the need to use 'force of personality' In 2000, a judge said:

> There is no chartered or professional institution of project managers nor a recognisable profession of project managers. In so far as it may be appropriate to accept expert evidence, the nature of the evidence that might be acceptable will depend on what the project manager has agreed to do.

Despite what the judge said, I have found the following organisations concerned with project management:

- Association for Project Management
- Project Management Institute
- Chartered Institute of Project Management
- Institute of Project Management.

However, the judge's point was not about whether there were or were not professional project management institutes, but that it is difficult if not impossible to categorise the duties of a project manager in the same way as one can say what an architect, building surveyor, quantity surveyor or engineer might do. The duties of a project manager depend on the construction professional who carries out that role and what the role is in a particular case. Moreover, the term 'project manager' is not exclusive to construction work, it refers to anyone who is charged with managing a project. The project might be the construction of a 30-storey office block or it might be the production of a new car or a type of toothpaste. It can be seen that simply labelling someone as a project manager does not adequately indicate what they do.

The only type of project manager I am concerned with here is a project manager involved in building construction and employed by the employer. It is impossible to say that all project managers are architects, although at one time architects were considered to be the obvious choice as the professionals most suited to lead the building team.

Professional Practice for Architects and Project Managers, First Edition. David Chappell.

Many project managers are building or quantity surveyors, engineers or people with a practical background in construction. Some contractors employ project managers but their roles are significantly different from project managers employed by the employer. If employed by the contractor they are often termed 'contracts manager' or 'commercial manager', but they manage the project for the contractor.

Types of Project Manager

There are basically two types of project manager:

- project managers (type 1) who act on behalf of the employer as an agent
- project managers (type 2) who administer building contracts.

What they do and, more importantly, what they are entitled to do are quite different. I cannot stress that too much.

Type 1 Project Manager

This type of project manager acts as the client's representative or agent (see 11: Agency). Usually, they act as agents for the client and they can do, in relation to the project, everything the client can do, depending on the terms of their engagement by the client. If a project manager is appointed, all the people likely to be affected are entitled to know exactly the extent of the project manager's powers. Many clients seem to think that the employment of a project manager in this way will ensure the completion of the Works on time and without any extra costs. That, of course, is misguided because the only sure effect of the addition of the project manager is an extra set of project management fees for the employer to pay. This kind of project manager does not manage anything. The employer may also have a sense that the project manager is keeping an eye on the other professionals involved to see that they are doing their jobs properly. The old question springs to mind: 'Who will inspect the inspector?' At some point, an employer who is unskilled in construction matters must place trust in someone; it is not clear why that someone is often a project manager rather than the architect, quantity surveyor, structural consultant etc.

The project manager has no power to verify or sign any certificates nor to recommend payment under building contracts unless the building contract expressly names and gives the project manager that power. The matter is confused because some standard form contracts refer to the project manager when what they clearly mean is someone akin to a contract administrator. To be clear, if this kind of project manager is appointed quite separately to the contract administrator under the building contract, the project manager will have no powers under the building contract. Any interference by the project manager in the running of the contract can be interpreted by the contractor as interference by the employer. Some contracts allow the contractor to terminate in those circumstances.

Under most standard form contracts this type of project manager has no greater right than the employer to enter site, nor to attend site meetings and certainly not to give instructions to the contractor. The contractor should not take instructions from this kind of project manager. The project manager has no status on site during the progress of the Works. Attempts by the project manager to organise, run or chair site meetings should be firmly resisted.

If we except the person appointed under some construction contracts whose contract administration role in those contracts is stated to be 'Project Manager', the type 1 project manager described above is the usual role performed by the person termed project manager. It does not replace or affect the contract administrator's role.

Project Manager Type 2

This type of project manager acts as a contract administrator in regard to the building contract and must be named in the contract. This kind of project manager obviously issues instructions and certificates, but is also responsible for co-ordinating the roles of the other construction professionals and must have the authority to do so. This is true project management. It is essential that the appointment documents reflect the situation. This type of project manager has authority over the contractor and all the consultants during the construction stage. This type of project manager is what a true project manager must be in order to function properly. Unfortunately, many project managers are appointed as type 1 but try to act as if they were type 2. If this confusion is not sorted out at the beginning, many problems will occur.

Final Comments

A true project manager must have the following skills to a greater or lesser degree depending on the project type.

- *Management*: Must have a thorough understanding of the theory and practice of people management.
- *Construction law*: Must have a thorough knowledge, including construction contracts; must be aware of the latest developments in this field.
- *Value management*: Must be able to deal with a client's requirements at the best value.
- *Value engineering*: Must be able to analyse a building in order to eliminate unnecessary costs and improve value.
- *Procurement*: Must have a thorough understanding of procurement routes and available contracts.
- *Project planning and programming*: Must be able to understand, create, and apply programmes to achieve the required result.
- *Briefing*: Must be able to develop client wants into client needs.
- *Cost control*: Must have a thorough understanding of the means of controlling a project in progress.
- *Risk management*: Must understand how to assess, eliminate, and control risk.

34

Net Contribution Clause

It can be quite difficult trying to explain why a net contribution clause is an essential clause to be included in the architect's terms of engagement. The RIBA and many other construction disciplines have the clause in their appointment documents, but solicitors representing clients commonly insist they are deleted. So, what is the reason for having this kind of clause? In order to understand, it is necessary to consider a situation where a client suffers some kind of monetary loss through some negligence on the part of consultants working on a project.

Let's say that the architect, the structural engineer, and the heating engineer are all separately contracted to the client and responsible in different ways and, importantly, to different degrees for the negligent action. In that situation the client is entitled to take legal action for damages against just one or all of the consultants responsible. It is obviously cheaper to sue one person rather than two or three, so most clients would opt to sue the consultant against whom there is most chance of success. Let's say the architect, and the architect can be held liable to pay the whole of the claim even if the other consultants were partly responsible. The correct name for this is joint and severable liability.

If you are the architect, you may be faced with paying 100% of a claim even though you are only 5% responsible. Then, as in this example, you would have to bring separate legal actions against the structural engineer and the heating engineer at great cost in order to recover their share of the claim. If one or other of the consultants was insolvent or inadequately insured, you (or more likely your professional indemnity insurers) would be unable to recover. The purpose of a net contribution clause is to ensure that the architect is only liable to pay the damages for which he or she is responsible. The best net contribution clauses include contractors and specialists as well as consultants as people who must share in the liability.

Clients or their solicitors will often say that the clause is unfair. That suggestion does not stand up to scrutiny because it must be fair that the consultants bear liability in proportion to their respective responsibilities for the client's losses. Clients will say that in a situation where the responsibility is shared between several consultants and possibly the contractor, it is unreasonable to expect the client to have to face the cost of bringing separate legal actions against each responsible person in order to recover their losses because the client is completely innocent. But of course, the client knew that when the appointment was signed.

In summary, the courts have said that a net contribution clause is widely used. It does not exclude or restrict liability, it is not unusual or onerous, and it is fair and reasonable.

Professional Practice for Architects and Project Managers, First Edition. David Chappell.

35

Warranties

Definition

Warranties go under several names. They are sometimes called 'collateral warranties', 'warranties' or, particularly where professionals are involved, 'duty of care agreements'. They all amount to the same thing: a contract which is collateral to, or running alongside, another contract. For example, a contractor or sub-contractor might be asked to enter into a warranty with the future tenant or purchaser of a project quite separately from the building contract. Architects might be asked to enter into a warranty in favour of a financial institution that is financing the architect's client, future leaseholders, a prospective buyer or just about anyone who might conceivably have any interest in the development. This chapter is only concerned with the warranties which architects may be asked to complete. It is quite complicated and a challenge for me to explain in simple terms.

The Purpose of Warranties

First, it is important to understand the purpose of a collateral warranty. The basic purpose is to establish a contractual relationship between two people or companies. Why would anyone want to do that? The blunt answer is that a contractual relationship makes it easier for one person to sue another. Although warranties have been around for some time, it is only comparatively recently that they have assumed real significance. At one time it was assumed that if someone who had no contractual relationship with the architect lost money as a result of some action of the architect, they could simply sue the architect for negligence. Take, for example, the position of the leaseholder who discovered that there were design defects in the building just leased from the developer. Some years ago, the leaseholder would have sued the architect for negligence with some hope of success. The legal position is now changed and suing for negligence in those situations is not easy.

Suing in negligence is not suitable for what are basically breaches of obligations about quality. Actions for negligence concerning building defects can only be successful if damage or injury is caused to persons or property other than the defective building itself, or perhaps if there is an imminent danger of damage. But most purchasers would be hoping to recover the costs of correcting the defective work. Therefore, actions for negligence have become virtually useless in such situations.

Professional Practice for Architects and Project Managers, First Edition. David Chappell.

As a result, a subsequent purchaser who wishes to be able to claim against the architect in appropriate circumstances must require the developer to make it a condition of appointment that the architect enters into a collateral warranty or duty of care agreement in favour of a subsequent purchaser and that the warranty must be able to be transferred, preferably, from the point of view of the purchaser, an infinite number of times. The problem is, of course, that although it is easy to say that no architect should ever enter into one of these arrangements, a refusal might mean loss of the job. That needs to be balanced against the fact that an architect entering into a duty of care agreement is taking on at least the same, and possibly a greater, liability to the third party as is already owed to the client. This is the nub of the whole problem and something which must be very carefully considered. There are many architects who regularly sign warranties without bothering to read them and think of them simply as bit of paper that has to be signed but which is not of much consequence. That is a really, really bad idea. Warranties must be avoided if possible and, if not possible, must be read carefully with a view to getting rid of all the nasty parts.

Can Architects Avoid Signing Warranties?

Looked at from a common-sense point of view, it is silly for any architect to enter into a warranty agreement. The pressures forcing an architect to sign such an agreement are very great and many, if not most, of the agreements now being offered to architects seek to impose unacceptable terms. The party taking the benefit of the warranty will principally be interested in the architect's professional indemnity insurance. Many architects enter into duty of care agreements with terms so onerous that the insurance would be repudiated by the insurers if ever a claim is made. Every warranty must be put to the insurers before it is signed or the indemnity insurance will be at risk.

One of the strongest arguments against the use of a warranty is that the architect is doubling the possible liability without increasing income. In other words, the architect is getting nothing out of it. Of course, for there to be a binding contract, both parties must 'give' something unless the warranty is in the form of a deed and warranties as deeds are becoming more common (see 23: Contracts). Execution of a warranty as a deed should not be countenanced if the architect's appointment document itself is only under hand. This would result in the architect having a longer period of liability to the third party than to the original client. It is not thought that such a provision would be nullified by the clause limiting the architect's liability to the third party to that which he has to the client because the act of execution as a deed would not increase the architect's liability, but merely extend the time period for bringing an action under the agreement. Another clause would be required limiting the length of the limitation period to the same as under the appointment.

The amount of money required to create a contract need not be great provided that it is of some value. This is to be paid by the client and it is often ludicrously small, e.g. £1. As a matter of principle, architects should demand a lot more. It will depend on what the market will bear, but the architect must think of the increased liability and the real likelihood that future insurance premiums will show an upward trend. Without the benefit of a warranty, the future purchaser will find it virtually impossible to bring any legal action against the architect for a design failure, so a warranty is a very valuable piece of paper to the client.

Typical Clauses

Clauses commonly found in warranties include:

- Reasonable skill and care
- Prohibited materials
- Step-in rights
- Copyright
- Professional indemnity insurance
- Net contribution clause.

Reasonable Skill and Care

There should be a clause which simply states that the architect will exercise reasonable skill and care in the performance of his or her duties, and contain a proviso that the agreement imposes no greater liability or extent on the architect than the liability already owed to the client. It is now becoming common for such clauses to be extended to include requirements about diligence and to make the standard what is expected of 'a properly qualified and competent architect experienced in carrying out work of similar size, scope and complexity'. Reject any references to 'all' reasonable skill and care. The 'all' is likely to extend the duty beyond what is usual.

Prohibited Materials

The architect often undertakes that he or she has not and will not specify certain materials in the project. This requirement was becoming less common following a case where the manufacturer of a product on the prohibited list successfully objected. The architect must avoid at all costs any clauses which place an obligation to 'ensure' that certain materials will not be used in the building. This is for the obvious reason that the architect can ensure no such thing, but only make sure that they are not specified. Indeed, an architect cannot 'ensure' anything. Dangerous clauses are those which are vague about what is being prohibited and phrases like 'materials generally known to be deleterious' should be avoided. They lead to one party believing something is banned and the other thinking it is permitted to use it. The difficulty in interpreting this kind of clause can be seen if one simply asks these questions: 'Generally known' by whom? Can it be said to be 'generally' known if it is not known by everyone or most? How can it be established how many people knew? What exactly is 'deleterious', are we referring to any material which is, even in the slightest degree, deleterious? Sometimes the 'generally known' provision is restricted 'to members of the architect's profession' or 'members of the construction industry'. The difficulty of establishing whether it is generally known are still there.

Step-in Rights

Sometimes, certain notices have to be given by the third party receiving the benefit of the warranty. This is common where the third party is a funder who may wish to take over the completion of the project if the original client backs out or goes into liquidation. A funder will wish to be protected. The notices may be given by the third party to the architect in the event that the agreement between the client and the third party is terminated. In such circumstances, the architect is often required to agree to accept instructions solely from the third party in regard to the completion of the development under the same terms as those of the original appointment. Moreover, and dangerously, there is often a clause by which the architect effectively agrees that all fees have been paid up to the date of the agreement and absolves the company for any liability to pay any fees which may be owing. In such cases, the third party's liability to pay fees usually begins when it serves the notice mentioned above. At that point it becomes liable to pay all fees, including those outstanding, but the liability is short-lived.

It is common for warranties to include a clause stipulating that, if the architect wishes to exercise the right to terminate the appointment or if the architect considers the client has repudiated the appointment or if, for some other reason, the architect wishes to stop work, 28 days' written notice must first be given to the third party. Within that period, the third party may in turn give notice to the architect to accept its instructions instead of those of the client. Agreements usually provide that the architect loses the right to terminate, accept repudiation or stop work at that point. One can understand why the third party would not want the architect to terminate the appointment, but it can seriously disadvantage the architect. It is better simply to prevent the architect from terminating the appointment for a reasonable period after receipt of the notice to give the third party the opportunity to rectify the reason for the proposed termination by the architect.

A potentially difficult situation could arise because in order to take instructions from the third party to the exclusion of the client the original appointment must be terminated. Receipt of notice from the third party usually can be relied upon by the architect as evidence that the agreement between the client and the third party is terminated, but that might not assist the architect in relation to the original terms of appointment. Most warranties attempt to overcome this problem by noting that the client is a party to the agreement for the purpose of acknowledging that the architect will not be in breach of the contract by complying with the obligation under the agreement.

Copyright

Warranties often include a clause protecting the architect's copyright in the documents provided, but which allows the company to use them for the purposes of the development, advertisement, letting, etc. Care must be taken with clauses of this kind. An architect should never, ever, sign a warranty which gives copyright to a third party or even to the client. The most clients and others can expect is a licence to use the architect's designs.

A particularly wary eye must be kept on the appearance of the word 'irrevocable' in conjunction with the licence because it means exactly that. Once an irrevocable licence is granted, it cannot be revoked. Otherwise, depending on the circumstances, revoking a licence may be an option if the architect is not paid. An alternative is to allow 'irrevocable' to remain but to insert 'subject to all fees having been paid' at the beginning of the clause. Third parties often complain about any attempt to insert that proviso saying that it is not their responsibility to pay the fees. That is a spurious argument because the third party is getting the warranty free of charge and should make sure that the client pays, pay themselves or forfeit the copyright licence.

A rather nasty clause has been finding its way into warranties of late. It is a provision whereby the architect is required to waive moral rights under the Copyright, Designs, and Patents Act 1988. That is something which no architect should do. The Act allows the architect to assert the moral right to be identified as the author of the work of architecture in question whenever it is published and, indeed, on the building itself if the architect so desires. This is not a right which any architect ought to relinquish. (see 6: Copyright).

Professional Indemnity Insurance

The architect may be required to undertake to maintain professional indemnity insurance for a sum to be inserted and for a period of years to be inserted. Warranties usually make the continuance of the insurance dependent upon the insurance being available at commercially reasonable rates. If, at any time, the architect considers that the insurance is no longer so available, he must notify the company. It is difficult to see what action the company could take if the architect had behaved unreasonably because, even if it could show that the architect was in breach of the agreement, it would have suffered no loss unless and until a claim was made on the insurance.

Increasingly, the words 'to architects with a good claims record' are added after insurance being available 'at commercially reasonable rates'. The effect of this is that provided the insurance is available at commercial reasonable rates to architects with a good claims record, the architect will be obliged to maintain it. This overlooks the fact that the architect in question may not have a good claims record and, therefore, the rate quoted by the insurance company may be well above the commercially reasonable rate to others. At the end of the day, it matters not what an insurance company is prepared to offer other architects, it is the rate to the architect who is the party to the warranty which is important. Therefore, these add-on words should be deleted and the words 'to the architect' substituted.

Net Contribution Clause

Every warranty and every appointment document should have a net contribution clause (see 34: Net Contribution Clause). The aim of this clause is to make the architect only liable for his or her share of any liability as though all the other parties had paid their shares.

Assignment

An invariable feature of warranties is the right of the person to whom the warranty is given to assign it to another person (see 22: Assignment). This is achieved by the insertion of a suitable clause. In the absence of a clause permitting assignment without the architect's consent, there would be no ordinary right to assign. Too often, the assignment clauses permit assignment of the warranty indefinitely. This is a big advantage to the client or third party, but very serious for the architect because each assignment changes and possibly increases the parties to whom the architect may be liable. If assignment cannot be entirely eradicated from the warranty, the assignment clause should be restricted so that the agreement may be assigned, once only subject to the payment of all outstanding fees and to the architect's consent and with a time limit of three years after practical completion.

Conclusion

No duty of care agreement is ideal. There are standard terms available, but a far greater number of warranties are specially drafted by the client's solicitors. In general, standard warranties are to be preferred over tailor-made versions, but no warranty is good. It must be remembered always that the main purpose of the warranty is to give the architect liability to more people than would otherwise be the case. Architects should consider having their own, reasonably innocuous version drafted so that they can offer it if asked by the client to give a warranty. For a client to object is for the client to admit an intention to firmly truss the architect in unnecessary legal obligations. Architects must be the only profession which persists in putting its collective head on the block in such situations. A few basic principles to ponder:

- A client cannot demand a warranty as a legal right.
- A client can only demand a warranty if it is stated in the terms of appointment that the architect will give a warranty.
- Even if it is stated, the architect cannot be forced to give a warranty in any particular terms and can give a warranty on the architect's own terms. The client has no right to object.
- It is only *if* it is stated in the terms of appointment that the architect is required to give a warranty *and if* the terms of the warranty are reproduced in the terms of appointment that the architect can be forced to give a warranty in specific terms.

I once drafted a warranty that any architect could give without worrying. It was modelled on the kind of warranty that many firms offer for installed systems and wrapped around with many onerous conditions which the client had to satisfy before the warranty became operable, such as that the client had to have a thorough survey of the building carried out on an annual basis.

36

Consultant's Certificates

What are Consultant's Certificates?

Consultant's certificates are not certificates issued by a contract administrator or project manager under the terms of a building contract. These are certificates which a professional is asked to sign to certify that the building has been constructed properly. Architects, surveyors, and structural engineers are often called upon to sign consultant's certificates. They take different forms and range from the so-called 'standard' certificates agreed by the RIBA, RICS, etc. to bespoke documents. My advice in respect of all of these certificates is: 'Don't sign them'. Although they take different forms, most contain similar information. Some of the problems are set out below.

Insurance

To put it bluntly, the main purpose of these certificates is to make use of your professional indemnity insurance if there are defects in the building after it has been occupied. It is important to understand that if you are the architect of the building, your obligation to the client will usually end when your client sells the building to someone. That is because your contract to carry out the design and possibly contract administration is a contract with your client, not with any subsequent purchaser. The subsequent purchaser is extremely unlikely to be able to take action against you for negligence nor to have any redress against your client because he or she will be deemed to have carried out their own investigations before purchase and the centuries-old principle of *caveat emptor* (let the buyer beware) applies. I know I said I wouldn't include any legal phrases, but you must have heard that one.

Effectively, once the purchaser buys the property, he or she is on their own. Astute purchasers or their solicitors will ask for some kind of guarantee. Warranties are available from some insurance companies and of course there is the NHBC Buildmark warranty for up to 10 years on new property. Most warranties, however, require the insurance be taken out before the construction begins. Also, warranties can be expensive for the

Professional Practice for Architects and Project Managers, First Edition. David Chappell.

developer. In short, many buildings are sold without having any kind of insurance against future defects.

In the minds of many purchasers, their solicitors, banks, and building societies the answer is the consultant's certificate. In the absence of some other kind of insurance, many purchasers demand a consultant's certificate to say that the building has been properly constructed. Two kinds of consultants are asked to provide these certificates. The usual kind is the consultant who designed the building and the client will often make the provision of a consultant's certificate a term of the consultant's engagement. The other kind is the consultant who is approached out of the blue by a client wanting a certificate because a prospective purchaser is demanding one. This might be a developer who is carrying out its own construction and simply wants the consultant to sign the form.

There is usually a clause in the certificate requiring you to state the minimum insurance you will hold to cover your liabilities. This should make you pause.

Site Visits

Most certificates expect you to have made site visits during construction and then certify that the building has been constructed to a satisfactory standard. The wording of the certificate is usually lacking precision. If a court has to consider the matter, it is unlikely that the lack of precision will be interpreted in favour of the consultant if the client is a consumer, which is often the case. 'Satisfactory' is likely to be interpreted as the standard which the person relying on the certificate is entitled to expect; not good news for the consultant I'm afraid. Many consultants are lulled into thinking that if the certificate qualifies your opinion by referring to a 'visual inspection' and using words like 'so far as I could determine', it is pretty safe to sign. The question for a future court might well be whether you ought to have carried out more visual inspections and what ought you to have been able to determine during those inspections if properly carried out.

Reliance

This is the key point. There will be a clause stating that your certificate 'is being relied upon' by the purchaser of the building. It will almost certainly say that the building society or the bank, whichever is lending the money to build, is also relying on the certificate. If you pass this in front of your professional indemnity insurers, as you must, at the very least they will require the wording to be changed to read that the purchaser and/or bank 'is entitled to rely upon' the certificate. This makes a huge difference to your chances of escaping liability if defects are discovered later. The second option leaves open the question of whether the purchaser did in fact rely upon your certificate or actually upon something else.

Time Period

There will be a clause requiring you to be liable for 6, or possibly 12, years from the date of the certificate to the first and all subsequent purchasers.

Liabilities

If you have agreed to provide one of these certificates as a part of your terms of engagement, I hope that you have already obtained the agreement of your professional indemnity insurers.

You may have been approached to provide one either because there is no professional already involved in the construction or because the building is nearly, or actually, complete. My best advice is that you should not sign. If you are the architect for the project or an architect approached specifically to sign the certificate, you can simply say that you have a policy of not signing this kind of certificate, or you can say that you have been expressly advised never to sign one. Of course, if you have already agreed in your terms of engagement to sign, there is nothing you can do but sign. I have heard architects say that surely they should be prepared to be responsible for their own mistakes. That is an extremely laudable sentiment but the question is 'responsible to whom?' To the client, yes, but not to a string of unknown future purchasers. That is just nonsense and very foolish.

The point is that the consultant's certificate seeks to impose on you greater liabilities than the ordinary law would do. That, of course, is the function of any contract, but the consultant's certificate is not a contract, it is you formally confirming your professional opinion and that the purchasers and/or building society are relying upon that opinion. The law says that if a person A possessed of special skills gives negligent advice to B knowing that the advice will be relied upon and if B does rely on the advice and, as a result, suffers loss or damage, B can sue A for the loss. It is immaterial whether A has received any payment.

Consultants say that they often amend the wording to protect themselves. The problems are, first, that any amendments should be carried out by an expert in this kind of work and, second, the wording cannot be amended enough to give you sufficient protection without removing the whole reason why your client wants the certificate.

Charging

Usually, a consultant will charge for the certificate but, in my experience, the charge is usually ridiculously small. If you must issue this kind of certificate, be aware of the risk you are running. Take the situation where the certificate turns out to be inaccurate to a degree that amounts to negligence. If a building society has advanced a substantial sum of money on a mortgage arrangement and the building is found to be worth far less than was anticipated, the building society will be looking to you to make up any shortfall if the building owner cannot keep up repayments and the building has to be sold for less than the valuation based upon your certificate. That could amount to many thousands of pounds.

Hopefully, your professional indemnity insurers will come to your rescue but the inevitable result will be that they will raise your premium and it will stay at the new level for the rest of your professional life. So, if you are 30 and you find that you are paying an extra £2000 annually after your claim has been settled, you are looking at paying perhaps an extra £80 000 – all because you signed an A4 sheet of paper. That is an enormous risk to take.

Most architects who have spoken to me about this admit that they tend to charge a modest hourly rate for the inspections and nothing for the certificate. Those asked to sign a certificate without inspection often talk about asking for £200 or £300. One said that he charged £30 a certificate. If you are providing a certificate for work that you did not design and act as contract administrator, your certificate is extremely risky and must be worth several thousands of pounds.

Summary

- If you designed the building and your client cannot sell it without a consultant's certificate, you may have difficulty in refusing it, but at least you will have the reassurance that, having designed the project and inspected the construction, there should be no serious errors.
- If you agreed to provide the certificate as part of your terms of engagement, you cannot later refuse to do so.
- If you are approached to provide a certificate for a building with which you have had no earlier involvement, you would be well advised to decline.
- If you agree to sign, always pass the document to your professional indemnity insurers first for vetting.

37

Conflict of Interest

What is Conflict of Interest?

In the context of construction, conflict of interest occurs when one of the professionals has an obligation or a desire to do one thing and at the same time has an obligation or desire to do a different thing and the two things are not entirely or partly compatible.

When a conflict arises, there are three options for the consultant:

- Remove the cause of the conflict if possible.
- Obtain the agreement of all parties affected that the consultant continues.
- The consultant withdraws from the situation.

A consultant who continues to provide services while aware that there is a conflict situation, but who does not reveal it to the other parties involved, is in serious breach of trust and guilty of unprofessional conduct. Depending upon the conflict, the consultant may become open to legal action by any party who has suffered loss or damage.

Conflict Examples

It is not common for an architect, quantity surveyor or engineer to have a conflict of interest, but it can happen almost without the consultant concerned realising it until too late.

The most common example of potential conflict is when novation or consultant switch takes place in the context of a design and build scenario. The only thing that saves a consultant from being in serious trouble is the fact that the situation is not only known but engineered by the employer and accepted by the contractor. In other circumstances, if a consultant was approached by a client to provide advice and other services which adversely affect another of the consultant's clients, the consultant must decline to act. The only possible situation where that might be acceptable would be if the consultant had ceased all services for the earlier client some time before. Even so, the consultant should proceed with great care and if in any doubt, should decline.

It is easy to see how a conflict situation could arise, actually is virtually inbuilt, in the case of novation or consultant switch. Novation, when properly done, is the termination of the contract between employer and consultant to be replaced by a new contract on exactly or virtually the same terms between the contractor and the consultant by agreement of all three parties (see 59: Novation). Consultant switch is when the contract

Professional Practice for Architects and Project Managers, First Edition. David Chappell.

between employer and consultant is terminated and an entirely new contract on different terms is entered into between contractor and consultant (see 58: Consultant Switch). In both cases, the consultant is first of all working for the employer and entirely in the employer's best interests. Then the consultant is expected to work for the contractor and entirely in the contractor's best interests.

Putting it very broadly, the employer is intent on getting the best building for the least possible outlay while the contractor is intent on producing the lowest and, therefore, cheapest building for the maximum financial return. Therefore, there is a serious conflict of interest between employer and contractor. Therefore, a consultant working for each in turn is a part of that conflict. The conflict is accentuated by the fact that the consultant working for the contractor will be doing so probably while privy to some very confidential matters which the employer has previous discussed.

The consultant must comply with lawful instructions given by the contractor even though the consultant knows that these instructions are contrary to what the employer wants. The position is complicated because the employer and the contractor will be in contract by which the contractor is obliged to comply with the employer's requirements set out in that contract. Usually, however, the consultant is not bound by anything in the building contract unless the consultant's terms of engagement as novated or the new terms under a switch arrangement specifically say so. So, the architect may be instructed by the contractor to produce construction drawings which the architect knows do not reflect what the employer wanted, contrary to the design and build contract. The architect may point that out to the contractor, but if money is at stake, the contractor is unlikely to listen.

What if the contractor decides to mount a claim for loss and/or expense against the employer? The contractor will certainly expect the architect and the quantity surveyor to assist in the formulation of the claim and they can hardly do that without making use of knowledge gained while engaged by the employer in the early stages of the project.

An even worse situation arises if for one reason or other the consultant is in the position of working for both parties at the same time. This sometimes arises when solicitors acting for the employer draft the novation agreement so that the consultant is in the position of having to report back to the employer about such things as progress and defective work. This usually affects architects who should never have agreed to that kind of clause. It is surprising that many contractors do not object to it either. I once had to advise an architect who found himself having signed a contract with the contractor while still being in contract with the employer. He was producing construction drawings for the contractor and inspecting the work on site for the employer. I told him he had a death wish. Needless to say, neither employer nor contractor were happy with him and both were considering taking legal action against him.

Despite all these obvious problems, novation and consultant switch appear to be alive and well and very common.

Conflicts sometimes arise if an architect is asked by two separate clients to carry out feasibility studies for different types of development on the same site, each client having it in mind to make an offer for the site if the feasibility study shows it to be attractive. Clearly, the architect must only act for one client even though it may be tempting to act for both so as to have a good chance of getting to design the project in due course.

Some contractors employ their own architect and offer complete design and build services directly to employers. Architects in that position must take care, when discussing potential schemes with employers, to make clear that they cannot give truly independent advice and employers must engage their own consultants if independent advice is required. The contractors concerned are usually not too keen on that approach for obvious reasons.

I was recently asked if there was a conflict if a client gave instructions to an architect to produce a design which the architect knew would be totally unsuitable. No, that would not be a conflict of interest in the sense I have been discussing. It would rather be the age-old problem of a client refusing to take the architect's advice. In those circumstances, the architect can simply confirm then carry out the client's express instructions or resign, depending on circumstances.

38

Consumers, Corporations, and Associations

Dealing with Consumers, Corporations, and Associations

Many professionals seem to be hopelessly confused when dealing with clients or with parties to a building contract. What follows is just a few remarks about one or two things that are important to bear in mind.

Consumers

Everyone knows about consumers in the sense that the word is bandied around frequently. The key thing to remember about consumers is that they are treated in a distinct way by the law, quite different from companies. There are Acts of Parliament dealing with consumers and their treatment with which every construction professional should be familiar. Essentially a consumer is not a corporation or commercial enterprise.

If you are a professional it is very important to decide whether your client is a consumer or a limited company. Contractors need to be sure about the status of the employer in building contracts. In essence, a consumer is given more protection by the law than a limited company.

The position can become tricky. For example, if a client requests the services of an architect to carry out extensions on their home, that person is treated in law as a consumer. It does not matter whether they are a couple in their 80s who have spent all their lives working as employees in the local shop or whether they are a couple in their 40s who have built up a sizeable fortune in commercial activity, they will be treated as consumers.

In one case which finished up in court, the architect lost his claim partly because the judge decided that he had not treated his clients as consumers. That was in spite of the fact that one of the clients was a very astute merchant banker and the other was an expert in economics. So, beware. I suspect that if the architect had been acting for a client, retired but with a strong background in construction, such as an architect, surveyor or a senior person in building contracting, that might have been taken into account depending on the claim, but that person would still be a consumer in the eyes of the law.

Professional Practice for Architects and Project Managers, First Edition. David Chappell.

Corporations

A corporation is an artificial legal entity. Examples are public and private limited companies, local and other public authorities, and the holders of certain offices, for example the Bishop of London. In the case of an office, it is the office and not the office holder that is the legal entity with which a contract is formed.

Most people understand when they are dealing with a local authority or a statutory undertaker and do not confuse these corporations with their chief executives. The difficulty tends to arise when dealing with limited companies, particularly small ones.

Some architects get confused when dealing with companies and they do not understand that a company is a separate legal entity (i.e. treated as a separate person) from its directors and shareholders. I once had a query from an architect acting as contract administrator. The contractor (a limited company) had gone into liquidation and all work on site had stopped. The former director and sole shareholder of the defunct company approached the architect and the employer, suggesting that the employer employed a new building company which he had just formed which could carry on the work under the same contract. The architect was enthusiastic about the idea because, as he said, it would save the trouble of getting a new contractor and entering into a new contract. He did not understand that the approach was from a brand-new company and, leaving aside any misgivings he ought to have had in regard to the commercial competence of the director and the financial standing of the new company, the previous contractor was an entirely different legal entity. In short, the architect, having been used to dealing with the director, was treating him and not the company as the contractor.

Some contractors are not limited companies and in that situation the contractor is the person who owns and runs the business. If the business goes bust, it is the owner of the business that goes bust or goes bankrupt to be precise. It is very important for an architect to know the status of the contractor: limited company or simply a business owned by someone. Architects should take the same care when dealing with clients. Limited companies can and do go into liquidation owing fees and the chances of recovering anything are negligible.

If the client is a person, albeit a company director, he or she could become personally bankrupt so long as they were commissioning the architect on their own behalf and not on behalf of their company. Although the chances of recovery fees from a bankrupt person are little if any better than recovery from a limited company in liquidation, a person at risk of personal bankruptcy is likely to take more care to remain solvent.

Associations

This is difficult territory. If an architect receives a commission to carry out work from an association, such as civic societies, local history societies, etc., and it becomes necessary to take legal action to recover fees, the architect will no doubt take a solicitor's advice. Nevertheless, it is useful to know who is legally responsible for any fees owing. In general terms, and it does depend on the constitution of the association, all the members are responsible. Therefore, legal action could be taken against any or all of them for the full amount. In practice, the action would probably be taken either against the chairperson and treasurer or against whichever of the members seemed best placed to satisfy the debt.

Section III

On with the Job

39

The Brief

Wants vs Needs

The process of drawing up a good brief involves listening to what the client wants and writing it down in the form of what the client actually needs. In many cases, clients will present a list of what they want included in the building. Sometimes clients will actually produce drawings of buildings as they envisage them. The role of the architect is often totally misunderstood. Clients sometimes consider that you are simply there to make it technically possible for their own designs to be constructed. Commercial clients in particular seem to be attracted to the notion of producing little sketches, while large organisations with their own estates departments will often present very detailed briefing notes to the extent of detailed lists of accommodation with areas included.

That same client may be in the habit of toddling along to his or her GP and asking for a prescription for a specific drug. Further investigations and tests may show that the problem cannot be solved by any drug but requires surgical intervention. Professional people, by and large, are there to solve problems. Architects are the prime problem solvers. The brief is really the very detailed setting out of the problem. Just as your client may ask the GP for cough mixture when what is needed is a resolve to stop smoking, your client may want a three-storey office block in the shape of the initial letters of the company when what is needed is a single-storey building with an open court in the centre. In both instances the path from initial requirements to detailed advice lies through an intensive investigation of all the relevant facts. Neither patient nor client is the best judge of the situation.

Getting the Brief

Sketches and detailed lists can be very useful in getting into a client's mind, but the danger of very detailed instructions from a client is that it is tempting to regard them as the brief. Whatever you receive from the client only becomes the brief after you have analysed it thoroughly and amended it in the light of your experience, your research into the building type, and research into the habits of your client. Often, the client's briefing document should be discarded because it rather prejudges the whole situation. On one occasion, I had a client who wanted a new factory and presented me with a layout of the factory process which looked extremely and unnecessarily complicated. On visiting his existing factory to see for myself how the process worked, I found that the

Professional Practice for Architects and Project Managers, First Edition. David Chappell.

factory consisted of a number of old houses that had been knocked together to provide very cramped accommodation for the processes. What the client had given me was the existing tortuous layout which had become 'the only way to do it' in his mind.

Rather than the traditional list of rooms with areas, the brief should normally take the form of a user requirement study or some development of that principle. The idea is that the architect analyses the client's needs in terms of activities and identifies in respect of each activity a number of key criteria, including direction of movement, areas, volumes, requirements for finishes, orientation and aspect, interaction with other activities and to what extent, numbers of persons involved, special requirements ancillary to the activity, and social and psychological needs. The result may be a world away from the list of rooms plus areas.

The amount of work involved will not be justified if the proposed building is a common building type. However, even if that is the case, you should be careful that the client has not simply become used to doing things in what is really an inefficient way and begun to think of them as indispensable parts of any brief.

The best briefs schedule the information in a logical way, supported by sketches if relevant. Inevitably there will be a lot of notes. Once you have assembled all the information from the client and elsewhere, you must re-write the brief in the form you believe best reflects what the client actually needs from the building. This should be sent to the client for approval before you embark upon the design process. Schedule a meeting with the client a few days after sending the completed brief so that you can explain it in detail.

In a great many cases, the brief is the result of sitting down and talking to the client, who may well have little real idea of what he or she wants. This may be the most fruitful situation because the client has no preconceived ideas and the brief will gradually emerge under your guidance. There are guidelines for the production of briefs and in the case of large developments you will certainly be well advised to develop your brief by the use of formal techniques. However, in all but the smallest commissions the general process of briefing is likely to follow this pattern or something very like it:

- Meet the client for a general chat about the project.
- Inspect his or her existing premises, if relevant.
- Obtain a brief in a reasonable amount of detail.
- Carry out research into the building type, the client's business, habits, etc.
- Meet the client for final tidying up of queries related to the brief.
- Present the finished brief to the client and go through it in detail.

Above all, you must resist the temptation to start designing the building before you have clarified the whole of the brief. The design must flow naturally from the detailed analysis of all your client's needs.

40

Feasibility Studies

General Points

Early on in most projects, the architect will have to produce a feasibility report for the client. Obviously, this cannot be carried out until the architect has obtained the client's brief. But the extent of the brief will be determined by the kind of feasibility required by the client. For example, if the client is a family who wants to know whether it is feasible to have the kind of house they want on a site they have in mind, the architect will probably need a very full brief indeed. However, if a developer is considering acquiring a plot of land on which to construct a residential development, only an outline brief may be necessary. In both these cases, it would be foolhardy to proceed with design work without carrying out a feasibility study.

It is the architect's job to present the feasibility report to the client in a way that makes it as easy as possible for the client to come to a decision. Nothing is more critical than deciding whether or not to carry out a project. Feasibility reports are necessary if the client requires one or if the client does not require one but the architect believes it to be important in the particular circumstances. Some clients see such things as simply another way that architects find to charge more fees. If the client refuses to commission a feasibility report despite your advice to the contrary, you must confirm these circumstances in writing.

What to Put at the Beginning

Near the beginning of the report, you must set out exactly what you are being asked to do so that the report can be read with that in mind. There must also be a list of the notes or assumptions being made so that certainties can be separated from assumptions. Typical assumptions relate to whether a survey or a structural analysis has been carried out and the situation regarding boundaries and site conditions. If other consultants have been involved, they must be recorded together with what they have done. If you have consulted authorities such as Historic England, highways, planning, education, and so on, they must be listed with the precise nature of their contributions.

Professional Practice for Architects and Project Managers, First Edition. David Chappell.

Headings

It is important to have a checklist in order to prevent the inadvertent omission of a significant item. The following is a list of headings which is not exhaustive, but simply a starting point. Every feasibility study will require its own specific list of headings.

Site location
Access
Shops
Health
Social and recreational
Education
Employment
Rights
Planning points
Licencing
Drainage
Architectural/historical
Geological factors
Statutory undertakings and services
Policy
Grants
Structural analysis
Access
Design possibilities
Estimate of cost
Programme
Conclusions
Approvals/decisions
Additional material

Remember that a feasibility study is little use unless every fundamental issue has been addressed and all options and potential problems have been properly considered.

41

Surveys

Types of Survey

'Survey' is one of those terms which can be used for a variety of activities. It is the kind of thing that is carried out by surveyors and architects. One thinks of measuring instruments and notebooks and laser techniques. I remember years ago having to carry out a measured survey of a plot of land. With a colleague I arrived on site to find that there was a thick fog in that area. Having with difficulty found the site, it was impossible to see from one side to the other. Those were the days of stretchable measuring tapes or dangerous hand-cutting metal tapes. Choosing safety over accuracy, we set to work shouting to each other to check that we were both in the correct positions.

You may also be asked to survey an existing building or a partly constructed building if the contractor has left site before completion.

A survey may yield precise measurements, but it may also be for the purpose of checking the condition of a building. Inspections may be carried out to identify defects and their causes, to determine the condition of a building before piling operations or underpinning, or to produce a 'schedule of condition' simply before the building is leased or a 'schedule for dilapidation' when the lease comes to an end. It is important to establish what kind of survey is required.

Do not waste time and money carrying out a very detailed measured survey of a site if all your client requires is some information while considering purchase. However, before purchasing, your client may want, and you may advise, a feasibility study. Obviously, a more detailed survey would be required and possibly some sketches to show what the site will accommodate.

Who Should Carry Out the Survey?

Most architects are capable of carrying out a survey and in some instances it is crucial that it is the architect who does so. That is particularly the case if it is a building that is to be refurbished or altered because there is nothing like the discipline of producing a detailed measured survey of a building to give a thorough understanding of its construction and little idiosyncrasies. That is especially the case when dealing with a historic building, where very accurate measured drawings are necessary. At other times, the additional skills of the surveyor may be indicated. If that is the case, the architect must always carefully brief the surveyor about what is required and the level of detail expected.

Professional Practice for Architects and Project Managers, First Edition. David Chappell.

Vital Points

The correct address is crucial. A colleague once surveyed the field next to the field his client was considering purchasing. Unfortunately, the mistake was not discovered until he was showing his client the finished drawing. It can be difficult if the site is out in the countryside and there are no distinguishing features.

If surveying a building, remember to get the keys first. Arriving at the building and realising that access is impossible is very irritating, particularly if the site is a long way from the office.

Before any kind of survey, whether of land or buildings, it is very important to obtain a plan showing the boundaries of the site.

Boundaries

Resist any suggestion that the boundaries are obvious on the site. If necessary, ask your client to get a solicitor to provide a drawing clearly showing the boundaries. Ideally, they should be shown by a red line. If the line runs alongside a wall or hedge, it is important to know which owner is responsible for the wall or hedge (usually shown by a little T sign). Do not be fobbed off with a red line running across an open area unless the distance from the nearest permanent object is shown. Where there are collections of old buildings it is common for the horizontal boundaries to vary between two buildings so that part of the floor of one ownership is over the ceiling of a different owner.

Solicitors may say that the boundary is uncertain and that you should use your experience to determine where the boundary should be. Many architects will obediently go to the site and come to very sensible, but entirely wrong, conclusions about the boundaries. If the boundary really is unknown, the client should be advised that the boundary line must be agreed between the adjoining owners. That is a task for the owners and their solicitors, with the architect or surveyor if appropriate for advice, to meet and decide. Forging ahead with even a rough sketch design when the boundaries of the site are uncertain is asking for trouble.

General Points

Existing old plans of sites and buildings are very useful. The old plan of one hilltop site I was to survey revealed that there was an old tunnel running underneath which had housed a long-forgotten private railway to carry goods from one factory process to another. Sometimes old plans show abandoned mineshafts, which may render a site unusable without great expense. Old buildings sometimes include unexpectedly thick walls, secret rooms and concealed columns, beams or even rainwater pipes in the walls: things that may be revealed on old plans. Clients sometimes have these drawings or they may be found as deposited plans in local authority files and local archives, deeds registries, and libraries of various kinds. Local inhabitants may be helpful in locating old wells and the like, but perhaps more useful in confirming that a well exists rather than where it exists.

Check the aspect, orientation, overshadowing from adjacent buildings, existence of services such as drains, water, electricity, and gas, and access to the public highway. Other features of the site must be recorded, such as levels, dimensions, benchmarks, positions and types of trees, existing buildings on and near the site and their character, overhead cables and poles, rivers, and ponds.

The first thing the architect should do after arriving at the site is to have a walk around the boundary and observe the surroundings, the trees and bushes, the boundary walls, and the fences and outbuildings. If an existing building is involved, before entering the architect should carefully examine the elevations.

Levels are usually taken around a building but floor levels inside the building, other than the ground floor, are often ignored. The level of every floor should be recorded and the floors themselves checked to see the extent to which they are out of level; most floors are not perfectly level and this can cause problems when careful details designed in the office do not seem to work on site.

If the survey reveals a serious problem, it will be necessary to take further instructions from the client before proceeding. There is no point in surveying a building which may have to be demolished.

Instructions from the client are also required if opening up parts of the building becomes necessary. In these cases, it is usual to employ a contractor to carry out the work. If the client does not actually own the building, opening up can only be carried out with the express permission of the owner.

All services must be tested and other consultants brought in to do this as necessary. Many old buildings have what can only be described as eccentric drainage systems. Although an architect or surveyor will have the necessary skills to trace drainage using dyes to colour the flow, it may be impossible to trace the various connections and the covers of inspection chambers are often covered in earth, grass or even paving. In these instances, it may be necessary to have a TV survey done. The possibility of unexpected cesspits and septic tanks should not be overlooked.

It is a mistake to think that a feasibility study can be carried out or a project can be designed without visiting the site. Just because the site or the building concerned is a long distance from the office, even in a different country, is no excuse. The architect must visit the site. There is no other way to understand the site or the building.

As part of the survey, a full set of photographs and videos should be taken, although it is a well understood and oft demonstrated fact that none of your photographs will show the very thing that you most want to look at when you return to the office.

42

Ground Investigations

Definition

A ground investigation is an examination of the ground to determine its type and character, including matters such as its bearing capacity, the presence of old mine workings, underground obstructions, services, and any existing contamination. The investigation is usually carried out first by visual inspection, then by means of trial pits, boreholes, soil sampling, and analysis and testing. Often a mixture of several of these methods depending upon the type of ground and what is known about its history (for example, the likelihood that structures with extensive underground works occupied the site) is used.

Practicalities

It is not usually practicable to require tendering contractors to carry out their own ground investigations, although it is sometimes included in the invitation to tender for design and build contracts. Realistically, to have different contractors entering upon the site to carry out their own investigations, boring holes and digging trenches in various places, is not desirable for obvious reasons.

Phrases in the specification or bills of quantities such as 'The contractor will be deemed to have carried out its own site investigations' will not be enforceable unless the contractor has been allowed to do this. In most projects, even design and build, the employer will have the site investigated at an early stage. In general, if the employer, as is usual, includes the site investigation report as part of the tender and contract documents, the employer will be liable to the contractor if the report is found to be inaccurate and excavation costs the contractor more than it would have done if the report had been accurate.

An employer cannot escape liability for an inaccurate report by adding a warning to the effect that the information may not be accurate. That is the equivalent of the employer stating that it is misrepresenting the situation.

Although architects are not usually qualified to carry out site investigations, they do have a responsibility to advise their clients about the need to have site investigations carried out.

Professional Practice for Architects and Project Managers, First Edition. David Chappell.

Ground Investigation Reports

Many architects believe that once the investigation report has been received and incorporated into the tender and contract documents, everything is under control – not so.

Years ago, I was involved in a project to construct three residential point blocks on a relatively flat site. A site investigation was carried out by geotechnical specialists randomly selecting a series of bore holes in every part of the site. When the report was received it showed that the site was unremarkable except for a top layer of demolished houses, which was as expected, and a seam of coal about 10 m from the surface. Each point block was to be founded on a set of large diameter deep reinforced concrete piles and drilling for the piles commenced. On reaching the coal strata it was discovered that it had been mined at some point and the records, if indeed there were any, had been lost. The mine workings which were found to be on the old pillar and stall method were flooded and the flood poured into the hole drilled for the first pile. It meant added cost because weighty steel sleeves had to be inserted to hold back the flood while the piling took place. From what could be seen of the old mine, it appeared to extend under most of the site. So why had the investigation not discovered it? The answer was that each bore hole, despite being located randomly, had gone down through a pillar or other unmined part of the site.

The moral is that site investigation reports may not tell you the whole story, no matter how carefully the bore holes are drilled, if the bore holes are in the wrong place. Nevertheless, in most cases a site investigation report is essential and gives a realistic view of the site. Always read the report with care, particularly the first and last parts, which usually contain disclaimers of responsibility if the report is inaccurate. The report will give all kinds of information. Some of the information will be deduced by the firm carrying out the investigations from the type of material revealed by the bore holes, e.g. the ground bearing pressure. But be aware that if the firm does not take responsibility for conveying a true picture of the site strata, you may not be able to rely on the conclusions the firm draws from it.

The sensible way to deal with all of this is to advise the employer to directly engage engineers to deal with ground investigations and to provide the information required to safely construct the building on the site.

43

Reports

What is a Report?

Most architects have experienced that sinking feeling when someone, be it client or senior architect, asks for a report. Different people mean different things when they ask for a report. Some people simply mean 'Come and talk to me about …'. Others mean 'Give me something that I can sit and read and carefully evaluate'. One is essentially an oral report and the other is essentially written. The *Concise Oxford Dictionary* defines a report as an account given or an opinion formally expressed after investigation or consideration.

There are two important parts of that definition: 'formal' and 'investigation'. A report is set out in a particular way and it is written or spoken only after some kind of investigation. The idea is to present findings as clearly and concisely as possible whether oral or written. What follows assumes that the report is a written report because, apart from the actual writing, an oral report should follow generally the same process.

Why do I always refer to 'oral' when you might say 'verbal'. The reason is that, strictly speaking, 'verbal' means 'concerned with words', although it is often loosely used to mean 'spoken words'. 'Oral' means 'spoken words' and it is, therefore, more precise and better than 'verbal'.

Why Write a Report?

Almost everyone has to produce a report at some time in their working life. So far as construction professionals are concerned, reports are an essential part of practice. When is it better to write a report than to write a letter or a brief note? There are only three reasons for writing a report:

- to give information
- to obtain information
- to obtain decisions or approvals.

Many reports combine all three reasons. At the end of the day, the decision whether to write a report or a letter will depend on the combination of a number of things:

- how complicated it is
- how long it is

Professional Practice for Architects and Project Managers, First Edition. David Chappell.

- whether diagrams or other illustrations are necessary
- why there is a need to write at all.

Reports have a lasting and formal quality which gives them a significance which letters do not usually have. Moreover, reports have a structure which is completely different from that of a letter. It involves building up the facts and forming conclusions.

The Reader

When preparing a report, the reader is the most important consideration. For example, if the material has to be presented to the board of a company, several copies will be required and the presentation will be very important. Some special copies may have to be produced summarising the main points for those who think they are too busy to read the full report from first page to last.

Unless the report is being prepared for people belonging to the same discipline as the writer, care must be taken to avoid technical expressions. It is easy to fall into the trap of using expressions and particularly abbreviations and acronyms unique to a particular profession in the mistaken belief that the recipient of the report will be impressed. He or she is more likely to be confused or irritated.

One of the essential qualities of a report is clarity. Often, the professional is trying to explain difficult processes or unfamiliar concepts to the relative layperson. If the phrasing is too technical, the recipient will not understand and the purpose of the report will be lost. It is a mistake to think that technical expressions are acceptable if a glossary is included. Glossaries occasionally have a purpose, but generally they should be avoided in a report, as should anything else which requires a lot of cross-referencing by the reader. It is a sign of failure in the writer if the report is not comprehensible in a straightforward read through.

There are times, of course, when to use the standard phraseology of a particular profession is desirable if not essential. Such an occasion would be when a report is being prepared for presentation to fellow professionals. It may shorten the report by removing the need for long explanations. However, there should be no traces of jargon. The use of jargon shows an inability to write well.

Often overlooked is the fact that a report may be read by people with conflicting interests. Few people will read a report totally free from bias, and most will have a preconceived notion of what they would like the report to say. A well-structured and factual report has a better chance than a letter of providing a convincing message in such circumstances.

The Report

Leaving aside those architects who effortlessly slide into report-writing mode, most of us waste time wondering how to start. I always think it is good to start at the beginning, although you may be surprised at the number of people who start a report with the conclusions and work back.

The aim of most reports is to guide the reader through a series of related facts, highlighting the options if any and closing with some recommendations or conclusions, with perhaps a request for a decision. Some reports, of course, are not like that, they are simply a presentation of the results of some research or survey. A report without a recommendation of any kind, however, is a rarity. Even if no action of any sort is required following a report, it is wise to say so or the recipient is left wondering if he or she should be doing something.

It is rare to produce a report entirely from first principles, and unnecessary. Most practices produce many reports of a particular type. In such cases, it is sensible to produce a format/checklist to speed up writing. It also avoids the danger that all reports will use exactly the same wording. I worked in one office where anyone tasked with writing a report was given a report that had been written years earlier and, for some reason, was considered to be the last word in reports. In a sense of course it was because no one had properly written a report since then. All subsequent reports were based on that model and the inevitable result was a cut-and-paste job. On the other hand, it is wasteful if every person in a practice starts from the very beginning every time. That is where formats are useful.

A format is simply a plan. The idea is to set out a framework common to all reports of a particular type. It will have a basic structure for general guidance and indications of options for hanging on the framework. It may seem complicated and it may take a little time and care in preparation, but it will repay the initial effort many times over. If the mind is freed from the drudgery of deciding how best to arrange the information which has been gathered, it can concentrate on the creative aspect – the actual writing.

Occasionally, it will be necessary to prepare a report for which there is no close precedent. In such a case, the basic principles of report structuring must be borne in mind:

- title page
- table of contents
- introduction
- possibly a bullet point summary
- the text
- conclusions/questions
- appendices.

The introduction is simply to state the authority for preparation of the report. More important is the summary. Not everyone agrees with the idea of having a summary. The arguments in favour are that:

- it enables the reader to grasp the key points quickly
- it is useful for the busy reader.

Arguments against a summary are that:

- it may tempt people to miss reading the full report
- it may give a poor impression of the full report.

The reader must be considered. A report produced for the benefit of a board of directors and some senior managers might well have several levels of information. It may be better to produce a full report, an abbreviated version, and a short summary each aimed at a different readership. Although a summary is usually unmistakable, a short version of the full report should always be clearly labelled to avoid misunderstandings. For some reason it has become the fashion to label all summaries as 'Executive Summary'. I am not clear what the benefit is of adding 'Executive' to the label because 'Summary' says it all. 'Executive' simply means relating to doing things. An executive is someone who does things. So, adding it to 'Summary' is just a waste of space.

The text contains the meat of the report. It is common to start by setting down the terms of reference used in preparing the report. This can answer many questions before they are framed.

It should state clearly what it is that the report sets out to do. Just what form the remainder of the text takes will depend on the subject matter, but it is usual to finish with a conclusion and some recommendations and, perhaps, a request for further instructions.

The appendices contain all the information which is not vital to understanding the main text of the report. Such things as graphs, photographs, plans, and statistics are often valuable adjuncts to the report, but not essential.

Fact and Opinion

The text of the report will be divided into fact and opinion. How far one or the other prevails will be determined by the subject. A fact is an incontrovertible statement relating to a particular situation at a particular time. Ideally, fact should be separated completely from opinion. In practice, it is not usually easy to do that and still maintain a clear exposition of the subject. The distinction, however, must be made clear to the reader and facts must come first in any particular section of the report. Opinions should be gathered together and put in the conclusion. That is a counsel of perfection which is difficult to achieve, particularly as in some kinds of report whole chapters may be very substantially opinion. There may be a thin dividing line between fact and opinion in some instances. For example, it would be opinion to state 'The best form of transport is the train', but it could be fact to state 'Over 50% of people consider the train to be the best form of transport'. A good report builds upon facts and reaches an apparently inevitable conclusion which may actually be opinion. A report is unconvincing if early opinions form the basis of later conclusions.

Style is important, but it will vary with the individual. Although eccentricities of style are to be avoided, a report is intended to be read and, therefore, a little character in the writing is not to be despised. On the whole, however, a fairly formal approach should be adopted and the third person used. A well-written report is the result of hard work and will emerge as a result of several drafts. The finished product should be crisply written and to the point. Grammar, spelling, and punctuation must be impeccable.

Presentation

Trash inside a nice cover is still trash. A good cover, however, is essential if the recipient is to be encouraged to look inside at what is hopefully an important piece of work. A practice which regularly produces reports as part of its business will usually have its own, instantly recognisable, cover.

The layout of text on the page is a matter for individual or practice preference, but there are one or two rules. Margins should be generous, especially at the spine. It makes binding easy and gives space for noting comments. A top margin should be a maximum of two thirds the depth of the bottom margin. It helps later referencing if pages are clearly numbered and the text is separated into numbered sections and paragraphs, each corresponding to a different topic or concept. The line spacing is traditionally double, but this combined with generous margins means the page begins to look rather empty. Single spacing is perfectly acceptable, but one and a half spacing is a good compromise.

It is best to avoid references if possible. If they are necessary, they are best gathered at the end of each section. Footnotes and side notes are not recommended, particularly if they occupy more space than the text.

Elaborate presentations are becoming common as means to deliver a theme to a group. Presentations of reports are often carried out with audio and visuals. Such presentations may indeed generate a lot of attention, just like the cover of the report, but the presentation is transient and afterwards the only tangible evidence will be the report. In such circumstances, the layout should be devised to trigger memories of the presentation, but it must also be capable of standing alone.

The report must be properly bound so that it can be opened flat.

Essentials of a Good Report

The essentials of a good report can be summarised as:

- clear purpose
- defined readership
- well structured
- clarity of language
- formal style with individual approach
- fact and opinion readily identifiable
- good presentation
- conclusion, recommendations, and/or request for decisions at the end.

Occasionally, a report is the final step in a process. The majority of reports, however, are to be looked on as a stage in a process. Very often, the calibre of a report is a crucial factor in determining whether the process follows one course or another, or even comes to an end.

44

Sketch Designs

Sketch design is a term which is loosely applied to any preliminary drawings prepared by the architect. Sometimes the drawings are rough sketches and at other times they can be highly finished presentations. Generally, when the phrase 'sketch design' is mentioned, one thinks of fairly rough drawings accompanied by outline perspectives. The idea is to have a proposal, or sometimes several alternative proposals, to discuss with the client.

Although sketch design sounds very casual, a great deal of effort is required to produce a good sketch design even if the project is relatively small. Where a large project is concerned, I would expect the sketch design to result from a meeting of all the consultants involved who obviously must be appointed at the very beginning of the project. The notable architect Sir Basil Spence was said to go on site with his sketch pad as soon as he received the brief. He would then sketch the site from all angles, inserting the kind of building he thought would look well. Armed with his wonderful sketches, he would call a meeting of all consultants to whom he explained the brief and showed them what he had drawn. Having fired up their imaginations the stage was set to do some valuable preliminary work to set the foundation for everything that was done from then onwards. I am not suggesting that the ideal way to design a building is to design the outside first, although it is clear that many buildings have been designed like this, including the only one of my student sketch designs to ever achieve a grade A1. The moral of my story is that before getting down to produce a sketch design (unless the building is very small) there should be a meeting with all consultants so that the sketch design can take everything into account albeit in a sketchy kind of way.

Professional Practice for Architects and Project Managers, First Edition. David Chappell.

45

Design Development

Definition

'Design development' is a much-misused phrase, usually by building owners. It has important fee implications.

It will not be found in standard contract definitions and it is not a phrase which is generally accepted to mean a particular part of the design process. It is a term which has to be viewed in context. It used to be the name of Stage D of the 2007 RIBA Plan of Work. There it was used in a very narrow sense, applying just to that stage. The definition of Stage D was:

Development of concept design to include structural and building services systems, updated outline specifications and cost plan.
Completion of Project Brief.
Possibly application for planning permission.

That actually gives the sense of what design development in a general sense means. When applied generally to the work which an architect carries out, it means the process undertaken by an architect to complete a design. Taking the process very briefly, the first step is the establishment of the brief, which should contain details of what the client requires from the finished building. From this, the architect prepares the outline of the design, sometimes called a sketch design or a concept design. At this stage the client can see the general disposition of rooms, spaces, and sizes, and some basic amendments may be made. The next stage is to add more detail, including services requirements and constructional considerations. The final stage is when all the details are finalised in respect of design, specification, construction, and cost.

The Key

The key thing about design development is that the design is developing throughout the process, but it is not changing. It is essentially the same design that the client agreed as the original concept but more detail is being added and slight adjustments made. If the client requires the design to be altered at any subsequent stage, it is not design development, it is design change. The word 'adjustment' is important. Changing the position of a washbasin may be design development or it may be a design change, depending on the circumstances. As a very broad rule of thumb, it is design development if the adjustment

Professional Practice for Architects and Project Managers, First Edition. David Chappell.

is necessary to make the design work, but it is a change if the design works perfectly well without the adjustment.

The Fee Question

An architect can be expected to carry out the whole of the design development for the fee quoted and agreed. However, changes to the design will normally attract additional fees. If the design is changed, the architect is entitled to a fee for carrying out the change. Many clients do not understand this. They assume that within the overall fee they are entitled to change the design as many times as they wish. This trend is observable whether the project is a small house or a large commercial building. Clients want to feel free to change their minds about aspects of the design without any financial consequences. The client should be firmly disabused of that notion.

What some clients don't want to understand is that if the architect designs a building in accordance with the client's initial requirements and produces a plan which satisfies those requirements, the architect has performed his or her side of the bargain and is entitled to be paid the agreed fee. If the client, on reviewing the design, decides to change the original brief, the architect is entitled to extra fees. In this regard, architects can be their own worst enemies because many architects are quite prepared to amend their designs several times until the client is finally happy. That is fine if the architect is working on an hourly rate, but not if it is a fixed fee.

Many architects seek my advice when they are finding it difficult to produce a design which satisfies their clients and wonder what they can do to make clients understand that they cannot go on forever amending the design at no extra cost. The consultation follows the same pattern. In each case, I ask the same questions: 'When you produced the first design, did it satisfy the client's brief?' The answer is usually that it did. 'Well then', I say, 'Why, when the client asked you to change the design, did you not explain that you would be charging an extra fee for the changes?' The answer to that is usually that the architect considered that it was part and parcel of the services to accommodate some changes required by the client in the early stages. I would then ask how many changes amounted to 'some changes' and if the architect had a clear idea of that, did the client have the same clear idea?

At this point, realisation begins to dawn that, by agreeing to alter the design several times without commenting on any fee implication, the architect has set a precedent, certainly in the mind of the client, that the architect will makes as many changes as it takes to get the client's final agreement even if the client has many changes of mind back and forth. When an architect gets into this kind of mess the only thing to do the next time the client looks at the design and suggests further changes is to point out that the initial design was produced in response to the brief carefully taken down by the architect and that the initial design fully satisfied that brief, that the architect has tried to deal with the considerable changes required since then but notes that after (specify the number) re-drawings later, the client is still having changes of mind. Regrettably, the architect will have to charge on an hourly basis for any further changes. Needless to say, at that point the client, having been lulled into a cosy feeling that the architect is game for changing and re-changing the design for as long as the client wishes, will feel let down by the architect. However, in those circumstances the architect has little choice.

Of course, one understands the architect's wish to keep the client happy, but it is more important that both parties are happy. The only certain way to get out of this mess is not to get into it in the first place (as one of my friends unhelpfully used to say).

The principle is the same if the contractor is employed on a design and build basis. The contractor will have produced his Contractor's Proposals in response to the Employer's Requirements document. The proposals have to undergo design development to produce the detailed drawings which enable the contractor to construct the building. But if the employer makes a change to the Employer's Requirements, that is not design development, it is a change to the brief as a result of which the contractor will have to change the design. The contractor will then expect payment of the design fee element as well as a valuation carried out in accordance with the contract in respect of the construction work.

46

Cost Estimates

Definition and Warning

The term 'cost estimates' is often misunderstood. In practice it is probably more often misunderstood than understood. This is despite the fact that it is commonly used throughout the construction industry. It means a 'probable cost' or a 'judged amount'. It is usually intended to be an approximate figure rather than a figure carefully calculated. This is the trap, because depending on the particular circumstances it may be taken as a firm offer which, if it is accepted by the person to whom it is submitted, would result in a legally binding contract.

This is most likely if the person submitting the estimate is a builder or tradesperson who is in a position to carry out Works or provide some kind of service. It could also apply to construction professional providing an 'estimate' of fees. Most people supplying an estimate assume that they are simply giving a figure which is approximate and liable to change. Therefore, if your plumber gives an estimate for refitting the bathroom at £7000, that same plumber would no doubt be astonished, as only plumbers can be, if you objected to a final bill amounting to £7500. The only safe way to proceed is to qualify the word 'estimate' by calling it a 'very rough and approximate estimate'.

Construction Estimates and Fees

Architects, working to a budget, are often asked to give an estimate to a client of the cost of the project as designed so that the client can make a firm decision whether or not to proceed. In such circumstances the architect should always refer the client to a quantity surveyor for an accurate estimate. The architect is obviously not offering to carry out the Works for that price. Such estimates by their nature cannot be precise and, therefore, the architect or the quantity surveyor should inform the client of a possible margin of error and other things which need to be considered such as inflation or whether VAT is included or excluded.

Estimates produced by an architect or quantity surveyor before the invitation of tenders must be more accurate than an estimate produced at feasibility stage: there is a vastly increased amount of detail available at the later stage. Clients tend to expect accuracy and, therefore, architects and quantity surveyors often err on the high side in order to avoid unpleasant surprises when tenders are opened. It is certainly a mistake to pitch an estimate too low. A subsequent failure to achieve that figure may result in a

Professional Practice for Architects and Project Managers, First Edition. David Chappell.

client claiming at least the return of the fees and possibly more, such as the additional overspend. If the word 'estimate' is used, it should have some foundation in calculation and fact. Something to bear in mind is that whatever figure you or the quantity surveyor gives to the client at the beginning of the project will be the figure that the client clings to throughout the remainder of the job. That is the case even though the client has instructed you to include many additional items and you have consistently warned that the cost is increasing. When the tenders come in much as you and the quantity surveyor expected, it will be the client who is appalled at the vast increase in cost from your original estimate; just a fact of life I'm afraid.

47

Cost Planning

Take Care

The first, and it could be the last, thing to say about costs is that the architect should stay as far away from them as possible. The quantity surveyor is the expert on costs. It should be made clear to clients that it is essential to have a quantity surveyor dealing with cost estimates on every job except the very smallest ones. It is a fact, not, as they say on all the health products, 'clinically proven', but none the less fact in my somewhat less precise world that your clients will always remember the first estimate of cost you give them, whatever else they forget.

That said, it is a very astute architect who can avoid being drawn into giving a client a rough estimate of cost. The client will set out what is required in the house, office, factory etc. and then ask if you can give an idea of the likely cost. If you do, this is the figure that your client will remember forever without any of the qualifications you may attach. If you suggest that now is the time to get a quantity surveyor involved, your client will remark that surely you can provide just a very rough guide. Architects are well known for jumping in with both feet when they should really stand well back from the edge. Most architects will feel well able to give a rough figure based on the client's brief turned into areas or volumes of building. Maybe you can, maybe you can't, but don't.

Some, possibly all, schools of architecture teach students how to roughly price the cost of a building by applying standard figures to the areas or volumes. The problem is that there are so many possible variables of specification, structure, finishes etc. that any figure you give will be far off the eventual tender. One has only to look at the great variation in tender price for the same project to realise that estimating is a difficult job. So, architects must not give even rough estimates, no matter how carefully qualified, because long after the client has increased the cost of the project by increasing the floor area, upgrading the finishes, and adding interesting little quirks in the design, that same client will be astonished at your incompetence if the project cannot actually be constructed for the original, well-remembered estimate you gave for a garden shed which has now become a well-appointed extension to the house.

If you must give your own estimate of cost, the only way to protect yourself is to notify your client in writing of likely increases in cost when your client asks you to add or upgrade something. This may assist you when your client eventually complains to the ARB that you are incompetent.

Professional Practice for Architects and Project Managers, First Edition. David Chappell.

The Budget

The key thing is to get a budget out of the client: how much can be spent, including the cost of construction and all professional fees. However much your client kicks and screams, you must get this figure. Even say that you cannot continue if you do not have a figure. The truth is that you cannot design something for your client if you do not know how much your client wants to spend. The budget is as much part of the brief as floor areas and usage of space. Clients hate to give this figure and it will be necessary to explain why you must have it. It is as though clients are wheeler-dealing with architects, completely misunderstanding their role. A client cannot treat engaging an architect to design a building in the same way as going to purchase a used car. In going to buy a car, one might not want to say how much one is prepared to pay until the process of walking around and looking at what's on offer for what price is completed. Then one sees the right car at roughly the right price and attempts to negotiate a cheaper price. Apart from a little time spent trying to get you to buy the car, the salesman has not wasted any time at all. If the same technique is applied by the client to the architect, the architect spends many hours devising a scheme to present to the client only to be told that it is too expensive. Therefore, you must get a budget figure before you do anything.

The Cost Plan

Armed with the budget figure and briefing information, the quantity surveyor can produce a cost plan which allocates a sum of money to each element of the design. Importantly, so far as the architect is concerned, the quantity surveyor can tell the architect what types of construction and finishes can be used even to the extent of indicating the range of types of finishes for walls, ceilings, and floors and the comparative cost of using different constructional methods. As the design progresses, the detailed cost plan can be updated and become more and more accurate. Not only is this very helpful for the client, it is invaluable to the architect, who is effectively being given a toolkit specifically designed for that commission.

We all know that even the most careful costing can result in a poor set of tenders if the tendering climate is not good. But cost planning by the quantity surveyor is the application of science and statistics to the problem of estimating, whereas most architects simply rely on a volumetric or, worse still, floor area system of arriving at a rough cost which is of no help in telling the architect whether to use polished hardwood narrow strip flooring or some kind of wood chip boards.

48

Amenity Societies

Always Involve Amenity Societies

Most cities, towns, and sometimes villages have amenity societies. The name is used here to describe all the many kinds of special interest, civic, and other societies that get involved in commenting, often quite loudly, about proposed new building work. They perform a valuable service to the community and act as watchdogs to see that proposed changes to the environment are for the better. Sometimes, of course, they can be a real pain. It is always a good idea for architects wishing to get planning permission for anything which could even loosely be termed a notable building to get the client's agreement to arrange meetings with the local amenity society. If the proposal involves refurbishment or changes or extensions to an old building, it is prudent to involve the local history society or at least ask if they wish to be involved.

Timing

Do not wait until the society lodges an objection to your proposal at planning application stage. By that time, views will have hardened and it will be difficult to persuade the society to change its mind. For some unaccountable reason, what are commonly known as u-turns seem to be something to despise when in fact they simply show a sensible willingness to reconsider a decision.

As soon as you have some idea of the likely appearance of the building, that is the time to discuss the scheme with the society members. Obviously, the client will have to agree, but there are dividends to discussing proposals with amenity societies at an early stage at the very start of the design process. They may make useful suggestions. At worst you will find out what they dislike.

Problems

One of the problems with amenity societies is that among the members there may be people with an axe to grind. The point may not be directly related to your building but your building is considered to be a good opportunity to raise some long-standing grumble. Needless to say, if the proposal personally affects one of the members, and

Professional Practice for Architects and Project Managers, First Edition. David Chappell.

particularly if that member is the chairperson or secretary or treasurer of the society, you will have an uphill struggle to secure the society's support. I will go further and say that you will have no chance of getting their support. I am aware of one such instance where the secretary of the society, who was also a person of some standing in the local authority, opposed a large development. The barely concealed reason was its proximity to his home. Being of an assertive nature, he easily persuaded the society to successfully object on other grounds.

Quite apart from instances of obvious self-interest, which should become apparent at any initial meeting, there is always the danger of an obsessive desire in some individuals to protect old buildings. If a development threatens anything old, which could be anything over 50 years, there could be objections. I know instances of attempts to protect lamp posts, wooden benches, a patch of stone paving, and a square metre of old stone wall. There are larger examples of decrepit old buildings of no architectural, historic, or other interest in danger of the collapse which would be a blessing to all concerned where societies fight tooth and nail to stop demolition. I think that sometimes they just need a cause to champion.

The moral of all this is that amenity societies should be treated with the utmost respect. They do wield considerable influence.

Offer a Presentation

If the client has commodious premises which are the subject of the proposal and easily accessible, it could be a good idea to invite society members along to hear a presentation and have light refreshments available afterwards. Otherwise, offer to go to one of their meetings. In making the presentation, perspectives and models are always an attraction. Do not simply rely on plans, elevations, and sections, which many people find difficult to understand (see 12: Presentation). Questions and views should be invited and it should be made clear before the members leave that it has been a very helpful meeting and all the views expressed will be taken into account. Importantly, with the client's agreement, a follow-up letter should be sent to the society with a promise to keep them informed of developments.

49

Building Control

A Few General Things

I am not going to say much about Building Regulations. You all know more about them than I do. Every architect or person who designs buildings should have a good working knowledge of the Building Regulations. There are books devoted to them so it is pointless to even attempt a discussion of them here. What I would like to do is to offer a few thoughts about building control as it affects the architect and client.

At one time, all building control was operated by local authorities. Now, of course, there are many private companies which offer the service of approved inspectors. Many of these companies are very efficient, helpful, and surprisingly competitive. Building Works or alterations to buildings usually require a Building Regulations application to be submitted. For some minor works a competent person may be engaged to design, install, and test the work. Some constructions are exempt from building control.

It is an offence to start construction without first depositing plans or a building notice with the local authority, giving at least two clear days' notice. If an Approved Inspector is involved, an Initial Notice of the intention to carry out the work must be submitted five days before work commences. Approval is not needed before work starts. Importantly, there is no deemed approval as some people believe. Even if there was, it would be irrelevant if there was a contravention of the Regulations because the applicant has an overriding duty to construct in accordance with the Building Regulations.

Completion Certificates

Although many architects refuse to issue a certificate of practical completion unless the local authority has issued a completion certificate under the regulations, those architects are misguided. The completion certificate issued by the local authority and final certificates issued by approved inspectors have no connection with the building contract. Building contracts do not normally say that the certificate of practical completion cannot be issued until local authority completion certificate is issued. It is true that most building contracts somewhere say that the contractor must comply with the Building Regulations, but those contracts assume that the architect will decide whether or not the contractor has complied. It would be a breach of contract for the architect to delay the issue of the certificate of practical completion until the local authority's certificate had been received. It must also be remembered that the criteria for the issue of the certificate

Professional Practice for Architects and Project Managers, First Edition. David Chappell.

of practical completion is not the same as for the local authority's certificate. Most work specified by architects ought to exceed the requirements of the Building Regulations. Therefore, the local authority's completion certificate is no guarantee that the Works *as specified* have reached practical completion.

Local Authority Fees

Local authorities charge a fee for processing applications and inspecting the Works. Many architects actually pay these fees themselves and then seek to recover them from the client. That is an exceeding bad practice. It means that the architect has to wait until the client pays the architect's fees which include the local authority fee as a disbursement. During this period, which may be longer than anticipated, the architect is losing any bank interest on the amount of the local authority fee. It is better practice that the architect requires a cheque from the client made out to the local authority for the amount of the local authority fee so that the architect can submit the cheque along with the application or notice. Architects should refuse to submit applications unless the client provides the cheque. If the client objects to being asked to provide the cheque, it is worth pointing out that it is no part of the architect's service to advance money to the client.

Withdrawing Applications

Several architects have asked me whether, after submitting Building Control, or indeed Planning, applications, and if the is client owing fees, they can withdraw the application and refuse to submit it again until all unpaid fees have been paid in full. This sounds like a great idea to compel payment if architects could do that, but they can't. The reason is that when they submit these applications, they usually do so as agent for the client. In other words, the client has submitted the application and only the client can withdraw it. Of course, the architect can write to the local authority and ask them to withdraw the application, but the authority will do nothing unless the architect clearly states that he or she is acting on behalf of the client and if the architect does that, it will amount to unprofessional conduct and fraud to say the least.

Building Control Officer's Instructions on Site

My final word on this topic concerns the situation which occurs when the architect arrives on site to be told by the contractor that the Building Control Officer has been to site and instructed the contractor to do something that is not in the contract documents. It may be excavating for deeper foundations or laying the damp-proof membrane in a different way or increasing the size of a padstone etc. Of course, the Building Control Officer has the right to point out contraventions of the Regulations and to demand that the problem is rectified. Mostly, the architect will decide that the instruction was sensible and simple confirm it as an architect's instruction. There lies the problem. The

Building Control Officer has no authority to instruct the contractor and the contractor has no authority to carry out the instruction. The contractor, and probably the architect also, may be grateful to receive a way out of the contravention rather than just being informed that there was a contravention and that it should be corrected. But only the architect can instruct the contractor. What if the architect, arriving on site is informed of the problem and that it has now been corrected in accordance with the instructions of the Building Control Officer and what if the architect, while accepting the problem, actually wishes to solve it in a different way? The contractor is in breach of contract because it has constructed work which is not in accordance with the contract despite the fact that it may now be in compliance with the Building Regulations. The architect is entitled to issue instructions requiring the contractor to remove the unauthorised work and vary the work in accordance with the architect's requirements. All this could be avoided if the contractor simply informed the architect of the Building Control Officer's 'instructions' before carrying them out.

50

Procurement

What does Procurement Mean?

'Procurement' simply means the obtaining of something by care and effort. In the construction industry it is used to refer to the way in which a finished structure is produced. There are many ways of getting from nothing to a finished building and new ways are being devised all the time. I say 'new ways' but usually the new ways are based on ways that have already been used successfully and the new way simply makes a few adjustments, not always for the better. It is surprising how many 'new ways' are essentially design and build. Very rarely, someone decides to look at the way buildings are procured in an entirely new way and it is sometimes referred to as introducing a new philosophy. But, when you have spent a great deal of time considering how to procure a specific building and whichever established or new procurement system you adopt, you must always keep the end goal firmly in sight. Whatever procurement system you choose, it is simply a means to an end not, as some people seem to think, an end in itself.

Choosing the Right System

One hundred and fifty years ago there was only one common system of procurement and that was not what we now term 'traditional' but more like what we term 'construction management', with a contractor plus separately engaged trade contractors for joinery, plumbing, bricklaying etc. We like to think that life was simpler then. Now you have seemingly endless systems from which to choose, but the choice must be made in the light of the criteria gathered from the employer during the early stages of the commission. The key things to be considered are detailed in the following sections.

Time

The majority of employers want the project to be completed as quickly as possible. This desire can be responsible directly and indirectly for many of the disputes which arise in regard to building projects. It is part of the architect's task to explain the possible consequences of undue emphasis on speed very plainly to the employer. Unfortunately, many architects allow themselves to be bullied into promising a timetable which is not achievable. If architects get themselves into that situation, I am afraid that they have only themselves to blame. Architects, unlike other professions, are not good at saying 'No'.

Professional Practice for Architects and Project Managers, First Edition. David Chappell.

If your employer was told by a consultant surgeon that after performing one procedure, he would have to wait for three weeks to allow his body to recover before the second procedure could be performed, it is highly unlikely that he would argue. If he did and demanded that the second procedure be carried out with only a week in between, the consultant would simply decline and, if pressed, would no doubt give him the opportunity to go elsewhere. In my experience, the reason that some architects don't refuse to be pressured into unrealistic timescales is because they do not want to offend the employer and thereby lose the commission. But the choice is really quite stark:

1. Accept a ludicrously short timescale in the certain knowledge that it is unachievable and will result in recriminations and possibly claims, or
2. Stick to a realistic timescale and the employer may, just may, respect the professionalism that refuses to be pressurised.

Design and construction processes are known to be lengthy. The time available will affect things such as the type of design and construction. If speed is vital, standard designs and construction techniques might be chosen which might not be compatible with high quality.

Identifying the absolutely minimum period for any particular project can be a problem. The period is directly related to other criteria so that economies in time can only be achieved by sacrificing in other areas: small simple buildings are quicker to erect than large complex buildings; after a certain point, speed becomes very expensive, high speed is often high risk for the employer. Those are just some factors.

In order to reduce time, it may be possible to reduce various operational periods. The greatest economies in time are usually achieved by telescoping the first period into the second so that the construction starts before all the design and production information is ready. That is usually called fast tracking. Early selection of the contractor is important. Fast tracking has risks and some consider it to be bad practice because if work on site begins before details are finalised the employer has less control over the project and cannot be certain precisely how much it will cost. The contractor will usually be involved in the design stage and that will probably mean a negotiated tender, which will generally be more expensive than competitive tendering. If speed is essential, it can only be achieved at the expense of other considerations.

Where speed is essential, organisation of design and construction work becomes more important. Should the organisation be left in its present state, fragmented between architect and contractor, or should it be in the hands of one or the other or indeed a third party?

The following are among the essential attributes of fast building:

- single purpose
- competent management
- interlocking working practices
- excellent communication channels
- effective quality control.

Often, the employer's priority is that a particular completion date is achieved. This is time certainty. It may not matter how long the design and construction takes provided that completion date is known from the beginning. Some organisations must plan for the opening of the building many months before completion because of other events taking place at the same time. A typical example is if it has been arranged for a notable person to perform an opening ceremony. A delay of even a few days may be disastrous.

One of the main reasons why contracts do not finish on time is because the employer has a change of mind at a late stage or even during the construction process. Another common reason is shortage of production information, which may, or may not, be due to employer changes of mind. An employer who desires time certainty must be made to understand that it is incompatible with changes of mind. If the employer settles the requirements, the architect produces full and accurate information, and there are no variations during the progress of the works, the contractor's principal excuses for not completing on time are removed.

With time certainty, control goes out of the hands of the employer, with most of the risk residing with the contractor; there is also certainty, but not necessarily economy, of cost. The quality, size, and complexity of the project should have no effect other than to fix the completion date nearer to or further from the date of commencement. These factors will not usually affect the chances of meeting the date when fixed.

Cost

If the cheapest possible building is required, some kind of competitive tendering is indicated. Open tendering usually results in lower tenders than selective tendering, but problems may be caused by the inclusion of unsuitable or unknown firms. Negotiated tenders can be economical if the project is one of a string of projects which the contractor is hoping to carry out. Other factors which tend to increase the cost of building at tender stage are:

- contract conditions onerous to the contractor
- requirement for high standards of workmanship and materials
- an unusually short contract period
- high liquidated damages
- very detailed tender documents
- complexity of work
- restrictions on working hours or space or sequence of working
- inadequate number of firms on the tender list prepared to give a proper tender.

Other things encountered during the progress of the Works may produce large cost increases on the tender sum:

- employer's changes of mind and consequent variations
- late supply of information from the architect and other consultants
- contract provisions for fluctuations in costs
- employer interference on site
- contractor's claims for loss and/or expense due to employer's actions or defaults
- type and amount of cash flow arrangements. Procurement methods can have a significant effect upon cash flow and, therefore, on the real cost to the employer. In appropriate circumstances, a straightforward cost reimbursement contract can be the cheapest way to build. The risk, however, is with the employer and there is no cost certainty. Appropriate circumstances include:
  - complex work of uncertain nature or extent where to request a lump sum price would result in the contractor loading its tender against the unknown factors

- effective cost controls and recording arrangements
- well-organised and competent contractor
- when contractors, generally, have full workloads.

At times, when there is a shortage of work, a form of cost reimbursement or management fee approach may prove to be an expensive proposition, although in times of low construction activity contractors are sometimes prepared to price the work with a low profit element and take the chance that nothing of significance will go wrong. In times of full workloads, the opposite tends to be the case and paying contractors their actual costs plus an agreed amount for profit may be a better financial solution.

The employer should always be advised on the long-term life-cycle costs of the building. This will affect quality considerations (e.g. high-quality construction using durable materials should require less maintenance and, therefore, less expenditure over a long period) and may influence the type of design and even the time spent in construction. Only after a full life-cycle costing exercise has been carried out and all costs expressed in terms of present costs can it be determined whether it is more economical in the long term to invest more in the capital cost of the building. Even if this is shown to be the most cost-effective option, the employer may decide that the necessary finance is not available.

An employer may be more concerned with certainty of cost than getting the cheapest cost. That suggests a lump sum contract with strict cost controls. It is not enough simply to stipulate that the contract is on a firm price basis. Certainty, unlike economy, of cost should be achievable without affecting or being affected by any other procurement criteria.

Control and Risk

There is some form of risk for everyone involved in a construction project. Risk need not be entirely monetary. It can involve time or quality. The results, however, are often translated into monetary terms. The amount of risk can be reduced, but it cannot be removed entirely. The chances of a building being constructed in a wholly satisfactory way are improved if an experienced contractor is selected.

Control generally goes with risk. In a fixed-price lump-sum contract, the contractor is shouldering most of the risk. It is gambling that the price quoted is enough to cover anything overlooked together with any inadequacies in its work process. If the contract provisions are onerous, if there could be problems with labour relations, the skill of operatives, the attitude of the clerk of works, and the architect, a point may be reached where the contractor is unwilling to tender at all because the risk is too great.

On the other hand, if a management contract is used, the employer will take most of the risk. It operates on a cost reimbursement principle. The risk that the price will be greater than expected will fall squarely on the employer because the contractor will be entitled to be paid costs plus a management fee.

Getting the contractor to take a risk will cost the employer money. Although it may seem in the employer's best interests if the contractor can be made to take virtually all the risk of a contract, it must be remembered that the contractor will price the risk and if the risk does not materialise, the contractor gains extra profit. If the employer is willing to take some risk, the result may be a very much cheaper project. Contract provisions which assist in assessing the allocation of risk include:

- type of price
- contractor's obligations
- workmanship, materials, and defects
- grounds for extension of time
- payment provisions
- loss and/or expense provisions
- termination provisions.

Quality

An employer seeking a high-quality building is looking for quality of design or of construction or, more commonly, both. Where design quality is paramount, an independent architect is clearly indicated. Where single-point responsibility is required, the employer has the option of:

- design and build
- design and manage.

In design and build, the builder is responsible for driving the contract to completion; in design and manage it may be the architect who designs and co-ordinates the building work.

Good-quality construction cannot really be separated from design. A design may be mediocre in an aesthetic and/or functional sense yet built of first-class materials put together in a thoroughly sound way. It is doubtful whether a contractor-led procurement system will automatically result in a better quality of construction, but it probably will result in improved buildability. Certainly, it appears to be the case that involvement of the contractor early in the design process can have marked advantages in securing the most suitable constructional system, which in turn should improve the quality of the construction. Factors which may tend to work against high-quality construction are:

- acceptance of the lowest tender
- short contract period
- risk on the contractor.

Positive factors are:

- sound design
- good specification
- full, accurate, and clear production information
- good supervision by the contractor
- proper inspection procedures by the architect
- competence, skill, and experience of the contractor
- skills of operatives
- motivation of the contractor and its operatives.

Size/Value

The size or value of a project alone is not a conclusive indication of the procurement or contract type most suitable. A relatively small building such as a clinic or laboratory may be so crammed with complex technology that it is a very expensive project, ideally suited to some kind of management or project management contract. A large simple building may be quite expensive, but suitable for a straightforward traditional procurement arrangement.

Therefore, size and value can be considered as giving an indication of the most appropriate procurement system, but these criteria may not be the key factors in terms of decision making. Larger projects may need a further tier of management. On smaller schemes this may be too cumbersome.

Complexity

Complexity may result from:

- the employer's requirements
- innovative design
- special construction methods
- the nature of the site
- complex phasing of site operations.

It will have an effect on:

- time
- cost
- control
- quality.

The more complex the project, the more important it is to involve the contractor at an early stage and, therefore, some form of two-stage negotiated tender is probably essential for highly complex work. A very simple project, such as a warehouse or other large enclosed space, is suitable for simple procurement systems such as traditional tendering or design and build. The employer may have little control over the complexity of the requirements, but the complexity of the procurement as a whole can be reduced by considering design and phasing requirements.

Procurement Systems

Someone once said that there are only six jokes and all the rest are variations on the six. The same is true about procurement. It seems to be fashionable to invent allegedly new systems of procurement. It is easy to get dazzled by the seemingly endless choice. How can you be sure that you have given proper consideration to all the choices? Well, the answer is that you can never be sure. Once you understand that, stop stressing and life becomes easier. All the procurement systems are variations on six, some might say four, systems. The detail may change and a 'new' system may appear in a welter of excited publicity, but if you examine it closely, you will see that it is usually an old system in a new outfit. It is important to understand the basic procurement systems so that you can recognise 'new' systems as they come along and understand what the key points are. These are the main systems:

- traditional
- project management

- design and build
- design and manage
- management contracting
- construction management.

These are the systems which differ from each other in significant ways.

Traditional

This is where the employer commissions an architect or other construction professional to take a brief, produce designs and construction information, invite tenders, administer the project during the construction period, and settle the final account. There may be other consultants for such things as structural calculations, cost control, and building services employed directly by the employer. The contractor has no design responsibility and will be responsible for constructing the building in accordance with the drawings and specifications produced by the architect and other professionals.

The key points are that the construction professionals are responsible for the design of the building and they are all contracted separately to the employer. The contractor is responsible for the supply of goods and materials and construction of the building. The contractor will employ direct labour as well as being in contract with sub-contractors and suppliers.

Project Management

In true project management, rather than the fudge that usually passes for project management (see 33: Project Manager), the project manager takes the lead. The project management system places most emphasis on planning and management. The project manager has the authority to manage and control the project, including organising and co-ordinating all consultants.

The key points are that the project manager and all the professionals are in separate contracts with the employer, but the project manager controls them all and is the only one entitled to instruct the contractor. The professionals are responsible for the design. The contractor is responsible for the supply of goods and materials and construction of the building. The contractor will employ direct labour as well as being in contract with sub-contractors and suppliers.

Design and Build

This is a simple system in principle which places responsibility for both design and construction in the hands of the contractor; a single point of responsibility for an employer. At its simplest and, I would say, its best, the employer is assisted throughout in preparation of the brief, selecting the contractor, and acting for the employer during the construction by an architect and the contractor engages its own architect to complete the design.

The key points are that the contractor is in contract with the employer and responsible for design and construction and enters into supply and sub-contracts. The contractor can start work from RIBA Stage 0 or at any other stage until commencement on site.

Design and Manage

This is not well established. It is the counterpart to design and build and it is sometimes referred to as design, manage, and construct. The system may be led by an architect, engineer, or surveyor. This type of procurement is ideal where relatively small projects as concerned and require strict control over every aspect of the design.

The key points are that the professional is in contract with the employer and responsible for design and construction, directly employs other professionals, and enters into contracts with suppliers and sub-contractors.

Management Contracting

This system requires the contractor to be selected at an early stage. The contractor is not normally responsible for carrying out any of the construction work. It simply has a management function for which a fee is paid.

The key points are that the works contractors are in contract with the management contractor. The architect and other consultants and the contractor are each contracted separately to the employer. The construction work is divided into packages, and tenders for the individual packages are invited as the Works progress and the employer pays only the management fee and the works contracts' costs without the addition of any contractor's overheads or profit.

Construction Management

This system has something of the flavour of project management and management contracting. The architect and other consultants are appointed by the employer. The management contractor is appointed and paid a fee, and it is responsible for inviting works package tenders.

The key points are that the management contractor, the consultants, and the packages form a number of separate contracts with, and are paid directly by, the employer but the management contractor is responsible for managing and co-ordinating the Works, including co-ordinating the consultants.

Some General Points

Design and build appears in several common guises and there is some confusion in the terminology. Some of the common names and a brief definition of each is as follows:

- *Design and build*: This is the basic system where a contractor carries out both design and construction.
- *Design and construct*: This is a broad term which includes design and build and other types of construction such as purely engineering work.
- *Develop and construct*: This is where a contractor takes a partially completed design and develops it into a fully detailed design.
- *Package deal*: This term is often used to refer to any of the above. Strictly speaking, it is when the contractor is responsible for providing everything in one package and it is particularly the case when an industrialised building is involved.

- *Turnkey*: This is a system in which the contractor is responsible for everything, including furniture and pictures on the walls if required. The idea is that the employer simply turns the key and begins using the building.

There have been many other variations on the same theme in recent years.

Few contractors have their own architects' department and will usually engage an architect, in the normal way, to assist them. Architects must not forget that they will owe a duty to the contractor, which will depend on the conditions of engagement agreed for the work. They will have no duty to the employer (the 'client' is the contractor in these circumstances) other than the ordinary common law duty to ensure that the design will not result in injury or death to the building owner, or those who will use the building, or damage to property other than the building itself.

Architects should be careful if they are asked to carry out work for contractors in a design and build situation. An architect's normal obligation is to use reasonable skill and care. But the normal design and build liability, unless altered by the contract concerned, is to produce a result which is fit for its purpose if that purpose is made known. Therefore, a contractor may attempt to engage an architect on 'fit for purpose' terms. Most architects will not be insured for that liability and they should reject it.

Of course, the employer may engage a design team to complete the design of the building and a great many production drawings in some detail before seeking tenders from contractors to complete the design and to construct the building. The stage at which the contractor is engaged is very flexible up to work starting on site.

In my experience, the best way to arrange things is if the employer appoints an architect to carry out all the initial work up to and including preparing a brief and an outline scheme together with a performance specification on which contractors will be invited to tender. The architect should continue to organise the tendering process and will act as the employer's agent throughout the construction stage and beyond. The contractor will engage its own architect to do the detail design development work and to produce the contractor's proposals to satisfy the performance specification.

It has become common for the design team to be appointed by the employer on the basis that they will transfer to work for the successful contractor after tender stage. There are two ways of doing this. In the first way, the architect or design team is engaged by the employer to do everything up to tender stage and at that point the appointment comes to an end. The successful contractor then enters into a contract with the design team to complete the work. This is called 'consultant switch' (see 58: Consultant Switch). The second way is called 'novation' (see 59: Novation). This is a procedure by which a contract between the architect and the employer is replaced by another contract on identical terms between architect and contractor. The agreement must be made between all three parties. The contractor takes on all the responsibilities of the employer to the architect as though the contractor had been a party to the contract instead of the employer from the beginning.

The problem with both consultant switch and novation is that the architect and design team are in a conflict situation as soon as they begin to work for the contractor client (see 37: Conflict of Interest). This is blindingly obvious. It can be argued that there is no real problem because all parties agree to the process but that is to ignore the practical reality. Many employers and contractors also do not really understand the implications until the deed has been done and the architect and the team have stopped working for the employer and started working for the contractor. At that point, the employer realises that there is no more design advice to be had from them and has to find another architect or construction professional to assist during the construction process. If the various agreements have been devised by solicitors, one may find that they have attempted to maintain a duty on the architect and team to report back to the building owner as the work progresses. This simply intensifies the conflict to a point where the professionals involved risk being in breach of their respective codes of conduct.

Management contracts are very difficult to administer properly. It may be for that reason that they are not as popular as in the days when every contractor decided to add the term 'managing' to its description. A wag in the office where I worked always used to insert the word 'just' before 'managing' in the headings of letters he received from management contractors. I cannot endorse the practice of writing things on received correspondence which is, at least, embarrassing in any future legal proceedings, but it was so very appropriate in many cases. The employer takes more risk under a management contract than would be the case under a traditional procurement system, but this is the price to be paid for greater control over the work. The contractor is not, as commonly thought, one of the design team under this procurement system. The management contractor is responsible for all the works contractors, therefore its interests are not the same as the employer's interests. This system is often called 'fast track'. Work begins on site as soon as sufficient production information has been produced to enable the first works contractors to start. That means that the architect and other consultants are in a constant race to produce the remainder of the drawings. A key danger is that work has to be redone because subsequent drawings reveal things that were not taken into account in the design of earlier work.

Construction management is a better system than management contracting partly because it does make the construction manager the hub of the design team and of the trade contractors. The key, and very important, difference between this system and management contracting is that the individual trade contractors are in contract directly with the employer. The system calls upon the same kind of fast track skills from the design team as required under the management contract.

Partnering

It is appropriate to say a few words about partnering here. An obsession with partnering has grown over recent years, probably triggered by the Latham Report. Like 'managing', many large contractors described themselves as 'partnering' as soon as Latham said it was a good idea. I will leave you to decide whether it is a good idea. Frankly, I do not think it makes a great deal of difference except in very special cases. Since Latham, it has been the fashion to pay lip service to partnering principles.

The idea of partnering is that employer and contractor and all the sub-contractors and suppliers should work together in a spirit of mutual trust and respect, in good faith and collaborating to the benefit of both. It embraces concepts such as incentives and rewards for all, continuous improvement, an open-book policy (where the contractor or sub-contractor allows access to its costs) and so on.

It proceeds on the fallacious assumption that the interests of the employer and the contractor can be brought together. It is, at best, wildly optimistic to think that this can be achieved in anything other than a superficial way. The reason is simple and I have given it elsewhere in this book, but it is worthwhile saying it again: the employer wants the best possible building for the least possible cost to the employer, but the contractor wants to construct to the lowest possible acceptable standard at the least possible cost to the contractor. Whatever either party may actually say, those are the bottom lines and they are not compatible. Money is at the heart of most problems on site. If the contractor is making an acceptable profit and the employer is not paying out much more than expected, things will go smoothly whether or not partnering principles are used.

No doubt most contractors would like to think that the employer is more than satisfied with the finished building. No doubt most employers would like to think that the contractor is making a reasonable profit. But these are inadequate grounds on which to base the partnering ethos.

There are two kinds of partnering. The first kind is where the parties to enter into a binding contract which includes some or all of the partnering principles noted above. Unfortunately for that approach, the courts have shown a reluctance to imply a general obligation of good faith into commercial contracts. One only has to consider such obligations as to show a spirit of mutual trust and respect to see that there is little hope of making these ideals legally binding obligations. Can one party seek adjudication or arbitration against the other on the basis that the other party did not trust them? I think not.

The second kind of partnering seems to accept that the partnering principles could be quite tricky to enforce and involves the parties entering into a binding contract but excluding the partnering principles. However, the partnering objectives are set out in a separate non-binding charter. This has the great advantage of separating the agreement which can be enforced at law from the other agreement which is simply an expression of how all parties want to work. This kind of partnering is characterised by attempts to make all the relevant people get to know each other during a day or two of enforced jollity at some remote hotel before the real work starts. No doubt it helps personal relationships or reinforces mutual dislike, but whether it has any lasting effect on the way the project proceeds is a moot point. I believe in keeping business on a business-like footing.

If all the people interested in getting a finished building on site were working in the same direction instead of constantly fighting, there should be benefits all around. I have tried to show that employer and contractor start off from basically opposing positions. The problem with partnering is that it seems to be trying to recreate the atmosphere of building before about 1970 when relations between all sides of the construction industry and employer bodies were much better in general terms than they are now. It is difficult to create something which ought to come naturally or not at all. Trust and respect have to be earned. Successful partnering probably occurs naturally, if at all, depending on the people concerned and what motivates them. If the contractor knows that there is the chance of further projects after the current one, this helps relationships enormously: that has nothing to do with trust and respect of course.

51

Contract Selection

Do Not Start Work Without a Contract

One of the key things which all clients expect is that their professional advisors are able to select the most suitable form of building contract for the particular project. A few years ago, an architect asked my advice on the correct form of contract for a huge engineering/architectural construction abroad with a contract figure of several hundred million pounds. It was unusual because each of the engineering, quantity surveying, and numerous other consultants were differing nationalities. Only the architects were British. The contractor and trade packages were also varying nationalities. The architect discussed these difficulties at length, Eventually I said that I would be happy to advise on a suitable contract if he provided various important criteria. I said I would complete the task in two to three weeks. 'When is the project due to start on site?', I asked. 'It started six months ago', he said. This story indicates two things very forcibly. The first is that the importance of having a legally binding contract in place before any work starts on site is frequently ignored. The second is that the larger and more complex the project, the more cavalier seems to be the approach. One suspects it is due to the employer demanding an immediate start on site on the basis that the cost of a delay in commencing a hugely expensive project will far outweigh any extra costs resulting from late execution of appropriate contracts. That can be a very costly error.

Although I know that there are some architects and surveyors who always choose the same, usually short, contract whatever the size or type of project, the only way to decide on the appropriate form of contract is to first get together all the criteria relevant to that decision. That may seem trite, but it is a constant surprise that decisions are reached about the most suitable form of contract without trying to marry the contents of the contract to the project criteria.

Standard Forms

The appropriate contract will perfectly fit all the criteria. But most contracts which are used are standard forms and may not fit all the criteria. Using a standard form is rather like buying a standard car or a standard house. There is a variation between models but the choice to be made is quite basic. Once the choice is made, the particular model must be accepted complete with disadvantages. The reason for the choice is, or should be, because the advantages of the particular model appear to outweigh the disadvantages.

Professional Practice for Architects and Project Managers, First Edition. David Chappell.

To take the analogy a stage further, a standard car can be 'customised' to more closely suit the customer's requirements. A contract can be amended (with care) for the same purpose. A car can, at some cost, be created for a customer. A contract can, but much more expensively than using a standard form, be specially drafted for a client. There are very good reasons for choosing a standard form of contract (see 52: Contract Documents).

It is unlikely that any standard form contract will be perfectly suited to a client's needs. Therefore, having put together the criteria, effectively the brief for the contract, you should be able to advise the client about any desirable amendments to the contract. Preferably, this is something for the architect to do, but certainly it should not be left to a solicitor until you have agreed with the client about the basic changes required and what you wish them to convey. Just giving a standard contract to a solicitor is inviting him or her to carry out wholesale amendments just because they believe them to be an improvement. I once met a client who had asked a contractor to price for a design and build job and to recommend a suitable contract. The contractor had recommended the eminently suitable JCT Design and Build Contract and handed it over to a solicitor for vetting. The solicitor proceeded to delete all references to contractor design, presumably because the solicitor had only ever dealt with traditional contracts. The result was that the contractor entered into a contract by which it was only liable for construction, but carried out the design also, leaving liability for design at best uncertain, at worst with the employer.

Criteria

Although certain projects may well throw up unusual additional criteria the main criteria to be considered when choosing a standard form contract are likely to be some of the following:

- speed of construction
- guaranteed completion date
- cheapest price
- certainty of price
- substantial control by employer, but greater risk to the employer
- substantial control by contractor, but greater risk to the contractor
- high quality of design required
- high quality of construction required
- medium to large size and cost of project
- small to medium size and cost of project
- complex project
- simple project
- traditional contract
- design and build contract
- prime cost contract
- management contract
- construction management contract.

It can easily be seen that some of the criteria conflict with others. This is just a list from which you can select your criteria and add any more before choosing the appropriate standard form. Obviously, there is a substantial collection of standard forms from which to make a choice. Every architect or surveyor involved in building procurement should have a reasonable working knowledge of the contents of every standard building contract to enable them to look at the criteria and have a fair idea of the likely contract or contracts. It is worth remembering that a person who advises the employer to use the wrong form of contract which results in the client suffering a loss may be liable to be sued for negligence.

Amendments

Once the basic contract has been decided, a further decision must be taken about the need to amend the contract to more closely satisfy the criteria. The following is a list of topics which are commonly amended for various reasons:

- priority of documents
- discrepancies
- instructions
- programme
- assignment
- sub-letting
- possession
- completion
- extension of time
- loss and/or expense
- time periods.

52

Contract Documents

Documents

We might as well start from the basic of basics because as soon as I talk about a 'document', there are many people in the construction industry who start to get that glazed look in their eyes which tells me that they are thinking 'Oh no, we are getting very legal now'. The problem is that one cannot work in the construction industry without hearing and having to understand what a document is. A document is almost anything, but usually something flexible like paper or plastic, on which marks have been made with the intention of communicating information, even to oneself. So, things such as drawings, writing, typescript, printing, computer printout, and photographs are all documents. The kinds of documents encountered in construction include:

- professional terms of engagement
- invitations to tender
- tenders
- sketch drawings
- presentation drawings
- production drawings
- specifications
- schedules of work
- bills of quantities
- employer's requirements
- contractor's proposals
- architect's instructions
- certificates
- correspondence
- applications for payment
- pay less notices
- payment notices
- final accounts.

This is not intended to be a complete list. It is just to give you the idea.

Professional Practice for Architects and Project Managers, First Edition. David Chappell.

Why Do We Call Some Documents 'Contract Documents'?

Putting the word 'contract' in front of 'documents' tells us that these are the documents which make up the building contract. In other words, it is the collection of documents which form the contract which binds the employer and the contractor together for the purpose of constructing the building. Most of the standard forms of contract clearly state what constitute the contract documents.

Typical contract documents for a small residential project might be simply a set of production drawings showing exactly how the building is to be constructed, a schedule of the work to be carried out which the contractor has priced, and the standard printed form of contract. On a larger project, there may be bills of quantities and production drawings. I have seen contract documents consisting of dozens of different documents.

Standard Form of Contract

You might ask whether it has to be a standard form of contract. The answer is that it does not have to be a standard form, but using a standard form is much cheaper than getting specialists to draft a form of contract for a particular project. Very often, when faced with the need to have a very large building constructed, an employer will be advised to get the form of contract especially drafted by lawyers. There will be times when there are things about the building, its construction or timing that necessitate having a bespoke contract, but that is not a common situation. The advantages of using a standard contract are:

- There are many kinds of standard forms from which to choose.
- Standard contracts have been prepared by skilled and experienced people.
- Standard contracts are quite cheap when compared to the cost of having a contract specially drafted to suit a particular project.
- Most of the forms are fairly flexible within their particular procurement area.
- Most of the forms are the result of development over many years of use and cover most eventualities.
- Architects, quantity surveyors, and contractors become used to the standard forms of contract and do not have to go through a severe learning process to understand a specially drafted form for which they will, or certainly should, charge.

Those six points are enough to persuade most people of the advantage of a standard form contract. There is another advantage but it is slightly more complicated.

The law assumes that both parties negotiate and agree the contract and, in those circumstances, the courts are reluctant to interfere with what has been agreed. However, we all know that very few building contracts are negotiated and, if so, it is usually only about the money, not the detailed terms. But if the employer, as is usual, simply puts forward the building contract to be used and eventually the contract is signed on that basis, any true ambiguities in the contract will usually be interpreted in favour of the contractor. (No, you don't want to know the name of the rule, it will just complicate things. Oh, alright then. It is called the *contra proferentem* rule, but please forget that.)

The important thing is that there are exceptions to this rather inconvenient rule. Many standard forms are treated as being negotiated and exempt from the rule because the form has been agreed by representatives of all sides of industry, actual or potential users. Many standard forms (for example JCT and ICE forms) fall into this category. Moreover, a standard form, with its years of development, should have less chance of containing ambiguities than a specially drafted building contract. A bespoke contract is not exempt unless it can be shown to have been freely negotiated and, in view of the reason for having a bespoke contract, free negotiation is unlikely.

Amendments

An employer may have a lawyer make various amendments to a standard form. This is much cheaper than getting a bespoke form and it does enable specific requirements to be accommodated. However, there are two dangers. The first is that the amendments will not be treated as freely negotiated and, therefore, any ambiguities will be interpreted in favour of the contractor. If the amendment is substantial, the whole form may not be considered as freely negotiated. The second danger is that it is very difficult to amend a standard form successfully. The reason for that is that an amendment may not take all effects into account. I have seen this situation many times, including one attempt to amend the payment provisions which only amended some of them and created a forest of ambiguity and confusion. My best advice is never to amend a standard form contract. If it is essential to amend, make sure that the client engages a real expert to do it.

Consistency is Essential

It is important that all the documents comprising the contract documents are consistent with one another. This is extremely difficult to achieve in practice even when the only documents are a standard form contract, some drawings, and priced bills of quantities. If there are many contract documents, consistency is virtually impossible. I noted earlier that I have seen contract documents composed of dozens of separate documents. The worst case I encountered was where there was a bespoke form of contract, a specification and a priced schedule of work together with two sets of pre-start meeting minutes, several letters, two memos about various agreements and a list of certain materials whose purpose was unexplained and not referred to elsewhere. Trying to establish the order of importance of these additional documents and their effect upon the bespoke contract was impossible for the participants and resulted in a substantial dispute. So, try to limit the documents and endeavour to make them agree. Too often in all kinds of contractual situations I have seen the parties try to overcome some problem by agreeing to include a letter, email, or memo as one of the contract documents without any thought about the effect, if any, on the other documents.

Finally

A final thought: if you want, and you should want, to be strictly correct, each contract document should be signed by the parties and identified as being contract documents, e.g. 'This is one of the contract documents referred to in the Agreement dated …'. The standard form will have its own wording and it will be the 'Agreement' referred to in the sentence above.

I do tend to have a final thought after my final thoughts and this is no exception. You may say that it should be up near the front of this chapter rather than at the end. I respect that view, but do not share it. Wherever the contract documents are mentioned in the contract or elsewhere, it is usual to capitalise the initial letters: Contract Documents. That is because they will be defined somewhere and anything defined in a contract is capitalised in that way so that you know.

53

Production Information

Definition

'Production information' is a term used to describe all the information which the architect has to prepare in order for the contractor to be able to carry out and complete the Works. It includes:

- detailed technical drawings
- drawn schedules
- work schedules
- specifications.

The term was first coined in the original RIBA Plan of Work as the name of Stage F and the tasks to be done were identified as the preparation of the final production information, i.e. drawings, schedules, and specifications. The latest edition (2013) of the RIBA Plan of Work seems to have dropped this term (perhaps it was seen as being too easy to understand) in favour of trying to describe the information in more detail in Stage 4. For many years, what is now still generally referred to as production information was simply referred to as 'working drawings', which was used as a generic term to encompass everything covered by 'production information'.

Schedules

I pick out schedules to mention in particular because this is a somewhat neglected aspect of production information. Possible schedules include:

- sanitary fittings
- precast concrete
- ironmongery
- doors
- windows
- lighting
- glazing
- floor, wall, and ceiling finishes
- colour schemes
- tiling

Professional Practice for Architects and Project Managers, First Edition. David Chappell.

- lintels
- architraves
- skirtings
- door casings
- plumbing pipe runs
- rainwater pipes, hoppers, and gulleys
- inspection chambers
- external paving.

Architects who prepare these kind of schedules for all their projects will learn a great deal about construction.

54

Bills of Quantities

What are Bills of Quantities?

The word 'bill' has several different meanings. It can mean a note of charges or a declaration or a draft of an Act of Parliament or a list of things. Bills of quantities are detailed lists of all the work, goods, and materials needed to construct a particular structure. Their purpose is to enable prices to be apportioned to each item so that the total of all the items is the total price for constructing the building. They also help variations to be valued and certificates to be prepared.

Preparing the Bills of Quantities

Bills of quantities are usually prepared by quantity surveyors (QS). Having said that, I must admit to working, as a young architect, for an architect who always prepared his own quantities to save quantity surveying costs. There are various established rules for measuring work (see below) but once these are mastered, the actual measuring and preparation is relatively easy, although tedious. The technical term for measuring quantities from a drawing before putting the result on the list is known as 'taking off'. The problem I had with my employer (well actually just one of many) was that he would often take off quantities before a drawing was done. This was particularly true of internal fixed furniture, such as ramped seating in a lecture theatre. On a good day, he would have done a little scribbled and dimensioned sketch so that I knew (roughly) what to draw. On a bad day, he would have had the detail in his head and subsequently forgotten so that I had to create the construction drawing from what he had listed in the bills.

Unfortunately, that is by no means an unusual situation, even where a QS is involved, if the architect has not produced the drawings by the time bills are required and the QS is asked to make a guess. On another occasion, I worked in a team of a dozen architects preparing construction details for a very large building complex. Bills of quantities had been prepared on the basis of (in those days) sixteenth of an inch to a foot drawings, tenders had been received, one accepted, and the contractor was well advanced on site. There was a great deal of fitted furniture and construction details to be drawn and the chances of discovering what the QS had measured for any particular item was negligible when such things as architraves, skirtings etc. were measured in thousands of feet. Obviously, all the drawings should be supplied to the QS before taking off is complete.

Professional Practice for Architects and Project Managers, First Edition. David Chappell.

It rarely saves time to finish the bills before the drawings are complete and never saves money because variations inevitably become the norm.

There is no particular rule about the circumstances when it is necessary to prepare bills of quantities. For example, if it is going to be a design and build contract, it would be most unusual for bills to be prepared by the quantity surveyor working for the employer, but they would have to be prepared in some form by the contractor before it submitted its price. Bills would rarely be prepared by the employer for small jobs, reliance being put on drawings and specification alone, but again the contractor would have to prepare a list of items in order to arrive at a tender figure. Where large buildings are concerned, bills of quantities are essential in order to form a basis on which to secure comparable tender prices.

Structure of the Bills

The bills of quantities are usually divided into the following parts:

- *Preliminaries*: These include all kinds of information for the contractor, such as details of the employer, QS, architect, site information, contract details, safety, health and welfare, water and lighting for the Works and so on. A full list can be found in one of the standard methods of measurement (see 66: Preliminaries).
- *Preambles*: This section amplifies the work by including detailed specifications of materials, goods, and workmanship.
- *Measured work*: This is the list of quantities, work, goods, and materials.
- *Provisional sums and dayworks*: These are sums for which the actual work and materials and, therefore, the price is not fully known at this stage (see 92: Provisional and Prime Cost Sums).

The measured work is divided into sections such as excavations, substructures, frame, etc. generally in the order in which the work is usually done. The list will vary depending on the kind of building. A large house and a multi-storey block of flats will have some different sections although many of the section titles will be the same. The list is set out in the order of the construction of the building.

Problems

A common problem is that the architect has not completed the drawings when the QS wants them. Put another way: the QS asks for the drawings before the architect has had time to complete them. There is no real answer to this other than for the architect to ensure that all the consultants, including the QS, are aware of the programme and accept it, and that all strive to get their parts done on time.

Unfortunately, there are many things, not least the client having changes of mind, which can delay the best laid plans which can mean that the architect has to redraw drawings or substantially alter them. This, in turn, may cause the QS to have to amend the take off. In those circumstances, it is not slightest use if the QS simply moans about its internal work schedules and delays. All the consultants should be separately engaged by the client and the QS can always complain directly to its client about the changes of mind. This rarely occurs because it is easier to complain to the architect. All the architect can do is to explain the position to the QS and if the QS decides that the delay is serious and possibly costly, it should be referred to the client by the architect if the QS declines to do so. All that may appear somewhat unlikely, but I can assure readers that I and many of my clients have experienced that situation.

Of course, in most instances, the QS understands that the delay is client induced and just gets on with things. It must also be recognised that some architects do fail to complete drawings on time because they have badly judged the time needed and do put the QS in the position of either waiting for information or, if the architect agrees, guessing what might be included.

Another common problem is that many architects fail to provide the QS with adequate specification notes. Indeed, some architects will say that they believe the responsibility for the specification lies with the QS (yes really). Clearly, the specification is an intrinsic part of the design process. It is very much the architect's job to decide upon materials, quality, thicknesses, fixing methods, and every little thing that goes into the construction of the building.

Standard Methods of Measurement

Throughout the construction industry, standard methods of carrying out measurement have been formulated over the years. This provides a set of rules which everyone can understand and to which everyone can work. These rules are essential when bills of quantities are sent out to tender because they enable each tenderer to understand exactly what is to be priced. The particular method of measurement used for preparing the bills of quantities must be stated.

If, for some good reasons, it is decided that the bills of quantities items are not to be measured in accordance with one of the generally accepted methods, this must be made very clear in the bills.

55

Specifications

What Really is a Specification?

There are two kinds of specification:

- a prescriptive specification
- a performance specification.

Prescriptive Specification

A prescriptive specification is a document which is separate from the drawings and which describes in detail the work, workmanship, goods, and materials required to construct the structure concerned. It tells you all the things that drawings alone cannot contain. There was a time when it was commonplace for drawings to be festooned with notes, commonly referred to as 'specification notes', which described all the materials and work on the drawings. Finding the right note could involve looking through many drawings. Thankfully, those days are long gone, although one still occasionally sees a drawing for a very small construction which contains all the information on the one sheet.

I am almost ashamed to say that as a student and later as a project architect I enjoyed writing specifications. I loved the terminology and the task of precisely stipulating the work to be done. I say 'ashamed' because all my contemporaries hated it. I loved the challenge every specification provided.

Performance Specification

A performance specification is a document which sets out all the criteria which must be met by the contractor. It is usually part of a contract where the contractor is to design and build, often referred to as the 'Employer's Requirements'. This kind of specification has some similarities to the brief which the architect obtains from a client before starting to design. However, the performance specification is usually a stage or two later than an architect's brief. It is often produced by an architect after obtaining the client's brief and preparing a sketch design although it could be prepared earlier than that if the contractor is going to carry out the design from concept stage. This kind of specification sets out how the building must perform. It allows the contractor to use initiative in complying with the specification and ought to produce a competitive price. The employer has no

Professional Practice for Architects and Project Managers, First Edition. David Chappell.

detailed control over the way in which the contract meets the specification, although if the employer definitely requires a certain method of construction or certain materials, those things can be made mandatory in the specification.

Writing a performance specification is a skilled task and it will usually take longer to produce than a traditional prescriptive specification if done correctly. Employers should be disabused of the notion that it is quicker to build on the basis of a performance specification than a prescriptive specification unless the employer is going to be satisfied with a poor-quality building. That is not because a performance specification is not good, it is because it takes much more time and care to draft than to draft the traditional prescriptive specification (see 56: Employer's Requirements).

Why is a Specification Needed?

The specification is essential to describe what the contractor must do. Everyone concerned with the building needs the specification, but they need it for different purposes.

At the beginning, it is needed by the architect who creates it, in order to be certain what is to be specified. That might seem strange, but if a team of architects is engaged on a large project, in fact any project where more than one architect is engaged, it is quite common for the architects to have different ideas about what materials or techniques are to be used. Drafting the specification in those circumstances requires the team to co-operate to arrive at the finally agreed specification. Building Information Modelling (BIM) can be very useful in that situation (see 18: Building Information Modelling).

If bills of quantities are to be prepared, the quantity surveyor must be provided with the architect's specification. I am very well aware that many architects simply leave it to the quantity surveyor to write the specification part of the bills of quantities. That is wrong on several levels. First of all, the specification is part of the design and, therefore, it must be prepared in detail by the project architect. Secondly, it is wrong to expect the quantity surveyor to guess what the architect intends to specify. In any event, the architect will eventually have to confirm what is in the bills of quantities. Thirdly, leaving the specification to the quantity surveyor is plain lazy and bordering on negligence. That is not to cast doubt on the ability of the quantity surveyor to produce a workmanlike specification, but it is just not the quantity surveyor's job.

The contractor's estimator needs the specification because it is essential if the project is to be priced properly. The specification should be clear and concise, and unambiguous for the estimator, who will sometimes quite wrongly base the pricing on the specification alone with just a glance at the drawings, even if there are no bills of quantities.

The contractor needs the specification in order to be able, first, to order the correct goods and materials for the project and, second, to be able to construct it.

The clerk of works needs the specification in order to check that the goods and materials arriving on site and the subsequent construction are in accordance with the specification and thus in accordance with the contract.

How is the Specification Used?

Specifications and drawings are often used for relatively small and uncomplicated projects. It is difficult to place an exact value on the work because the simpler the project, the higher the value for which a specification can be tolerated. I would tentatively suggest that work up to a value of about £200 000 at 2019 prices would be appropriate and there are some standard form contracts which would be suitable for use with specification and drawings up to double that value so long as the Works are relatively straightforward. The problem with using a specification as the key basis for pricing is that tenderers will, of necessity, have to take off their own quantities and if, say, four contractors are tendering, that is an awful lot of fruitless work for three of them. The cost of preparing this kind of tender is usually included in each tender. Moreover, the job of comparing tenders becomes difficult as the price will be submitted in different ways and some contractors may make mistakes in measuring the work.

Where the project is being constructed on the basis of some kind of management or construction management system, it will be necessary to invite tenders from works or trade contractors on a package-by-package basis. The individual trade contractors often have to prepare tenders from drawings and specifications with similar problems to contractors tendering for smaller but complete projects.

Drafting Specifications

I have already said that I used to enjoy drafting specifications. That was when every specification was drafted virtually starting from a blank sheet of paper. Of course, most offices developed their own template for fairly standard projects. In some cases, the template was a rather high-class name for a dog-eared old specification drafted by some long-forgotten architect in the practice and which everyone later used as the basis for their specification. Of course, from time to time people added a few clauses of their own devising or what they had gleaned from another specification which came into the office.

In recent years, it has become possible to draft excellent specifications by using the libraries of standard specification clauses which are available, usually by subscription. Care must be taken even with professionally drafted clauses to draw from because your particular specification may require you to amend some of the standard clauses to suit your project. Simply clicking on an item and expecting it to be what you want will sometimes provide hilarious or expensive results if the contractor takes the specification at face value and gets on with it.

When working for a contractor, I once had to deal with a specification like that. Among the vary many inappropriate clauses was one specifying a large quantity of reinforced concrete. There was no obvious place for it within the confines of the very small bungalow we were building. Several similarly odd clauses later, the architect under pressure admitted that he had simply picked up an old specification, gone through it quickly with a biro, crossing out and scribbling in here and there and then given it to a typist to be reproduced as the specification for our project. 'I am just so busy', he said. As his specification bore only a passing resemblance to what, according to the drawings, we were trying to build, his busyness cost his client quite a lot of extra money in the cost of work having to be redone for various reasons connected with the appalling specification.

When working from standard clauses or a template, it is so easy to include something which should not be there or forget something which should be there. When drafting a specification, you should do what the contractor should do: construct the building in your mind looking at the drawings and then see what needs to be in the specification. There are different views about whether a specification should or could include quantities. Be aware that some standard forms of contract state that if there are quantities in the specification, they must take preference instead of what is on the drawing. That would mean that if the drawing showed 15 hat and coat hooks but the specification showed only 10, the contractor would be correct in only pricing for 10. Of course, some standard forms say that the contractor must price for everything taken together. If that was the case with my example, the contractor would have to price for the most expensive option, i.e. 15 hat and coat hooks. It is very misleading to try and include quantities for every item in the specification because it would resemble bills of quantities but not actually be so. Therefore, on balance, you should only include quantities in the specification if it is absolutely essential for some reason. Otherwise simply stick to clearly describing the work or materials.

Specifications cannot just be thrown together. When finished, thorough checking by someone other than the project architect is indicated.

56

Employer's Requirements

What are Employer's Requirements?

Employer's requirements are the employer's instructions to the contractor. 'Employer's Requirements' is just an easy and self-explanatory term. They are used when the contractor is required to design as well as build the project or part of it. In traditional construction, the architect designs the building and then produces drawings and other information so that the contractor can build the project exactly as the architect intends. Therefore, part of the information produced by the architect will be the specification. In traditional construction, it will be a prescriptive specification, leaving no room for the contractor to make use of its own ideas about materials and construction.

The Employer's Requirements are quite different. They are a performance specification, which is something like the brief an architect will produce in conjunction with the client before commencing the design process, although in the design and build scenario, a sketch design is often included to which the contractor is obliged to work. The Employer's Requirements should specify the criteria, in contrast to the traditional prescriptive specification which specifies the particular way in which criteria are to be satisfied. Therefore, the document may specify a particular durability, colour, feel, and other qualities such as slip resistance for floor covering which the contractor can satisfy by using different materials and combinations of materials. In traditional work, the actual materials and workmanship of the floor covering would have been specified. If the Employer's Requirements are wrong in some way, the contractor may propose the wrong material or construction method.

Things to Consider

Design and build is not an easy option for the employer. If all that is required is a very simple building the Employer's Requirements can be brief. However, usually at least as much effort must be given to producing the performance specification as would be needed for producing a traditional specification. It is usually much easier to produce a prescriptive specification.

Part of the idea behind the performance specification is to allow the contractor to decide on methods of construction and materials that may result in a cheaper

Professional Practice for Architects and Project Managers, First Edition. David Chappell.

building than might be achieved by traditional methods. Certain mandatory things may be included, such as particular colours or finishes, but the fewer mandatory items included, the greater the opportunity for the contractor to use cheaper materials. On the other hand, the employer will not want to sacrifice good quality for price. That is the secret behind producing a good performance specification: the ability to write the specification so that the contractor has scope to make savings while a minimum quality standard is maintained. If the Employer's Requirements are very brief and any drawings are very simple sketch plans, the employer will have little control over the end product. Put another way, the more that is left to the contractor, the greater will be its chance to save money and put forward an attractive tender figure, but the less control will lie with the employer.

The extent of the contractor's liability for design will very much depend upon what it says in the design and build contract. It is important to understand that, if nothing is mentioned about design liability, the contractor will be responsible for checking that any design already carried out works properly and for design of the new work. In that context, the contractor's duty will go beyond that of the reasonable skill and care of the professional person and be the duty to ensure fitness for purpose.

Care must be taken in wording the Employer's Requirements. There will have to be a preliminaries section dealing with overall matters such as the identities of anyone acting for the employer, the terms of the contract, site restrictions and so on (see 66: Preliminaries). But among them may be what are known as representations: in other words, statements by the employer on which the contractor is entitled to rely. A good example of a representation is a description of underground conditions. If they are incorrect, they are probably misrepresentations and the contractor may have a claim for any additional costs incurred. Some employers try to avoid that danger by adding the comment that the contractor must check that the statement is correct. Unfortunately, that is the same as the employer saying that the statement is a misrepresentation, for which the employer would be liable. It is difficult for the employer to avoid liability for statements in the Employer's Requirements and any attempt to do so should be drafted only after receiving proper advice.

Variations

Most design and build contracts allow the employer to instruct variations, often referred to as 'changes' in this kind of contract. Usually, the only variations or changes that may be made are changes to the Employer's Requirements. The employer cannot normally give instructions to the contractor in regard to the actual design itself. For example, if the Employer's Requirements for an office block include nothing about a built-in reception desk and the employer now realises that one is required and of a particular design, the employer will not be able to simply get the architect to issue a detailed drawing. The matter must be dealt with by a written instruction amending the Employer's Requirements to include the desk and the specification of the desk must be very clear. Having said that, many employers in this situation do get the architect to issue a drawing and the contractor will rarely object. Nevertheless, it is usually wrong to issue change instructions in this way and best to be aware that difficulties can arise. One of the difficulties is that the contractor might successfully argue that it is not liable for errors in part of the design that was specifically instructed by the employer.

Planning Permission

The employer should obtain planning and any other necessary permissions before any tender is accepted. Of course, it is possible to make the contractor responsible for obtaining planning permission, but getting permission can never be guaranteed because it depends upon the planning authority. Therefore, the contractor might apply unsuccessfully for planning permission or even if successful, the permission may take some time before it is finalised. This may result in the contractor being able to claim extensions of the time for the delay and possibly claim loss and/or expense resulting from the delay. The employer could take steps to make the contractor responsible for obtaining all necessary permissions and for the consequences of failure, but it is likely that there would be a substantial addition to the tender price even if contractors were prepared to tender.

Contents of the Employer's Requirements

The following are some of the things which should always be included in the Employer's Requirements:

- details of the site, including the boundaries
- details of accommodation requirements
- purposes for which the building is to be used
- any other matter likely to affect the preparation of the Contractor's Proposals or its price
- statement of functional and ancillary requirements:
  - kind and number of buildings
  - density and mix of any dwellings and any height limitations
  - schematic layout and/or drawings
  - specific requirements as to finishes, etc.
- details of any provisional sums
- statement of planning and other constraints, e.g. restrictive covenants, together with copies of any statutory or other permissions relating to the development
- statement of site requirements
- the extent to which the contractor is to base its proposals on information supplied in the Employer's Requirements
- access restrictions
- availability of public utilities
- essential details to be included in the contractor's programme
- the method of presentation of the Contractor's Proposals:
  - drawings, plans, sections, elevations, details, scales
  - any special requirements, for example models, computer animation, video, building information modelling (BIM).

  - layout of specialist systems
  - specification requirements
- requirements regarding submission of the contractor's drawings
- the records to be kept by the site manager
- details to be included in as-built drawings which the contractor must supply
- details of functions to be carried out by the employer's personnel
- any details required by the contract being used.

57

Contractor's Proposals

The Contractor's Proposals should answer the Employer's Requirements. If the Employer's Requirements are rather vague, it leaves scope for the contractor to fill the gap with something appropriate. The Employer's Requirements document is simply a performance specification, although it may have some specific items included. For example, if the Employer's Requirements simply state that adequate natural lighting is to be included, this gives the contractor enormous scope to provide adequate natural lighting in any form: traditional single windows, curtain walling or rooflights. Such vague statements in the Employer's Requirements are not a good idea because the employer may get a shock when the contractor's proposals are received. Deciding to change things at that stage will cause delay and be expensive.

On receipt of the Employer's Requirements, the contractor, quite understandably, will look to see the cheapest way to satisfy the Employer's Requirements in order to arrive at the lowest tender price. Usually, the contractor will submit a detailed specification covering all the work and materials it intends to use to complete the project.

A very common problem is that the contractor submits proposals which do not quite comply with requirements. Design and build contracts do not always make provision for dealing with that situation. Some contracts say, with more optimism that common sense, that the employer should make sure that the Employer's Requirements and the Contractor's Proposals do not include any divergences. On reading that kind of unhelpful statement one immediately thinks, 'Ah, but what if they do contain divergences which are not noticed until the contract is signed?' Well, I would immediately think that at any rate. Fortunately, the way that most design and build contracts are worded makes clear that in such a case, the Employer's Requirements take precedence. Generally, one has to carefully read the contract to arrive at that conclusion. How much easier and straightforward it would be to simply state that if there are any divergences or discrepancies between the two documents, the Employer's Requirements will take precedence over the Contractor's Proposals. After all, a contractor that submits proposals that do not comply with the Employer's Requirements is not complying with the contract.

Sometimes there may be excellent reasons to cause the contractor to wish to include a material or a detail which does not comply with the Employer's Requirements. In that situation, the contractor ought to notify the employer before submitting a tender, explain the reason for the non-compliant proposal, and ask if it would be acceptable. There are two reasons for this. The first and most important reason is that it avoids a discrepancy between the two documents, as noted earlier. If the employer accepts the non-compliant proposal, the Employer's Requirements must be amended before signing the contract

Professional Practice for Architects and Project Managers, First Edition. David Chappell.

in order to remove the discrepancy. The second reason is that the contractor making the proposal should be tendering on the same basis as other contractors. Therefore, the employer must notify all tenderers of the accepted change. As an alternative, but slightly risky, approach, the contractor may simply include the non-compliant item as an alternative and subject to a stated price adjustment. The risk is that, if the invitation to tender says that alternatives are excluded, the whole tender could be rejected.

The Contractor's Proposals should not contain any provisional sums unless they are in the Employer's Requirements. If the contractor feels that a provisional sum must be included, although not requested by the employer, the employer's attention again must be drawn to the sum so that it can be included in the Employer's Requirements document before signing the contract. Moreover, the attention of the employer should be drawn to the provisional sum before the tender is submitted.

58

Consultant Switch

What is Consultant Switch?

There are a few terms and phrases which tend to get confused. 'Consultant switch' is one of them. It gets confused with novation (see 59: Novation). I have to own up to being the originator of 'consultant switch' as the name of the process sometimes employed where there is a design and build contract. It is ridiculously gratifying to see that it has moved into accepted terminology.

It is unfortunately common for a consultant (architect, engineer etc.) engaged by the employer to stop acting for the employer and to start acting for a contractor on a project, all with the agreement of the employer and the contractor. The 'switch' usually takes place when the design and build contractor's tender is accepted by the employer. It is essential that two separate agreements are signed; the first agreement must come to an end before the second is signed. Usually what happens is that the consultant enters into an agreement with the employer for the first part of the project, on the understanding that the consultant will enter into a new agreement with the successful contractor. During the first agreement, the consultant will carry out all the necessary services for the employer. For example, if the consultant is an architect, the architect will be involved in putting together the Employer's Requirements document and probably preparing an initial design to obtain planning permission. Preparing a list of tenderers and inviting tenders on behalf of the employer may be another service required. Contractors tender on the understanding that the successful tenderer will enter into an agreement with the consultant. Although the first agreement comes to an end before the second agreement is signed, unlike novation, the consultant and employer remain liable to each other in respect of the services performed and fees paid (or unpaid) during the first part of the project.

During the second agreement, the consultant carries out the services specified in the agreement for the contractor and the contractor pays the consultant whatever is agreed under the terms of the agreement.

Novation is a completely different process in which the employer and the consultant sign an agreement for the consultant to carry all the services during the whole of the process from initial briefing to completion of the construction. When the contractor's tender is accepted, a three-party agreement is signed which effectively transfers the agreement between employer and consultant into an agreement between contractor and consultant just as though the contractor had been in the place of the employer from

Professional Practice for Architects and Project Managers, First Edition. David Chappell.

the beginning. Novation is sometimes used instead of consultant switch, but neither novation nor consultant switch is to be recommended.

Advantages

An advantage is supposed to be that the consultant on starting to work for the contractor, completing the design and production specification and, if an architect, the drawings, will be able to develop them for construction while ensuring that the original concept is safeguarded in its detail. This idea ignores the fact that each consultant, whether switched or novated, will owe a duty to the contractor, not to the employer, for the completion of the production information. This means that the consultants are obliged to comply with the contractor's instructions. The contractor may instruct the consultant to produce a scheme which is inexpensive to construct, and possibly not what the design team and the employer originally had in mind. Much depends upon what it says in the agreements.

Conflict

It is difficult to see how either procedure can avoid a potential for a conflict of interest so far as the consultant is concerned (see 37: Conflict of Interest). That is because, in broad terms and whatever so-called 'partnering' (see 50: Procurement) arrangements may say, the objectives of the employer and the contractor are opposed. An employer wants the very best possible building in every respect for the cheapest possible price, but a contractor wants to use the cheapest possible materials and least amount of labour because that costs the least amount of money. The situation is sometimes made worse if the agreement with the contractor requires the consultant to report back to the employer about defects and progress after the switch. Moreover, the consultant may be placed in a difficult position if asked by the contractor to reveal things about the employer which are a breach of confidentiality.

Far better for the employer to keep the consultants as advisors and let the contractor get its own people on board. If an architect, the consultant would be ideal to act as the employer's agent. Far better than expecting someone totally new to the work to adopt that role while the architect goes off to work for the contractor, which makes no sense.

59

Novation

What is Novation?

Novation is not, as often described, the replacement of one party to a contract with another. It is the substitution of a new contract for an existing one. It can only be undertaken with the consent of all parties concerned, usually three. Unlike assignment (see 22: Assignment), which involves a transfer of rights or benefits, novation consists of cancelling existing rights and obligations between two parties and then creating a another set of rights and obligations in their place between one of the parties and a third party. The new contract is often on precisely the same terms as the original contract or with such adjustments as are necessary to reflect the changed circumstances. Novation agreements are invariably executed as deeds because of the difficulty of proving consideration between the parties if executed as a simple contract.

A novation agreement must be differentiated from consultant switch (see 58: Consultant Switch) with which it is often confused. Consultant switch needs two contracts and does not transfer rights and does not require a three-party agreement to achieve. The two contracts are often on substantially different terms.

Novation can be used to effectively replace one contractor with another on a project, e.g. where an insolvency has occurred. However, it is more commonly associated with design and build contracts. Often one or all of the design team are initially engaged by the employer to do preliminary work and then 'transferred' to the design and build contractor to undertake the detailed design. The consultants are expected to enter into novation agreements to create new contracts between each consultant and the design and build contractor. This procedure has given rise to the incorrect use of novation as a verb as in 'the architect was novated to the contractor'.

Conflict

Where a consultant enters into a novation agreement so that the contract between employer and consultant is replaced with a contract between contractor and consultant, there is the possibility of an actual or potential conflict of interest (see 37: Conflict of Interest). The only saving point is that all parties are aware of the potential conflict and, therefore, may be considered to have accepted it. It is essential that the novation agreement brings the relationship between employer and consultant to an end. It is regrettably quite common to find a clause in the novation agreement which requires the consultant to continue some kind of reporting duty to the employer. It is a truism that no person can serve two masters and consultants who execute novation agreements in these terms potentially face significant conflicts of interest and may be in breach of their professional codes of conduct.

Novation agreements are complicated to effectively draft and best left to lawyers. Usually novation documents are expressly drafted for a particular situation.

60

Schedules of Work

Basic Thoughts

A schedule of work is a list of the work that has to be done in order to carry out the project. Although referred to as a schedule of 'work', it will usually also include materials and goods. Its use should be, but not always is, confined to relatively small projects. It can be used together with a specification but care must be taken not to confuse the two or, much worse, have conflicts between them. Discrepancies between documents comprising the contract documents have to be resolved before contracts are signed if possible. If the discrepancies are not found until later, resolving them will usually involve deciding which document takes precedence and often results in additional costs.

Particularly if the project is fairly large, a schedule of work can often look very like a bill of quantities. Sometimes a schedule of work really is a bill of quantities by another name. But whereas a bill of quantities is produced in accordance with accepted methods of measurement, there are no official rules about a schedule of work. Often, a schedule of work will not include everything. Even when used with a specification there may be things missing from both documents. It is a good idea to make some very clear and obvious reference in the contract to the fact that the contractor must include in its price all the work and materials taken in the contract documents as a whole. This avoids the problems that I have often seen where the contractor simply prices what is listed in the schedule of work, believing that it contains everything that needs to be done.

What is the Purpose of a Schedule of Work?

That is a tricky question to answer. The contract documents taken as a whole are supposed to tell the contractor everything that it needs to know about constructing the project. So, if the schedule of work is to play its proper role, it must tell the contractor something that, without it, the contractor would not know.

That bring us to the real point that if there is a proper specification including all the things that should be in the specification (a thorough description of all of the work to be done, the materials and goods to be used, including such things as quality, location, and size, and a good set of drawings showing detail of the sizes, locations, appearance, and the way the components fit together), a schedule of work is unnecessary and, as indicated earlier, can be confusing.

Professional Practice for Architects and Project Managers, First Edition. David Chappell.

Where there are drawings and a specification, a schedule of works is sometimes provided as the document which the contractor has to price. That is acceptable only if it is clear to the contractor that the schedule is simply a convenient pricing device and that the contractor must take care to include everything shown or described in the contract documents as a whole. But it is normally preferable to have the contractor price the specification.

In certain kinds of contract, the work described in the specification might need to be broken down into packages for the purpose of obtaining prices. A schedule of work in that form may be useful, but in general a schedule of work is best avoided.

61

Activity Schedules

Quick Description

An activity schedule is a list of activities which is used to value the work completed by the contractor at various stages through the progress of the Works. It is an alternative to valuing the Works by using bills of quantities. The Works are divided into different activities and a price allocated to each one. In this respect the activity schedule has much in common with a standard bar (Gantt) chart plus costs. The idea is that if an activity is priced at, say, £9000 and the contractor has carried out a third of it, the payment due in respect of that activity would be £3000. It may sound convincing but that could be too simplistic a view.

Some Problems

This kind of valuation tool presents problems if the valuation and payment of the contractor is as usual on a monthly basis and one or more of the activities concerned spreads over several months. If the electrical installation or heating installation is represented as a single activity, the contractor will either be receiving too much money too early or the reverse because the value of work done will be evenly spread over the length of the activity. In cases like these, the activities should be divided up into sub-activities to make tracking and valuation easier.

Some people think that the activity schedule is rather a blunt instrument when trying to value the work carried out, whereas others believe that it produces a more accurate representation of the value of work done.

It is not quite correct to say that when each activity is priced the total of the activity prices equals the contract sum because there are some costs which go towards making up the contract sum which are not activities. Therefore, to arrive at the contract sum it is necessary to add on preliminaries, provisional sums, and the contractor's profit.

It is not practical to include approximate activities to replace approximate quantities. Therefore, if an approximation is required for tender purposes to be firmed up later as the Works progress, it is still better to use approximate quantities.

It is argued that inviting tenders on the basis of activity schedules rather than quantities enables easier comparison of the tenders received. That may well be so if speed is all that matters, but activities schedules possess none of the detail that bills of quantities

Professional Practice for Architects and Project Managers, First Edition. David Chappell.

provide and which is important if it is necessary to try to reduce costs when tenders exceed the budget.

An activity schedule may be prepared by each tenderer and submitted as part of the tender documentation, allowing an easy although not a detailed comparison of the tenders received. Alternatively, it could be submitted by the successful tenderer for use during the contract period, e.g. preparation of interim payments. This could be a dangerous thing to do in a financial sense because it allows a contractor to effectively front load payments.

Finally

Good activity schedules must contain an adequately detailed description of activities and apportionment of prices, particularly in the subdivision of schedules which exceed one month, otherwise proper valuation will be difficult. These schedules are very attractive in theory, but for the reasons outline above considerable reflection is needed before deciding to proceed on the basis of an activity schedule.

62

Implied Terms

General Rules

Architects, employers, and contractors are fond of saying 'It must be implied that … '. There follows whatever the architect, employer or contractor thinks is a good idea. Let's be clear right from the start: the law will not imply a term into a contract just because it seems like a good idea or because it would be a reasonable thing to do.

The clauses written in the contract (or stated if it is an oral contract) are called 'express terms'. Some terms can and will be implied, but there are rules which it is useful to remember. A term may be implied if the following are satisfied. It must:

- be reasonable and equitable ('equitable' means 'fair and just') and
- be necessary to give commercial effectiveness to the contract or
- be so obvious it goes without saying and
- be clearly expressed and
- not contradict an express term of the contract.

Examples of Implied Terms

There are a lot of terms which are easily implied into contracts. Here are some examples:

- If there is a custom specific to a particular locality, it will be implied into contracts in that locality provided that everyone knows about it and it is generally accepted.
- If in a particular trade, profession or business there has been an invariable and long-standing usage or practice which is well known in that trade, profession or business which is clear and not ambiguous, and if it is used by normal professional or tradespeople, e.g. 'reduced brickwork' meaning brick 9 in. (225 mm) thick and possibly 'compo' meaning the mortar used in bricklaying, but probably not 'snagging', which is capable of two meanings, inspecting and looking for defects or carrying out remedial work to defects, it will be implied into contracts used in that particular trade, profession or business.
- If both parties use language with a meaning different to the common meaning, but if both understand the different meaning with certainty, it will be implied into contracts between those parties.
- If an Act of Parliament says that terms must be implied, they will be implied, e.g. under the Housing Grants Construction and Regeneration Act 1996 (as amended)

Professional Practice for Architects and Project Managers, First Edition. David Chappell.

which provides for the implication of terms in different types of contract and clearly states that the Scheme for Construction Contracts (England and Wales) Regulations 1998 (as amended) applies as a default implication if the provisions agreed by the parties do not comply with the Act.

- Terms may be implied at common law, for example in construction contracts (i) a contractor will supply good and proper materials and will provide completed work which is constructed in a good and workmanlike manner, of materials which are of good quality and reasonably fit for their intended purpose, and (ii) an employer will not prevent completion and do that which is necessary to bring about completion of the contract.
- The courts will often be prepared to imply a term where the contract is otherwise complete, but needs a particular term in order to give a contract commercial effectiveness. This is commonly referred to as 'business efficacy'.
- If a term can be said to be the intention of the parties, the courts will apply what is known as the 'officious bystander test'. That test is that if, when the parties were agreeing their terms, an officious (that is a nosy and interfering) bystander had been asked if they were including the term in question, they would have irritably said 'Oh, of course'. It is sometimes referred to as being a term so obvious that 'it goes without saying'.
- A term may be implied if there is a previous course of dealing between the parties. A 'course of dealing' means that if parties have dealt with each other many times about the same things, always using the same terms and they enter into another similar agreement but forget to enter into a formal contract, the same terms as used before will be implied into the new agreement.

It must always be remembered that there can never be an implied term to give business efficacy to a contract if there is already an express term dealing with the same matter. This principle does not apply to those terms which are to be implied by law, i.e. under an Act of Parliament or at common law.

63

Tendering

Competitive Tendering or Negotiation

The first thing to say is that this is not to be read as an exhaustive consideration of all the contractual procedures surrounding tendering. Standard tendering procedures are described in many other books. The purpose of this section is to try and highlight a few of the important things to bear in mind.

For some projects it is simply not worth inviting tenders. These tend to be small jobs of domestic alteration and extension. The kind of small contractor who would be interested in this kind of work might be a single operative or at least a very small contracting firm. Most architects who work in this field will know one or two of these kinds of contractors. Projects which are larger in size, such as two-storey extensions to domestic properties and above, usually warrant inviting tenders.

Sometimes, a client has a favourite contractor that they have used before and insist on using the same one for the new building. That is not usually a good idea unless you know that the contractor is reliable. The contractor must still submit a tender and a breakdown, and it is advisable for the client to engage an experienced quantity surveyor to check the prices. A negotiated tender will never produce the lowest price for the project and the client should be made aware of that. If an investigation of the contractor shows that it is financially shaky or if enquiries among its past customers indicate that defective work is a problem, the client must be informed and strongly advised to seek tenders from among reliable contractors.

If the client is still determined to have a negotiated tender, the contractor must be chosen on the basis of its past record. Negotiated tenders often arise when there is a series of projects and a competitive tender has been accepted for the first project. Further projects in the series are often negotiated with the successful tenderer for the first project if the first project has progressed well and on time with no serious instances of defective work and the contractor and architect have a good working relationship.

Regrettably, there are too many instances where a client insists on using a so-called contractor, particularly for a new house, on the basis that the contractor did a 'very nice job' on the client's boundary wall or drive or other odd jobs. This kind of contractor will submit an unfeasibly low price and, if employed, will cause enormous grief to all involved. If the client will not be moved despite advice, the architect must seriously consider whether to continue.

Professional Practice for Architects and Project Managers, First Edition. David Chappell.

Tenderers

Most architects will have a list of contractors that are suitable for various kinds of project. In the first instance it is the architect, sometimes with the assistance of the quantity surveyor, to select the contractors who are to be invited to tender. Sometimes the tendering process is made open to any contractor wishing to tender, although that is not common. Nor is it a particularly good idea because the tenders obtained will be from contractors of markedly varying sizes and abilities. Your initial letter will be to a number of seemingly suitable contractors, asking if they are prepared to tender and giving them an idea of the size and scope of the project. When the construction industry is booming, you may have to send out several batches of enquiries before you get enough contractors willing to tender. It is important to do a check on each of these contractors even if you are currently working with them because a contractor's financial position can change very quickly. The kind of things to check include the following:

- names and addresses of all directors
- address of the registered office
- share capital of the firm
- annual turnover during the last three years
- number and positions of all office-based staff
- number of site operatives permanently employed in each trade
- number of trained supervisory staff permanently on site
- number and value of contracts on site
- the creditworthiness of the contractor
- address, date of completion, and value of three projects of similar character and size to that for which tenders are to be invited and which have been carried out by the firm recently
- names and addresses of clients, architects, and quantity surveyors connected with the projects noted above and to whom reference may be made.

You could write directly to the contractors concerned for most of this information and you should certainly take up references. At the time you suggest contractors for the list to the client, they may be provisional and subject to your enquiries. Be careful not to 'recommend' any of these contractors because if you do, your client may try to hold you responsible if one of your recommendations turns out to be a bad choice. Your client has the right to add contractors to the list, but all these additions must be checked out. It is a huge waste of the resources of the construction industry if you habitually send out tender information to six contractors. Producing a tender is a very expensive process for anything other than the smallest job. Ideally, tender lists should not number more than three or four contractors and a maximum of six under any circumstances. All the tenderers for a particular project should be of equal status.

All the above is fine in regard to fairly substantial projects. Realistically, there are many projects which are very small and very small indeed. When dealing with those, an architect will not get very far by submitting long questionnaires to the type of contractors that do small work. Here are a few thoughts about those contractors:

- Small contractors and small works divisions of larger contractors are not of the same status. Smaller contractors may be slower, but possibly more committed to carrying out local work.

- All contractors can only be judged on past performance, hence the need for tight control on site.
- Small contractors will not answer questionnaires, but the busyness of a small contractor often speaks for itself.
- Many small contractors are reluctant to work under any kind of formal contract. There is no real answer to this except to choose one of the very short, easy-to-understand, contracts. Certainly, never advise a client to deal with a contractor without a form contract of some kind.
- Building control officers, quantity surveyors, and other consultants can be a good source of information if a new small contractor is being sought.

Tender Documents

The composition of the tender documents depends on the size and character of the project. If the contract is going to consist of bills of quantities and drawings, the documents sent out to each contractor are likely to be simply the bills of quantities with appendices including things like ground investigation reports and some small-scale drawings to give the tenderers an understanding of the layout of the building and its relation to the site. If the contract will be based on specification and drawings, the tenders will each have to prepare their own bills of quantities in order to price the project. Therefore, a full set of drawings must be provided together with the specification and possibly schedules of work.

In situations where only a few drawings are provided, it is usual to inform tenderers that a full set of construction drawings are available for inspection at the architect's office. Anecdotal evidence suggests that relatively few tenderers bother to inspect the drawings and that those who do inspect the full set of drawings rarely secure the contract. That is attributed to the probability that those who take the opportunity to look at all the drawings are looking for problems and usually find some. Hence, they submit higher tenders than those who remain in blissful, but possibly costly, ignorance.

The Process

Many clients are under the impression that tenders for even the most complex of buildings can be obtained within a week and that the process can be expedited if they bang the table a few times and use words like 'stuff and nonsense'. That kind of client often reaps the expensive result of untoward haste by getting a contractor on site without a price or even a contract, for which situation the architect is usually held to be responsible. Realistically, the tender period should be as long as can be managed. Four weeks is a minimum except for the smallest of tendered work. That is simply because of the time the contractor needs to get its own sub-contract and supply tenders in and to correlate everything.

The invitation to tender takes the form of a letter and, as well as the invitation, it should set out the particular process which will be adopted where tenders contain errors, if the lowest tender is not to be accepted etc., and give a list of enclosures and a date and place for delivery of tenders. It is important state the criteria for a successful tender, whether and to what extent, lowest price, shortest contract period etc. will be important. What follows assumes that the employer is looking for the lowest price. It should also say whether the site of the Works is open for inspection and if so how to arrange a visit. Sending out tender invitations is often left to the quantity surveyor, especially when bills of quantities are being used, but there is no good reason why it should not be the architect who sends out the invitations and good reasons why the architect should send them out. If the architect is providing a full service, that will include putting together all the tendering information and sending it to tenderers. If tenderers have comments or questions they should be sent to the architect, who will circulate the questions and answers to all tenderers.

Tenders are usually to be returned to the offices of the architect and occasionally to the client. Delivery to the client is common when the client is a large corporate body or a local authority.

It is always wise to open tenders with witnesses present. If opened at the client's premises, it is sensible to have the architect, quantity surveyor, and client present. If opened at the architect's office the quantity surveyor would be a good witness. A list of tenders must be prepared together with the prices in price order for the client's benefit.

Care must be taken that all tenders comply with the rules set out in the invitation to tender and that all compliant tenders are treated equally. The client may take some convincing that this is essential, especially if a late tender is found to be the lowest. After the date and time fixed for the return of the tenders, tenderers normally telephone each other to find who is the lowest. That enables the higher tenderers to get on with other things and not hope to be successful. A late tenderer may know the other prices and have adjusted its own tender to suit. Therefore, late tenders must be excluded. Clients who insist upon accepting a late tender must be made to understand that the other tenderers may well be able to claim the substantial costs of tendering from the employer. The lowest of the other tenderers may even be able to claim damages consisting of the profit it would have made if it had been awarded the project on the grounds that the employer was in breach of the agreement made between employer and each contractor who properly submitted a tendering in accordance with the rules. Had the rules been properly applied, the lowest tenderer should have been awarded the contract.

If you are wondering how all the tenderers know who is tendering, simply consider that there will be goods and materials specified in the tender documents for which most if not all of the tenderers will have to seek prices from the same suppliers. Many suppliers are always ready to divulge to an enquirer that they have already received other enquiries for the same quantity on a particular site.

I have never experienced contractors forming a 'ring' to decide who got the next tender. That is something that allegedly used to happen, although it is quite illegal of course. I did hear of one interesting situation. When contractors are invited to tender, they generally dislike having to say no. That is usually because they want to keep in the architect's 'good books'. Therefore, when the time comes to actually submit a tender, a contractor who does not want the job (contractor A), but wants to be seen as having submitted a price, may telephone one of the other tenderers (contractor B) and ask for a 'cover price'. When contractor B has calculated its price, it will telephone contractor A and give him a price which is higher than its own price, but not so high as to seem ridiculous. When the architect receives the tenders, contractor A is seen to have submitted a price, but not one low enough to be accepted. I heard of a contractor who found it was the only true tenderer because all the others telephoned it for a cover price. In that case, the architect would not receive a true competitive price (far from it) but would not suspect because, although the lowest price might seem high, all the others were higher and in the same cluster.

Tenderers will often insert qualifications to their tenders. Whether qualification will be considered depends on the rules chosen to govern the tendering process. Often, the invitation to tender will contain a prohibition on qualifications, simply because it is almost impossible to compare tenders submitted on different bases.

When tenders are invited from a selected list of contractors, the lowest, or potentially lowest, should generally be accepted. If a particular tender is not suitable or there is doubt about the contractor's suitability then it should not have been invited to submit. All tenderers go to a great deal of trouble and expense to prepare a tender, and the object of such a tendering approach is to decide which amongst a number of acceptable contractors is to do the work at the lowest price. If the lowest tender is significantly below the others then there may be doubts about whether the contractor has made an error or misjudged the nature of the Works. If such doubts exist then an appropriately structured interview of the lowest tenderer could help clarify the situation. There is usually no legal obligation to accept the lowest or any tender. A contractor's tender is simply an offer which may or may not be accepted.

When a tender is accepted, the other tenderers should be notified, although they probably know already. When notifying the unsuccessful tenderers, it is good practice to set out the contractor's names in alphabetical order and the prices in ascending order, so that the prices cannot be related to the tenderers.

Tenders Which are Too High

This is always a difficult situation. Architects who have insisted that their clients employ quantity surveyors to estimate likely costs and to prepare a cost plan should not experience this situation. If they do, it is likely to be a result of particular circumstances affecting tendering, possibly in a certain locality, and usually suggests that suitable contractors in the locality have plenty of work. There are two things which can be done. The first is simply to re-tender the project to another group of contractors, at the same time asking if the original contractors want to keep their prices open or tender new prices. The quantity surveyor, who ought to have an ear to the ground on these matters, should be able to advise whether it is worthwhile re-tendering. If it is not worthwhile because the prices obtained are a good indication of the current pricing levels, it may be necessary to advise the client that the specification should be examined and amended so as to obtain a cheaper tender. This is usually carried out during the course of meeting between architect, client, quantity surveyor, and lowest tenderer. Once this is agreed, the quantity surveyor usually prepares an addendum bill of quantities to deal with the changes.

Exceeding the Budget

Clients often blame architects for tenders being too high. A very common scenario is that the client, after many requests by the architect, eventually provides a budget cost for the whole project, including professional fees. The architect, with the aid, perhaps, of the quantity surveyor's cost plan but on small jobs unlikely, will produce a design in line with the budget costs. This will be discussed with the client and changes will be made, usually by the client improving the specification or wanting to enlarge the size of some rooms and so on. As time goes on, the client may well add more and more cost to the project until tenders are obtained. This is the point at which the client, overcome with righteous indignation, will ask the architect just what exactly has been going on and why has the architect not designed to suit the budget provided and and and ... fill in the rest.

The only way to avoid being held responsible for the cost overrun is to point out face to face, but also in detailed emails, every time the client wishes to add things that the changes will substantially increase costs. If there is a quantity surveyor, make sure that the quantity surveyor is informed about every single instance so that the effect on costs can be calculated.

64

Letters of Intent

General Points

Clients generally want construction to start on site long before it is wise to do so, before the drawings are ready, and certainly before such 'unimportant' matters as preparing the contract documents are concluded. A client will say, 'Can't we just send a letter of intent'? The architect will probably say something along the lines of, 'Well, I suppose, possibly we could, although perhaps better to wait, I could look into it'. In due course, something with the optimistic title 'Letter of Intent' will find its way to the contractor.

The words 'letter of intent' is not a phrase which can only mean one thing like a 'building contract' or a 'barrowload of bricks'. There are all kinds of letters sent out under the, often mistaken, impression that they are letters of intent. The clue is in the title, but just putting the title at the head of a letter is meaningless, like writing 'Oranges' on a bag of potatoes.

Letters of intent usually result in small contracts for perhaps some of the total Works. They are often what are commonly known as 'if' contracts because they are put to the contractor on the basis that 'if' the contractor will carry out the work indicated, the employer will pay a reasonable sum. It is an invitation to carry out the contract. There is no contract until the contractor accepts the invitation by starting work.

The classic letter of intent is sent by or on behalf of the employer. It acknowledges receipt of the contractor's price for carrying out a specific project. It says that the employer intends to accept the price but cannot do so now. It then invites the contractor to start to carry out the project on the basis that the employer will pay for the work usually up to a specific figure. The letter may go on to explain how the payments are to be decided and paid, sometime reference is made to the payment provisions in the, as yet unsigned, contract.

The letter must actually amount to a letter of intent, not simply say that it is. Among the many kinds of letters wrongly sent out as letters of intent are the following:

- The letter may state a future intention to enter into a contract and invite the contractor to start work on site without reference to any payment or other obligation or liability. That is not a letter of intent. At best, it is what is commonly known as a 'letter of comfort'. It may include meaningless assurances such as informing the contractor of the usual highly ethical conduct of the employer and refer to the employer's usual policy. If the contractor carries out any work in response to this kind of letter, it should be aware that the work will be done at risk.

Professional Practice for Architects and Project Managers, First Edition. David Chappell.

- The letter of intent may ask the contractor to do some limited work in return for payment when the Works proceed. If the Works do not proceed, the contractor will be entitled to some payment for what has been done, but not necessarily in accordance with the contract, which of course has never been agreed.
- The letter may instruct the contractor to proceed with the project to completion on the basis of the terms in the letter. The terms may reflect the full agreement reached by the two parties, which effectively may be the whole contract. It never is very clear why, in those cases, the parties do not simply sign the contract.

Dangers

There are all kinds of dangers when using letters of intent. For example:

- Letters of intent are often badly worded and ambiguous so that the parties are uncertain whether or not they have concluded a binding contract.
- It may be unclear as to whether any disputes can be referred to adjudication.
- The wording may be such that the courts consider that a full binding contract has been created when that was not the intention of the employer.
- The employer may have agreed, without really understanding, to pay contractor's costs even if the contract for the Works does not proceed.
- The formal contract documents may never be executed by the parties.
- Once a contractor is well advanced with the construction under a letter of intent, the contractor may be reluctant (i.e. may make all kinds of excuses why it has not quite got around to signing the formal contract) to sign the contract. A common reason for that would be if the contractor is in delay and the proposed liquidated damages are substantial. In those circumstances, it may be impractical or, at least, very inconvenient for the employer to bring the work to an end and employ another contractor to complete the Works.
- Many letters of intent are so worded that the contractor is entitled to walk off the site at any time without liability or the employer may, without liability, be entitled to stop the contractor working.
- If the contractor is not certain about the amount of work to be done, that will adversely affect the contractor's capability to enter into supply and sub-contracts, which normally reflect, or at least acknowledge, the terms of the main contract.
- A letter of intent will not protect the employer to the same extent as a properly executed contract.

I have seen letters of intent drafted by solicitors which are almost as long as the contract for which the letter of intent is supposedly a temporary expedient. If half the time spent drafting a letter of intent was spent in preparing the actual contract, there would be a lot fewer problems in construction. If you use one of the commonly available standard form contracts, it should be possible to fill in all the blanks in a couple of hours, even for the uninitiated. Obviously, things like drawings and specifications take longer, but presumably you are not going to invite the contractor to start work before the drawings and specification are completed. Yes, I know that is often done (it used to be called 'fast track') and I have seen the sorry mess which often results. In fact, sorting out sorry messes is how I have made my living for many years.

There are two ways to send a letter of intent. The best way is for the employer to sign the letter. The other way is for you to sign the letter. If you do, you must make clear that you are acting on behalf of the employer otherwise you may become liable to the contractor. In both instances, the letter must be carefully drafted by someone with experience in drafting good letters of intent and the employer must see it and give you his or her authority before it is issued.

When to Issue

It is not wrong to issue a letter of intent. What is wrong is to issue a badly worded letter of intent without carefully considering the situation. These are four of the key questions which ought to be answerable in the affirmative:

- Is the work to be done and the price to be paid agreed or is it clear how they will be agreed?
- Are the contract terms agreed or likely to be agreed?
- Are the start and finish dates of the project agreed?
- Is there a good reason to start work before the contract documents are finalised and signed?

65

Preparing the Contract Documents

What are the Contract Documents?

The first thing to be clear about is what is meant by 'contract documents' (see 52: Contract Documents). Many architects think that the 'contract' is simply the printed form filled in and signed by both parties. Actually, of course, the building contract is a whole bundle of documents which are usually referred to as the 'contract documents'. Having said that, the confusion probably arises because it can also be correct to say that the printed form is the contract. The JCT Standard Building Contract with quantities 2016 has 'Contract' in the title, but a quick scan through that document will show that it is of little use without other documents to support it.

In theory the contract documents can consist of anything, but in virtually all building contracts, the contract documents consist of the contract drawings, the specification and bills of quantities or schedules of work, and whichever printed form is to be used with them. If the contractor is to design a portion or all of the Works, the documents will also probably include a detailed performance specification and the contractor's proposals for satisfying the performance specification.

How are the Contract Documents put Together?

All the documents, other than the printed form, which comprise the contract documents must be signed by the parties on the front cover of each document and on every sheet of drawings to identify them as contract documents. For example, 'This is one of the contract documents referred to in the Agreement dated …'.

In addition, documents other than the printed form itself must be made part of the contract by what is called 'incorporation'. To do this, it is necessary to clearly state in the printed form that these documents are to be incorporated in the contract. There is usually a space near the beginning of every printed contract form where the other contract documents can be listed.

The employer must not be given free rein to incorporate whatever takes his or her fancy. It is unfortunately common for document-happy employers to try to incorporate all kinds of other documents besides the absolutely necessary drawings and specifications etc., things like emails and letters passing between employer and contractor after

Professional Practice for Architects and Project Managers, First Edition. David Chappell.

tender stage, odd lists of prices or quotations for various things. Usually, the inclusion of extraneous pieces of correspondence as part of the contract only confuses matters if a dispute arises later and may even be a cause of the dispute. If any of these bits of paper are so important, the contract documents should be amended accordingly.

Don't Do This

Sometimes, an attempt will be made to incorporate the whole of a contract simply by reference to it in a letter, e.g. 'on the JCT Standard Contract terms and conditions'. That can never work because it overlooks the fact that there are many blanks in the printed contract which must be filled in before the contract makes any sense. The practice ignores the fact that there may be different editions and versions of a contract so that it is impossible to say with certainty which version is intended to apply. The result is usually chaos, which is only good for people like me who earn their livings by dealing with disputes and other problems.

What are Articles?

Articles are the formal opening parts of a contract which set out the essential elements that are agreed and made subject to the rest of the contract terms. For example, the articles include the names and addresses of the parties and the professionals involved with the contract and set out the contract sum to be paid by the employer and broadly what is to be done by the contractor.

What are Recitals?

Recitals usually explain the background to the contract and set down what the parties intend to do and sometimes what they have already done, such as that they have entered into another contract about a related matter. They are not usually essential to the contract and they will not override the rest of the contract if it is clear. However, if some parts of the contract are ambiguous, the recitals can be important if they clarify the ambiguity.

Completing the Printed Contract Form

This is a job for the architect or other professional who will actually administer the contract. Many architects leave it for the quantity surveyor to complete, but that is quite wrong. The quantity surveyor can be called upon for advice and assistance if appropriate. But it is not a task for the quantity surveyor alone, still less for the employer's solicitor, who may or may not have a full understanding of the most appropriate form of contract to use, but who will certainly not have experience in administering a building contract in progress.

It should be noted that although the preliminaries section of the specification or bills of quantities state how the contract form is to be completed, most of that information must be provided by the architect to the quantity surveyor. This means that the architect is effectively completing the printed form when providing that information. In theory, when an acceptable tender is received, the architect simply copies the information in the bills of quantities into the contract form. In practice, the process of accepting a tender may not be straightforward, various things may be changed and the transfer of information from bills of quantities to the contract form may not be easy.

Some Key Points

- The date of the agreement should be left blank until the last party signs even if this is after the project is well advanced on site or even completed. It should be obvious that every effort must be made to have the contract signed before work starts on site. It becomes more difficult afterwards as one or other party sees advantages in withholding signature.
- It is essential that the contract drawings are exactly the same as the tender drawings. Any post-tender amendments should be shown by means of an addendum attached to the contract.
- The words 'to be agreed' or sometimes 'TBA' should be avoided. The best chance of agreement is always before, not after, the contract is signed.
- Leaving an entry blank may trigger a default position which may not be what is required. Most of the entries are self-evident.
- There must be a date when the contractor is entitled to take possession of the site. There must be another date by which the Works should be completed or a method of calculating the date for completion, e.g. '20 weeks from the date of possession'.
- There must be a total sum for the contract or a method of calculating it.
- There must be a means of calculating periodic payments to the contractor and when they are to be paid.
- The extent and quality of the Works must be clearly set out.
- Decisions about levels of insurance and the like should be the subject of discussion between the employer and an insurance expert such as an insurance broker. Few architects have any degree of expertise in insurance matters and should not advise the employer other than to get proper insurance advice.
- The methods of dispute resolution must be stated. Contracts which do not involve residential work for owner occupiers must provide for adjudication.

Attestation

The attestation pages are simply the pages on which the parties to the contract sign to signify their agreement to the contract terms. 'Attestation' means the witnessing of an act or an event. When the parties attest, they are said to 'execute' the contract. There are two basic options. One option is to execute the contract under hand (referred to as a 'simple' contract). The other option is to execute the contract as a deed (referred to as a 'specialty' contract) (see 23: Contracts).

Are Some Documents More Important than Others?

The documents which comprise the contract documents are not all as important as each other. It is therefore vital to understand what might be called the 'pecking order', but is usually called the 'hierarchy of documents'. No matter how much care is taken in preparing the contract documents, it is almost inevitable that there will be instances where the documents conflict in some respect. That is particularly the case when they have been assembled in a hurry, perhaps after a long and difficult negotiation following tender stage.

Sometimes the printed form gives a clear indication of which documents are most important. If not, there are various rules which can be applied. For example, a document which is typed will prevail over one which is printed and one which is handwritten prevails over all. There are many other rules which can be used.

Some contractors like to pick out a clause in the contract which seems to confirm their argument and then rely on it to support a claim. I used to know a solicitor who used that technique frequently. He did not know much about building contracts, but he depended on the other side knowing less than he did. He was very successful in face-to-face negotiations, where he kept stabbing his finger on the clause, saying: 'It's as plain as the nose on my face'. I doubt whether he would be as successful today. Unless they are in conflict, all the parts of the printed form must be read together because some clauses may qualify others. For example, the employer's entitlement to liquidated damages for delay must be read with the clause which requires the architect to give an extension of time in certain circumstances.

Section IV

Dealing with a Building Contract in Progress

66

Preliminaries

What are Preliminaries?

Preliminaries are commonly referred to as 'prelims'. They are the first part of the bills of quantities or the specification which describes the Works in general terms and lists the contractor's general obligations. What exactly is contained in the preliminaries varies according to the method of measurement or the particular ideas of the architect or the quantity surveyor drafting them. Typical headings include, among other things, the following:

- location of the project
- names and addresses of the consultants
- list of drawings
- description of the site
- the form of contract and any amendments
- employer's requirements and limitation of hours of work etc.
- name boards
- management
- site accommodation
- services
- temporary works
- specialist sub-contractors and suppliers
- work or supply items by or on behalf of the employer
- statutory authorities
- provisional sums
- daywork.

It is useful to include certain essential controls in the preliminaries so such things as quality standards, control, security, safety, and protection should be there.

Pricing

The preliminaries is a most important part of the contract documents and conveys information to the contractor not present elsewhere in the documents. The contractor will price the preliminaries. Sometimes the pricing will be item by item and sometimes the contractor will simply insert a weekly price or even a total amount to cover all the

Professional Practice for Architects and Project Managers, First Edition. David Chappell.

preliminaries costs for the contract period. Very often the preliminaries are priced as a percentage of the costs of the Works. When a contractor writes asking for its 'prelims', it is not wanting you to send another copy of the specification. It is wanting to be paid the price it put in the preliminaries per week. Contractors often try to claim prelims (meaning money) as loss and/or expense if they suffer delay. As explained elsewhere, that is not the way to claim (see 99: Financial Claims).

Pricing on an item-by-item basis is by far the best way because you can see exactly what the contractor is charging and, importantly, what is not being charged. A preliminaries item for which the contractor is not charging will either simply have a line against it or it will say 'incl.' (meaning 'included'). It is bad policy for a contractor to mark any item as being included without charge because if that item suddenly becomes important, it may cost the contractor money. I recently saw preliminaries in which the contractor had written 'included' against scaffolding. Presumably the contractor was confident that the amount of scaffolding was fixed. As the work progressed, it became clear that scaffolding would be required for other parts of the Works but it could not be charged because it was included. Of course, if the reason for the extra scaffolding had been because the architect issued an instruction for additional work which required scaffolding, that would have entitled the contractor to extra payment.

Extension of Preliminaries

One often hears the term 'extension of preliminaries'. This refers to the way in which the quantity surveyor will adjust the monthly valuation of preliminary items if the project is delayed in a situation where the contractor has no additional financial entitlement. In such cases the quantity surveyor will often reduce the monthly amount of preliminary costs so that the total preliminary costs for the project are extended over a longer contract period.

The situation is different if the contractor has grounds for claiming loss and/or expense due to the delay. In that case, the preliminaries remain the same for the contract period and additional costs are added to replace the preliminaries for the overrun period. Although many contractors and quantity surveyors will just add the weekly preliminaries multiplied by the number of weeks overrun, that is not the correct way to do it. For any overrun period for which the contractor is seeking additional costs, the contractor must show that the costs have actually been incurred. Reference to the preliminary costs in the bills of quantities or specification is not sufficient because those costs are simply what the contractor estimated at tender stage and they may be too high or, indeed, too low. In the case of a financial claim, the contractor is only entitled to the amount of preliminary costs which it has actually lost or incurred.

67

Possession of the Site

What is 'Possession'?

Many building contracts refer to a 'date of possession', some merely refer to the 'commencement date'. Most architects think they know what these terms mean: they mean the date on which the contractor may start work on site. But what do we mean by 'possession'. To have possession of a piece of land is to be on the land. That of course is not the same as ownership. The law says that if someone has possession of land that person has a better right to it than anyone except the true owner of the land. That gives rise to the interesting situation that, in principle, the contractor in possession of the site may refuse access to anyone except the true owner. Therefore, building contracts usually make clear that the architect has the right to go onto the site and to authorise any other person, such as the clerk of works, to enter the site.

How does the Contractor get Possession?

Even if the building contract says nothing about possession, it will always be implied into every building contract that the contractor must have possession of the site in sufficient time to allow completion of the Works by the contract completion date. Therefore, if the contract simply refers to a commencement date, the contractor must have possession of the site in order to commence and carry out the Works. It is very obvious that if the contractor cannot go onto the site, it cannot even begin to construct the building. Therefore, if nothing is said about possession of the site, once the contractor is appointed, it has the right to possession.

The law would say that the contractor has a licence to occupy the site. The employer has no right under the general law to remove the contractor from site, but most contracts allow the employer to do so for a good reason specified in the contract. The degree of possession is important and, in most cases, unless the contract specifically states otherwise, a contractor must have complete possession of the site to be able to carry on and complete the Works. I once had to deal with a contract under which a local authority had agreed with a contractor to refurbish about 100 council houses. There was a date for possession and the council thought it could get away with just handing over the houses into the contractor's possession a maximum of 12 houses at any one time. The idea was that when practical completion was certified for a house, the contractor received another house in exchange so that work could continue, theoretically at the same rate.

Professional Practice for Architects and Project Managers, First Edition. David Chappell.

It was useful for the council who need only provide alternative accommodation for a maximum of 12 families at a time. Unfortunately for the council, the contract did not adequately spell out exactly what degree of possession the contractor would have and it was able to argue successfully that it required possession of the full 100 houses in order to properly progress the Works on site.

Make Things Clear

Many avoidable disputes occur simply because the architect or the quantity surveyor or the employer does not make crystal clear in the contract what is intended or required. You cannot get away with introducing things at the pre-start meeting (usually erroneously called the 'pre-contract' meeting) which are not agreed in the contract. Many architects just do not appear to understand that. They call a pre-start meeting and, at that meeting, they try to introduce all kinds of extra rules with which they expect the contractor to comply. I once heard an architect tell the contractor that he expected to receive the contractor's application for payment seven days before the certificate was due and if he did not receive the application, the contractor would not get a payment certified that month. That was quite contrary to the particular contract in use which left it entirely to the contractor whether or not it submitted an application and made clear that the duty of issuing the certificate lay entirely with the architect.

More than One Party in Possession

If a domestic property is to be refurbished or extended and the owner of the property wants to stay in it, it can be written into a contract, but it is not a good idea. Every architect knows that having the employer based actually on the site is a recipe for trouble. Quite apart from the fact that the employer and contractor may become bosom buddies to the exclusion of the architect, the presence of the employer may hinder the progress of the Works because employers seldom seem to understand that it is essential to comply strictly with the contract, which means that the employer must do exactly what he or she has agreed to do with the contractor.

For example, it may be in the contract that, at the request of the contractor, the employer will move from occupation of one part of the dwelling and take rented accommodation until the Works are completed. When the time comes to move, the employer may regret agreeing and refuse to move, entering into some unworkable ad hoc arrangement with the contractor which, to the contractor's delight, will provide it with lots of opportunities for claiming extra payment for disruption. Sometimes, ad hoc arrangements do work but living in a house which is partly a building site is never a good idea and where there are children it is positively dangerous.

Normally, the contractor will have exclusive possession of the site. In plain terms, that means that the contractor alone controls the site and anyone who comes onto the site. When sub-contractors are engaged by the contractor, they do not have exclusive possession because they have to work alongside the contractor's operatives and other sub-contractors.

Failure to give Possession

Some contracts allow the employer to postpone the date for possession. Sometimes this is referred to as deferment of the date. Whatever it is called, there will be consequences. The contractor will be entitled to an extension of time, which may have to be longer than the postponement period itself. That is because, if the contractor is geared up to start on a particular day and the day is postponed for, say, three weeks, the likelihood is that the contractor, having stood down operatives and equipment, will not be able to start exactly on the new date. Moreover, the contractor will almost certainly be entitled to successfully claim loss and/or expense because it will undoubtably cost it more money if possession is postponed. Even where a contract allows that kind of postponement, a maximum period of postponement is usually stipulated, otherwise the employer might try to postpone the date of possession indefinitely.

If the employer fails to give possession on the date specified, then, unless the contract allows the employer to delay possession, the contractor is entitled to claim damages and the date for completion may not be enforceable. Many architects think that if the contract allows them to issue an instruction to postpone the Works, that allows them to effectively postpone the date for possession. That is wrong. Possession of the site and the carrying out of the Works are two entirely different things. An architect has no power to change the date for possession, which is something either agreed between the two parties or implied by law. The contractor will want to fence off the site and establish materials storage compounds, accommodation, and health and welfare facilities before actually starting to carry out any of the Works. To do these things the contractor needs and is entitled to possession of the site (see 73: Postponement).

Failure by the employer to give possession to the contractor will amount to a breach of contract entitling the contractor to damages. It is part of the architect's job to make this clear to the employer in plain terms. Default in giving possession is a breach of a significant term of the contract. Prolonged failure to give possession may entitle the contractor to accept the breach as repudiation of the contract and to sue for damages, which would include the loss of the profit that it would have earned if the contract had been completed. That would be a catastrophe for the employer. Fortunately, contractors rarely take that course and usually decide to treat the breach as a minor matter and to claim damages for any loss actually incurred.

68

Dealing with Difficult Contractors

First Things

I am often asked how an architect should deal with difficult contractors. The first thing to establish, of course, is whether it is the contractor or the architect who is being difficult. A contractor's agent seeking clarification about a drawing may be perfectly justified in doing so because you have failed to give all the information that the agent needs. On the other hand, a contractor seeking the detail of the wooden skirting down one side of a room when there is a detail existing showing the skirting down the other side is probably being difficult.

The thing that must always be borne in mind is the need to have a project completed on time (there's a hope), to the Contract Sum (mmm), and in accordance with the drawings and specification. There are difficult contractors and there are very difficult contractors. The same can be said about architects, quantity surveyors, engineers, and so on. There are still many contractors who are keen to do a good job for a fair price, but they may be difficult to deal with. It must be remembered that the same result will be achieved irrespective of the behaviour of the contractor provided firm steps are taken to enforce the terms of the contract and only to certify work properly carried out. Obviously, the specification and drawings must be correct, relevant, and comprehensive. An old architect I knew used to caution against 'spoon-feeding' contractors. He believed in providing only small-scale drawings, whatever the project. Little wonder that he had continual problems.

In my early days as an architect, the contracts manager of a particular contractor insisted on asking me question after question along the lines of 'I see that you have hardwood on your drawing, could we use softwood instead at a cost saving'? Each successive question was asking me to stretch the specification a little bit further. Some were helpful, some were decidedly unhelpful and purely in the contractor's own interests. Eventually I just said 'No' without further elaboration and shortly afterwards, he stopped asking. A couple of years later when I had used that contractor on various projects and I was about to move away, the contracts manager got me alone on site and said that I must have thought that he was a difficult man when I first started working with him. 'Yes, I did', I said. He said that he had just been testing me to see how far he could go. When he established that it was not very far, he knew the score and just got on with things. In my subsequent experience many established contractors work on that basis.

Professional Practice for Architects and Project Managers, First Edition. David Chappell.

Next Things

Many architects make the mistake of trying to make friends with the contractor right from the beginning. If the contractor sees the architect working hard to establish a rapport with everyone, that architect will be labelled a 'soft touch'. In other words, here is an architect who will try very hard to avoid confrontation which might be unpleasant even to the extent of agreeing things which are not really in accordance with the contract.

The architect is not there to make friends with the contractor or with anyone else for that matter. The architect is there, like all the other consultants, to do a professional job. If you do not have that firmly in mind from the beginning, there is no use you reading any further in this item. There is an old saying, 'Start as you mean to go on' and that saying is absolutely on the nail so far as dealing with contractors is concerned. Let me be clear that I am not suggesting that all contractors are rogues and vagabonds, as an old architect I knew was fond of saying, although obviously some are. You must start dealing with every new contractor as if it was competently managed and dedicated to running the project with a keen eye on time, cost, and quality. Insist on complete adherence to the specification unless it could be demonstrated that the specification was wrong in some way.

If from the start the contractor is left in no doubt that you expect it to comply with the contract in every respect, you immediately lessen the chances of the contractor becoming difficult. Contractors are not usually difficult just for the hell of it (although some are). If they are difficult, there is usually a good reason. It may be that the contractor is getting short of money because the tender was under-estimated or that some of the workforce are underperforming or causing delays. It may simply be that the architect, eager to show how easy-going and friendly he or she can be, gives the appearance of being easy to influence and the contractor's agent on site, thus encouraged, sees how far the architect will go. If from the beginning you make clear that you will not put up with any nonsense, you will be unlikely to get any. The agent will realise that there is no point in trying to get you to lower standards or certify more money than earned or substitute other materials, so he will not waste time trying.

A Couple More Things

Contractors' agents constantly used to tell me that they have never 'done it that way before. You're the first young (in this context they mean "woefully inexperienced") fella who's asked me to do that'. 'It' appeared to embrace everything from laying concrete to installing plumbing. It was always said with a shaking of the head in disbelief that I could be so clueless as to suggest something which they were not happy to do. I became quite used to contractors telling me that I was the first architect they had known to issue Architect's Instructions, have regular site meetings, stop building in frosty weather or insist upon buildings being pretty near complete at 'Practical Completion'. The answer to an agent who says that it is the first time he has been asked to do something is to simply say that it will be useful for him or her to do something new for a change.

Some contractors bombard the architect with many unnecessary lengthy letters or emails, sometimes as many as 10 or 12 each day. They are calculated to stress the architect into spending hours each day dealing with them. Deal with them by rapidly scanning the content and highlighting anything that requires an immediate answer. Then write 'Thank you for your 12 letters/emails dated [*insert date*] which I will deal with in due course. The answers to your urgent questions are as follows': Then fire off the answers actually required. If none of the letters are actually asking sensible questions requiring immediate answers, simply write the first part. Nothing is more irritating to a contractor than to attempt to tie up the architect in fruitless letter writing only to find that the fruitless letter writing is actually being done by the contractor.

Contractual Difficulties

Many of the difficulties with contractors can be easily settled by looking at what the contract says and putting it into effect. Every building contract should give precise details about the way in which the contractor is to be paid and how that is to be calculated. The contract will also say that you can give instructions and that the contractor must carry them out, that the contractor cannot just stop work or go slow and if that happens what the architect can do about it. Contractors know that architects, for the most part, are not especially interested in building contracts. Most architects become architects because they want to design buildings. Therefore, contractors like to lob loaded questions at the architect like, 'Even though the project is late, you must still release half the retention on the date it should have been completed'. This can throw the architect into a panic. A proper understanding of the particular contract in use can easily dispose of this kind of nonsense.

Summary

One can summarise how to deal with difficult contractors by saying that the most important thing is that you must make clear from the beginning that, although you are obviously prepared to listen to any questions or suggestions that the contractor may have, you are not prepared to tolerate nonsense. Know your way around whatever contract you are using and be ready to use all the remedies in the contract if the contractor delays, ignores instructions or produces poor work. Consider carefully everything the contractor says and then be decisive. Do not engage in useless argument. If you are confident that you are correct, do not be afraid of the contractor's threats to walk off the site or to go to adjudication. If you are not confident, get some good advice, then you will be confident. Respect the contractor's chain of command. Do not give instructions directly to individual members of the workforce. Understand your contractor and its motivations. Most contractors' threats are simply that: threats.

69

Advance Payment

The Problems

It seems that more and more small contractors are asking for a payment up front before they start work. This seems to be particularly the case for domestic work. It can happen with larger projects but, in my experience, it is not as common. The principles are the same whether the project is large or small. Employers sometimes seek advice from the architect. Employers will sometimes simply give the contractor a few thousand pounds and mention it to the architect in passing, often just before or after the building contract is signed. I have had many panicky calls from architects who find themselves in that position and do not know how to deal with it. Should it be referred to in payment certificates? Should the employer issue a pay less notice? What if the contractor does not continue with the Works?

This can be quite a worrying problem unless it is handled correctly. The first thing to do is to look at the principle. Obviously, it is not a good idea for the employer to give any money to the contractor until the contractor has done something to earn it and the architect has certified the amount to be paid. On the other hand, setting up the site, ordering materials, and paying wages may require an outlay of cash which a small contractor just does not have or cannot easily borrow. If the contractor is asking for money up front and the employer is willing to provide a payment in advance of any work being done on the site, it is important that there is some way of protecting the money paid out. The employer does not want to pay out a sum only to find that the contractor becomes insolvent soon after starting the project. Another danger is that the contractor may become insolvent or just stop working and walk away a few weeks before the Works are complete even though the sum paid in advance is equal to the value of the work remaining to be carried out.

Solutions

The usual way to deal with this is twofold. The contractor must provide a bond (see 21: Bonds and Parent Company Guarantees) to cover the cost of the advance payment so that, if for any reason the work is not done or the contractor does not otherwise repay the payment, the provider of the bond (known as the Surety) will reimburse the employer. At the same time, the contractor must agree to repay the advance payment to the employer in instalments spread over the first months of the contract period.

Professional Practice for Architects and Project Managers, First Edition. David Chappell.

Some of the more elaborate building contracts make provision for advance payment and include a sample bond suitable for the contractor to use. But building contracts for smaller Works rarely include that kind of provision and there is no alternative for the employer but to seek legal advice to draw up the bond and the repayment agreement all to be signed and provided together with the signature on the building contract itself. Architects should not get involved in trying to draft a suitable agreement. A simple exchange of emails between contractor and employer is virtually never satisfactory and can be quite dangerous. It is not the architect's job to get the legal advice. To do so would make the architect liable to the employer for something for which the architect will have no professional indemnity cover.

Where this arrangement is carried out, whether as part of the building contract or as a separate agreement, the payment certificates must deduct the relevant instalment from the amount to be certified for payment. For example, if the employer advances £10 000 and the agreement is that the contractor will repay the amount in instalments of £2000 each month, the certificates will show £2000 deducted in the first month, £4000 deducted in the second month, and so on for five certificates until the full amount of £10 000 has been deducted and then that will be the figure deducted from the gross amount certified until the final certificate.

Unorthodox Payments

If the employer has simply paid money to the contractor as an advance payment without any proper agreement being signed, the employer is in a difficult situation. It is one of those situations from which the architect should stand well back and advise the employer to immediately seek legal advice. If the contract has yet to be signed, it may be that the employer's solicitor can draft an addendum to the contract with the contractor's agreement.

This is the problem. The contractor may not agree. It may simply say, 'Thank you very much for the payment, I am not signing anything'. Try not to step in at this point with some very clever solution. You are not being paid, nor are you insured, for finding clever solutions to the employer's ill-advised actions (to give them a polite name). The correct person to sort this out is the employer's solicitor at the employer's cost.

Until some agreement has been recorded in writing, you cannot acknowledge the payment in any way. In particular, you cannot deduct it from any certificate. That is because your powers, such as they are, depend upon what the contract says and if there is nothing in the building contract and no other agreement to cover the situation, you have no power to do anything other than what is in the building contract. This is something which many architects, and contractors also, do not understand. There is no 'divine right of architects'. I had a friend who admitted that he never had a copy of any contract in his office. I asked him how he knew what he was entitled to do in any given situation. His answer was that he just did what architects do: issue instructions, certificates, extensions of time, and that kind of thing. Clearly, he did not believe that the devil was in the detail. The only way you know what you can do under a particular contract is to read it and perhaps highlight all the places where it says that you 'may' (meaning 'may if you wish') and all the places where it says you 'shall' (meaning you 'must').

So, the short answer is that advance payments should not be made unless there is special provision for it in the building contract or unless the employer's solicitor has drafted an agreement. If the employer simply pays some cash to the contractor, advise the employer to engage a solicitor to sort out the mess, but otherwise ignore it.

70

Retention

Definition

Retention is a sum of money retained by the employer from amounts earned by the contractor so that if there is defective work or materials which the contractor will not rectify or if the contractor fails to complete the project, the employer can use the money to help to deal with the problem. The sum is deducted from each payment certified by the architect and the growing amount is usually called the 'retention fund'.

No Automatic Right to Retention

It is important to understand that there is no automatic right in law to deduct retention. This is often misunderstood by architects, contractors and, particularly, employers. In short, unless the building contract states that the retention can be deducted, the amount earned each month must be paid in full without deduction of retention. It is surprising how many architects deduct retention in their payment certificates without even checking to see if retention is permitted and at what rate. That often occurs if the architect is arranging for a relatively small job to be done and no formal contract (oops!) has been executed. An employer might engage a contractor to replace some rotting windows in a private house. The employer asks for a quotation, the contractor provides one, the employer accepts and when the invoice arrives after the work is done, the employer pays all except 5% which he or she mistakenly retains for six months in case there are any problems. The contractor is entitled to the full amount of the invoice unless retention has been agreed when the employer accepted the quotation.

The Mechanism

Most, but not all, contracts provide for retention to be deducted. Some contracts do this in a reverse kind of way by stating that each month the architect must only certify 95% of the amount the contractor has earned. That, of course, is virtually the same as saying that 5% must be deducted each month. If the building contract allows retention to be deducted, it usually also states that half the retention is to be released to the contractor at practical completion and the rest when the final payment is made.

Professional Practice for Architects and Project Managers, First Edition. David Chappell.

The amount of the retention need not be 5% of course. In practice, it can be whatever the employer and the contractor agree to put in the contract.

What happens to the retention fund before it is released depends on whether or not it is stated to be held in trust for the contractor and what the contract says about it. If the contract says nothing about how the retention is to be kept, the employer can simply keep it with the rest of the employer's money in the bank or building society.

If the contract states that the retention is to be held in trust for the contractor, it must be kept in a separate bank account whether or not the contract says so. Some contracts say that the employer must put the retention in a separate bank account *if* the contractor requests it. If the retention is held in trust, it must be held separately whether or not requested. That is because the employer has what is known as a fiduciary duty to keep the fund safe. If the employer went bankrupt or, if a limited company, it became insolvent and the retention was not in a separate bank account, the trustee in bankruptcy or the official receiver could use the fund as part of the employer's money to satisfy creditors. By putting the fund into a separate bank account, properly designated as being money belonging to the contractor, the trustee in bankruptcy or the receiver cannot use it as part of the employer's money and it must eventually be returned to the contractor.

It is also arguable that, under the legislation concerning trust funds, the employer is obliged to invest the retention fund for the benefit of the contractor. However, that is a matter for the employer to be advised by financial and legal advisers, not by the architect or quantity surveyor.

Retention Bond

Some contracts allow the contractor to provide a bond instead of having retention deducted. The wording of the bond is designed to allow the employer to have recourse to the bond in a similar way that the money in a retention fund could be used. If the amount of the bond falls below what the retention fund would have been, perhaps because of the addition of work, either the bond must be increased or the additional retention must be deducted in the usual way. Contractors are said to prefer a bond because it means that the full amount of the valuation is released each month. Although the contractor will have to pay for the bond, it will be taken into account in the tendering process.

71

Contractor's Programme

Basics

If a contractor is to carry out construction successfully there is a need to perform the correct operations at the right time and, most importantly, in the right order. If this is not done, chaos will result. The programme is the schedule showing each activity that is to be done and how it relates to all the other activities and to the time available for construction. The simplest form is a Gantt (bar) chart. The activities are listed down the left-hand side and the time is indicated in weeks and days across the top. The contractor will produce a programme for its own benefit, even if neither the contract nor the architect ask for one. Even the simplest construction jobs require a programme. A kitchen extension has to be planned, admittedly in not quite the same way as an airport terminal building, but some kind of programme of work must be figured out before construction actually begins.

There are obvious things such as the need to dig a trench before pouring contract foundations or the need for foundations before building a wall. But there are lots of other activities which go on and it is important to know which must be done first or at the same time. Not all of these things are immediately obvious. It is no good plastering walls and then having to cut out a grove to hold electric cables and other services. That is fairly obvious but still occasionally confused. In a project of any size, it is essential to know how all the trades must interact.

During the three years that I worked for a medium-sized builder, I learned many things, not all of them welcome. One day the managing director asked me to prepare a programme for the contract scheduled to begin in a few weeks' time (20 houses). I said that I had no experience of preparing such a programme because in my view it was something for an experienced builder. 'It's alright', said the MD. 'My lads won't take any notice of it. It's only for the architect; he won't know any difference. Just get the operations roughly in order and sloping down from left to right on the chart. Remember that it takes about a third of the time to build the shell to weathertight and the rest to do the interior.' Armed with these criteria, which I vaguely knew already, I duly produced a programme in the form of a bar chart and sent it to the architect. I was surprised, actually shocked, to find that the architect not only accepted the programme but attempted, unsuccessfully of course, to track progress on the chart at each site meeting, but not once was its validity questioned.

There are now several different sophisticated computer programmes which are capable of calculating and producing construction programmes assuming, of course, that the

Professional Practice for Architects and Project Managers, First Edition. David Chappell.

correct information is inputted. Contractors building anything of any size are advised to use these programmes to avoid silly mistakes in calculating the total time needed to complete a project. The computer can produce a network analysis which, as the name implies, consists of a series of interconnected lines and arrows showing how the activities relate to one another. The total time required will depend upon the critical path or paths. This is the longest string of dependent activities starting from the beginning of the time period and extending to the end. It is called 'critical' because if any of these activities takes longer to carry out than planned, the whole project will be delayed by that amount. Other paths through the programme are not critical because in those paths some or all of the activities will take less time to carry out than the time available in the programme.

Float

A word here about 'float'. This is a really simple thing which by dint of a great deal of hard work and obfuscation on the part of programme planners and others has been made extraordinarily difficult to grasp. Contractors are heard to remark that they 'own the float'. I might just as well say that I own the air. In both cases, the words describe what is there when there appears to be nothing else. Float is the difference between the time allowed on the programme for doing something and the time it will take to do it. There, that is it.

There is no float in the critical path because all the activities are lined up end to end with no time in between. That is why they are critical. If the programme allows five days to excavate foundations and it will only take three days to do it, we say that there is a float of two days. In other words, the excavation can be delayed by two days or, put another way, it can take two days longer to do and it will not affect anything else. Therefore, no one can 'own' float. This is quite different from saying that the contractor allowed for excavating foundations in three days and, because of architect's instructions, it took a total of four or five days.

Computer-generated Programmes

There are a few things which contractors and particularly architects should bear in mind. There is nothing magical about programmes produced by a computer. They can simply do many thousands of calculations in the time it takes a human being to do one. It is popularly but wrongly thought that if the computer-generated programme shows a particular sequence in time, that is the end of the matter. Contractors often use these programmes to show that they are entitled to extensions of time.

The truth of the matter is far more mundane. Everything, but everything, depends upon the way in which activities are linked to each other. The start of one activity can be linked to the finish of another activity or to its start. It can be made to start immediately on the finish of the preceding activity or not until a day or two have elapsed. It can be made to start before the preceding activity has finished. So, not only must each activity be linked to the correct activity or activities, each activity must be linked in the correct way. What may start out looking like a perfectly normal bar chart may soon change its appearance when any kind of delay causes the manner of the linkage to become obvious.

If properly produced, this kind of programme can be very useful. The contractor can use it to plan its work and to demonstrate why delays have occurred. The architect can use it to check progress and to calculate extensions of time. The critical activities can be highlighted.

It is important that the preliminaries section of the specification or bills of quantities (see 66: Preliminaries) must require the contractor to produce a computerised network analysis using software compatible with the architect's software so that the architect can put it onto a computer and examine it carefully. Everyone should beware of certain professional programme planners. The good ones can be very good indeed, but there are some around who are not so good. Inevitably, programme planning has developed into a distinct profession with its own mostly incomprehensible jargon to describe something in a complex way which should be relatively straightforward.

72

Acceleration

What is Acceleration All About?

The contractor is not obliged to accelerate the progress of the Works for any reason unless the building contract specifically states that the contractor must accelerate in certain circumstances. This is not understood by many what I term 'take no prisoners' architects. There are some architects who quite forcibly, but wrongly, instruct the contractor to accelerate progress, some even instruct the contractor to put more operatives on site. These are usually the same architects who fail to supply necessary details and then refuse to give an extension of time on the basis that the contractor can easily make up the lost time if it puts more operatives on the site or works overtime at its own expense.

Is it Best Endeavours?

No. Many building contracts have a clause stating that the contractor must use 'best endeavours' to prevent delay and some have a clause which states that the contractor must do everything reasonably required to the architect's satisfaction. The 'tnp' architects often refer to that as an acceleration clause. It is nothing of the kind of course. The key word is 'reasonable'. Unless the contract specifically says that the architect can order acceleration, it would not be reasonable, on any view, to order it. Even if 'reasonable' was not expressly stated, it would certainly be implied. All that the contractor can be expected to do under those kinds of clauses is to continue working regularly and diligently, and if the architect suggested some programme changes to assist the situation the contractor must try to comply, always provided that these measures did not involve the contractor in additional costs. Most contracts which include something about acceleration need the contractor to agree to it.

Building contracts will have a start and a completion date or at least a contract period. If not, the law says that the contractor must have a reasonable time in which to carry out the work. That is almost, although not quite, the same as saying that the contractor can have as long as it takes. It is the same as saying as long as it reasonably takes (see 26: Reasonable Time). All building contracts have an extension of time clause which must be operated if the employer, or anyone for whom the employer is responsible, causes delay and sometimes for neutral reasons such as adverse weather conditions.

Professional Practice for Architects and Project Managers, First Edition. David Chappell.

Constructive Acceleration

If a contractor believes that it is entitled to an extension of time and the architect refuses to give it, the contractor, fearing that liquidated damages will be levied if the completion date is not achieved, may institute acceleration measures to finish on time despite the delay. After doing so, the contractor may then try to claim the cost of the additional operatives, plant etc. as 'constructive acceleration'. The argument behind this is that the contractor had no choice but to accelerate in order to avoid liquidated damages in the absence of the extension of time which should have been granted. That kind of claim has no chance of success. The contractor did have a choice. It could simply have used the dispute resolution processes in the contract to get the proper extension of time and, if necessary, a refund of wrongly deducted liquidated damages. The argument that the contractor might be out of pocket in the interim does not usually impress a court.

Cautionary Tale

Some years ago, I was engaged to advise on a dispute concerning a supermarket. The opening date had been decided to be within a few days of practical completion being certified. A well-known TV soap star had been engaged to perform the opening ceremony and the date could not be changed. Inevitably it was realised when the opening was only a few months away that the Works were delayed by about three weeks. The employer was a supermarket chain and, without seeking advice, had taken it upon itself to agree acceleration measures with the contractor for a substantial extra payment. It was agreed that the contractor would put extra operatives on site and work overtime and weekends. This was done and after a further month, the delay had increased to four weeks, which was when I became involved.

The employer had made the classic mistake. The executives dealing with the project had become so panic-stricken at the thought of missing the much-advertised opening that they had rushed into the agreement without asking the architect whether the delays were caused by the contractor. If that was the case, the contractor would have had a duty, in any event, to use its best endeavours to prevent the delay and would face liquidated damages which ought to have been calculated to cover the costs of re-arranging the opening. More importantly, even if the delays were not the fault of the contractor, but it was just essential to meet the opening date, any agreement to pay the contractor extra should have been in return for the contractor meeting the original completion date. It is of no use whatsoever agreeing simply that the contractor would work overtime and weekends and put extra staff on. That should not have been the object of the agreement. An acceleration agreement must, I repeat MUST, provide that the contractor meets the required date or gets no extra payment. It may be said that no contractor would agree to that proviso. I think most contractors would agree if the extra payment was enticing enough and if achieving the required date was actually possible, and it often is if the will is there.

Final Warning

If an architect instructs a contractor to accelerate and there is no clause in the contract expressly allowing such an instruction, the contractor should refuse to comply. The architect's power to give instructions (or to do anything) depends on what is in the contract. If the contractor does comply, it may not be entitled to any payment for accelerating. If the instruction comes directly from the employer, the contractor may (but is still not obliged) to comply and is probably entitled to payment on the basis of an implied contract.

73

Postponement

What is Meant by Postponement?

Postponement is when the architect, or in some cases the employer, instructs the contractor to stop doing something that is part of the work. For example, the architect might instruct the contractor to stop work on the staircase construction in an office block. The reason might be because the employer has just decided that a different material would look better or it might be because there seems to be an error in some dimensions and the problem must be solved before work can continue. For our purposes, it does not really matter why the instruction is issued. It does not matter much to the contractor either. What matters to the contractor is that the work is being held up and the postponement will inevitably have a knock-on effect to other parts of the building, causing delay and additional costs. If the architect has to instruct postponement of the whole of the Works, the delay and extra costs will be very much greater. The architect might not actually issue a postponement instruction in these circumstances, but even if it is simply an instruction to vary the work, if its main result is to compel the contractor to stop work on one part or the whole of the building, it is likely to be considered as a postponement instruction by a judge, arbitrator, or adjudicator.

So What?

A long delay to any part of the building will have consequences for the employer as well as the contractor and a delay to the whole building could be a serious matter. The contractor will be entitled to an extension of time as a result of the delay and there will probably also be a claim for additional costs. If the contractor is delayed from getting on with the whole of the Works for a long period, say a month or two, most contracts allow the contractor to terminate its employment and claim substantial costs. Even if a contract says nothing about termination after a long postponement, after a reasonable (or perhaps I should say an 'unreasonable') period, the contractor will have the right to treat the postponement as a repudiation, accept it, and claim the profit it would have made if the contract had not been postponed indefinitely (see 100: Termination).

Professional Practice for Architects and Project Managers, First Edition. David Chappell.

Power to Postpone

Many architects think there is an implied right, one might almost say a 'divine right', for an architect to do various things in connection with the contract. If you are one of those architects, you might think that, as an architect, you can postpone the Works whenever you wish. Sorry to disappoint you but you cannot do that. You have no right, divine or otherwise, to postpone the Works unless the contract says that you can. The employer has no implied right to postpone either. If you or the employer tries to postpone the Works and there is no clause in the contract to allow you to do that, it will be a breach of contract. Something to bear in mind: if, by issuing an instruction about something, it inevitably follows that work is postponed, it will be treated as a postponement instruction causing delay and extra costs. Finally, remember that the power to postpone work does not allow you to stop the contractor taking possession of the site. That is entirely different (see 67: Possession of the Site).

74

Insurance

General

Insurance is a very complicated topic. Architects come into contact with insurance in many different ways. For example, every architect must have professional indemnity insurance. If you are a partner or director of a practice, there will be insurance for the office property and contents, third party liability, and so on. Probably all the partners or directors will take out joint insurance against the inability of any of them being unable to work. If a partnership is involved, the remaining partners will need insurance to cover the cost of paying out the capital of a deceased partner.

Subrogation and Joint Names

These terms confuse many people. Subrogation is when a person or thing is substituted for another person or thing. In insurance, it occurs when an insurer compensates a policyholder for a loss. The insurer is then entitled to 'stand in the shoes of the policyholder' in order to recover the money from whoever was responsible for the loss. So, an architect taking a post as an employee should check that the company's professional indemnity insurer has relinquished its right to do this (called a waiver of subrogation). If the insurer has retained the right, it means that if it has to pay out on a claim against the company, the insurer may then stand in the shoes of the company to sue the employee who was negligent.

Most insurance clauses for the Works in building contracts say that the employer or the contractor must take out the insurance in joint names. That is to prevent the insurer being able to exercise its right of subrogation. Insurance in joint names means that both employer and contractor are named as the insured parties. Thus, if under a joint names insurance the contractor is at fault and the employer claims the cost from the insurer, the insurer cannot exercise its right of subrogation and recover what has been paid out from the contractor. Obviously, insurers are not thrilled about joint names insurance.

Building Contracts Damage to Persons or Property

What seems to cause architects most trouble is the provision for insurance in building contracts. Exactly what is contained in each contract may differ and some contracts leave

Professional Practice for Architects and Project Managers, First Edition. David Chappell.

all the detail to be agreed. But, generally, there will be a clause that the contractor must insure against causing injury or death to any person and causing loss or damage to any property other than the Works by negligence. It is important to understand that if the contractor fails to take out this kind of insurance, it will still be liable for the injury or death or loss or damage. The absence of insurance might mean the contractor cannot meet the cost of meeting its liability if an incident should occur.

If you fail to check that the contractor has insurance against these liabilities and the contractor causes damage to other property, the contractor would still be liable to pay for the damage caused, but if the damage was substantial and the contractor had no money to meet the claim, the contractor could simply go into liquidation and the employer may be left to foot the bill. If you had not checked that the insurance was being maintained, the employer could well sue you for the money. More about checking shortly.

Damage to Other Property for which the Employer is Responsible

Another kind of insurance that is sometimes in contracts is the insurance taken out by the contractor against liability, loss, or proceedings etc. which may be incurred by the employer if injury or damage to property other than the Works was caused by collapse, subsidence, heave, vibration, or removal of support arising out of the carrying out of the Works but not caused through the contractor's negligence. Whenever damage is caused by the contractor to other property, it is likely that the owner of that property will claim against the employer. If the damage was caused by the contractor's negligence, the employer should be able to get the cost from the contractor or its insurers. However, this kind of insurance is useful where the contractor is not at fault, but the damage still occurs. Sometimes damage is unavoidable or very likely. That can be the case where the contractor is working on property which abuts other property on either side. Vibration caused by drilling or piling could cause damage even though the contractor has taken all reasonable precautions.

Insurance of the Works

The other kind of insurance in building contracts is insurance of the Works and of the existing property if the Works are refurbishment or extension to existing property. An important point is whether it is the employer or the contractor who must insure. Different contracts take different approaches. It is common, but not inevitable, that the employer has to insure existing property and any Works done to it and the contractor insures new Works. Usually, the party not taking out the insurance is entitled to ask the other for evidence that the insurance has been taken out and is being maintained. The job of checking whether the correct insurances have been taken out by the contractor is usually left to the architect, but see below.

If damage occurs, there may be disputes about whether the damage amounts to bad working practice on the part of the contractor or whether it is something that ought to be claimed under the insurance provisions. That is particularly the case if the insurance has been taken out in joint names.

The Architect's Responsibility

The building contract may make the architect responsible for receiving policy details from the contractor. The architect (or possibly the quantity surveyor) is responsible for entering the changeable insurance details into the building contract. Few architects or surveyors are skilled in insurance matters. Other than understanding the insurance clauses in the contract and how they are to be applied, it is foolhardy to attempt to give advice to the employer. An employer needing insurance advice in regard to the contract must be directed to an insurance broker or other expert. If the architect requests the contractor's insurance details, the architect has three choices:

- An architect with sufficient expertise and experience (very unlikely) can advise the employer whether the contractor's policy complies with the requirements of the contract.
- The architect can seek expert insurance advice and pass it to the employer.
- The architect can send the documents to the employer with advice that the employer should obtain specialist advice about its conformity with the contract.

There is no doubt that advising the employer to take his or her own insurance advice is by far the safest and most sensible option. Think of an insurance consultant in the same way as a structural engineer. You would not try to design complex engineering structures. You would advise the employer to retain the services of consultant engineer. Treat insurance matters in the same way.

75

Maintaining Standards On Site

Definition

Maintaining standards on site embodies the technique of ensuring that the quality of materials, goods, workmanship, and finished building are of the standard required by the specification and drawings. The architect can reject work and materials which are not up to the specified standards but the architect cannot demand a higher standard than that.

Some Basics

Maintaining standards on site is primarily the task of the contractor. But, if left to its own devices, the standard of many contractors will diverge from what is required in the specification and drawings. The task of maintaining standards on site should commence at design stage and continue until the building is complete and handed over to the client. Before any system of control can be exercised, it is essential to set standards against which the achieved quality can be measured, so it starts at design stage or earlier because, in order to maintain standards, the required standards must be clearly stated.

It is likely that different projects will be constructed to different standards. Nevertheless, there should be a minimum standard that even the humblest project will achieve. 'Start as you mean to go on' is an effective policy. Right from the initial client discussions, it is important to get this clear with the client and subsequently with the contractor.

One of the important parts of writing the brief is that the architect ascertains from the client exactly what standard the client expects or needs. In working through the stages up to the point at which tenders are invited, the architect must keep in mind the standards so that all the drawings, especially the detailed drawings, reflect the standard required. A good way to preserve high standards is to make use of libraries of specification clauses on a subscription basis. This is not the place to try and explain how to write a specification, but do avoid any all-embracing sentence such as 'Unless expressly stated to the contrary, all materials, goods, and workmanship are to be to the satisfaction of the architect'. It is a common sentence but there are some pitfalls:

- It does not give the contractor an objective and clear statement of the standard required.
- The law will say that reasonable satisfaction is implied.
- The actual standard is wide open to disputes.

Professional Practice for Architects and Project Managers, First Edition. David Chappell.

- Many contracts state that if the specification or drawings have required materials, goods, and workmanship to be to the architect's satisfaction, the issue of the final certificate is conclusive evidence that all materials, goods, and workmanship are to the architect's satisfaction. This can have serious consequences.

Architects will be concerned with maintaining standards in a very broad sense in their offices. What I am saying is that an architect who has a shambolic office routine will be in no position to either specify clear standards (high or low) or to get to grips with enforcing it on site. In the office, the architect will set up systems and procedures to enable efficient working. The architect must also keep a sharp eye on the contractor's organisation of the site. Just as clear construction standards are unlikely to emerge from a chaotic architect's office, a poorly organised and messy site does not provide the correct atmosphere and background likely to result in proper observance of specified standards in the construction work.

General Points

Although control is exercised on site primarily by the contractor, it will have a complex network of site agents, trades foremen, and chargehands in supervisory capacities. However, the employer, the architect, and the clerk of works have important duties of inspection to check that the required quality is being produced. Visits to site should be unexpected and certainly when important elements are being constructed. As an aid to controlling standards, tests are often employed. A wise course of action is for the architect only to instruct opening up the Works or testing if there is a suspicion that the work is sub-standard. That is because most contracts state that if the architect instructs opening up or testing and the work is found to be in accordance with the specification and drawings, the employer has to pay the cost of the investigative work and the cost of reinstatement.

The client is interested in obtaining the best possible standard for the money. The contractor wishes to produce the lowest acceptable standard because the higher the standard, the greater the cost. 'Acceptable standard' is the key phrase. The only acceptable standard is the standard in the specification and drawings.

A final word about tolerances. Everyone understands that it is impossible to construct a building so that everything is exactly the size specified or drawn. There are nationally recognised tolerances specified for all kinds of construction work. Many of the tolerances, when closely examined, often seem excessive. It is worthwhile learning the tolerances allowed, for example, by British Standards and in appropriate cases making a clear note in the specification that the project requires a tolerance which is more exacting than normal.

76

Coming to Blows

Have you ever had a fight with your contractor? I do not mean simply a rather heated argument but one in which one of you tries to inflict physical damage on the other. I think it is probably quite rare, but I have been consulted twice about physical assault in somewhat different situations.

The first concerned an architect who, after inspecting the building, refused to certify practical completion, leaving the contractor liable for substantial liquidated damages. The site agent pursued him to his car and then attempted to throw a punch at the architect's face through the open window. Fortunately, he missed. The second situation was rather more complicated. The architect was following the site agent, who was following the client as they walked through the almost finished house. The architect was several yards (I suppose I should say 'metres' but 'yards' seems so much more expressive somehow) behind the site agent, who followed the client into one of the rooms and the architect heard a scuffle. On reaching the room, the architect saw the client getting up from the floor and accusing the agent of attacking him. The agent, standing apart with arms raised in surrender, vowed that he had never hit the client but merely manhandled him to the floor – so that's alright then! So, what, if anything, should the architect have done in those situations?

In the first instance the architect wisely sat in his car with the doors locked and the windows closed and rang the police. When the police arrived, the site agent denied any attempt to punch the architect. The police gave a general warning about keeping the peace and left while the architect quickly sped away. In the second instance, the architect checked that the client was not actually hurt and then all three left the site in separate cars. The client subsequently criticised the architect, saying that she should have instructed the director of the contractor firm who was also the site agent to exclude the site agent from the Works, but she argued that there was no reason to do so.

I advised the first architect to issue an instruction under the contract excluding the site agent from site together with a letter to the contractor briefly stating why and requiring (i) that a replacement agent be appointed and (ii) for an assurance that such an incident would never occur again. What happened was that the site agent did leave site, but so did all the operatives together with their equipment. They never returned and the employer eventually terminated the contractor's employment. It seems clear that the contractor did not leave site as a result of the incident or the instruction, although the instruction was cited as being the reason. The real reason was that the contractor was very much delayed and facing substantial damages, but it did not have the ability to quickly finish the project so chose to abandon the Works.

Professional Practice for Architects and Project Managers, First Edition. David Chappell.

My advice to the second architect was that she should write and advise the client that she had not witnessed the alleged assault and that it did not affect the contractor's or the site agent's performance, therefore she had no grounds for excluding him from the Works. However, the client should not venture onto site unaccompanied but should notify the architect, who would accompany the client around the site and on those hopefully rare occasions the site agent would be absent. She should also write to the contractor setting out the position briefly and making clear that she had not witnessed the incident but that clearly something had occurred and, therefore, when the client wanted to visit site, the agent should arrange to be away for a short period. As already noted, the client was unhappy with this, but there was nothing else the architect should or indeed could do.

Most building contracts contain a clause allowing the architect to instruct the exclusion from site of any person employed there, but either the contract will say that the architect should not act vexatiously or unreasonably or the general law will imply that. If the architect comes under direct attack from one of the contractor's operatives, whether sub-contractor or site agent, it is perfectly reasonable and certainly not vexatious for the architect to instruct the exclusion of that person from site because that person is potentially preventing the architect from doing his or her job properly.

However, where the attack is on the client, whether or not the architect actually witnesses it, it cannot reasonably be said that the continued presence of the site agent will affect the Works other than for the better unless as well as being violent the agent is also incompetent, in which case he should have been excluded earlier. Where a contract administrator is involved, there is no real reason why the client should ever need to speak to the site agent and far better that all communications and instruction go through the architect as all building contracts make clear. Therefore, it would be unreasonable, although not perhaps vexatious, to exclude him. Of course, that does not prevent the client reporting the action as a criminal assault or bringing a civil action and, if the architect did witness it, the architect could give evidence. One would expect that the contractor would fire the agent in those circumstances in any event.

77

Meetings

Before You Have a Meeting

The best meetings are when two people who have the power to decide things meet to decide something. A clear decision is very likely. Where there is an aversion to that kind of meeting it is generally because one or both of the people who would be involved have great difficulty in making firm decisions. The fact that I have encountered a wide-ranging aversion to one-to-one meetings is worrying for that reason. The effectiveness of any meeting can be measured in inverse proportion to the numbers attending. I used to work in a large office where meetings were the order of the day. The joke was that anyone with nothing to do could always find a meeting to attend. Attendances of two dozen people were not unknown and there were always people in a meeting who had no clear idea of its purpose. The conclusions of such meetings tended to amount to 'We have had a full and frank exchange of views and we are now in a position to have a further meeting to look into the matter in more detail.' That was, and still is, quite frightening when one thinks that it is not an episode from a TV sitcom but what actually happens in real life.

Before any meeting is convened, the first thing to do is to decide what question the meeting has to answer. That seems obvious, but many meetings occur simply because no one seems to know what the question should be and they assemble on the basis that something useful must emerge from the meeting. No, nothing will emerge from such a meeting except the urgent need for another meeting.

After deciding the question, the next thing to do is to decide who is best placed to answer it. That may just be one person. In that case a quick informal meeting with that one person is bound to be effective and produce, if not the answer, at least the way to the answer.

If there is no one person, but there are two or three people who are likely to know part of the answer, a meeting with those people is indicated.

If the question is actually 'What question should we be asking ourselves in this situation?', that indicates the kind of people who should be brought together: probably people with a flair for getting to the nub of any problem, but note that they are still answering a question.

What must be avoided is asking people to come to a meeting just because they have some involvement in the project. That is sheer waste of resources.

Professional Practice for Architects and Project Managers, First Edition. David Chappell.

Site Meetings

The most common meeting for members of the construction industry is the site meeting. Let's see how the principles of that meeting work. It is a fact of construction life that it is impossible to make all the necessary decisions before work starts on site. Anyone who tells you that on a well-run project all the decisions will have been made before the start on site has obviously only a tenuous link with reality. Clients have changes of mind or just cannot decide things, some things are overlooked, and, dare I say it, errors in the drawings and other documents are found. All these issues need attention. Many architects insist on weekly or fortnightly site meetings which the architect, clerk of works, all the consultants, possibly sub-contractors and the contractor's director, contracts manager, and site agent attend. Sometimes even the employer is present, which is never ever a good idea although some architects like to have the employer on hand to make decisions, but this is rather like asking a patient to assist the surgeon amputating his leg. The employer is not in the right state of mind to be at such a meeting where technical matters are discussed and there may be delicate issues to sort out with the contractor. Employer decisions should be the subject of meetings just with the employer. Because the role of most project managers is to act as the employer's agent, it is a good idea to exclude them from site meetings or insist that they attend purely as observers. Good luck with that (see 33: Project Managers).

Vast amounts of money are expended on site meetings which can last for hours. Some consultants will be there just in case they are needed. Yet there are few things done or decided at such regular meetings that could not be more efficiently done or decided outside the meeting. The most common topic is progress, which should be closely monitored by the architect at all times assisted by the contractor, which should notify possible delays (there never seem to be notifications of improvements on the programme). Contractor's queries should not wait for site meetings but should be, and usually are, communicated to the architect immediately they arise. In a similar fashion, the architect should not wait for the meeting to answer. One can see the need for a pre-start (often referred to incorrectly as a 'pre-contract') meeting when everyone should be present to get acquainted and basic matters should be set out. After that, site meetings should only be held if there is no other way to deal with something.

Having said all that, I know that many architects do feel that a regular site meeting is useful so that the architect can inspect the Works, check progress, and hear the contractor's concerns in one session. When dealing with small projects, regular site meetings can be valuable for focusing the minds of smaller and less business-like contractors on progress and on the need to comply exactly with the drawings and specification. If regular meetings are to be held, it is important to limit the attendance and frequency and to inspect the Works at random times outside the regular meetings.

Other Meetings

There are lots of other meetings which might be held. Meetings such as those with the design team or with the client are usually arranged individually for a particular purpose.

Design team meetings will usually involve the whole team. They will be relatively frequent in the early stages of a project and the main purpose is to share information and to ensure that all the team are working to achieve the same design results. If the architect has a good personality, they provide the opportunity to make everyone feel like a vital contributor because of course each member of the team is exactly that. Once the project enters the construction phase, there ought to be less need for design team meetings unless there is a major problem. The likelihood is that the architect will have occasional meetings with specific members of the team to deal with particular issues.

Meetings with the client will usually be called by the architect in order to explain something or get the client's agreement to something. Although we all tend to talk about 'the client', that may be a number of people, for example a board of directors or the committee of an association such as a civic society. The architect will have met the whole board or, in the case of an association, will have met the key people such as the chairperson, secretary, treasurer, and the committee at the time of appointment. After that, someone used to making decisions and with full client authority should be nominated to deal directly with the architect. That will ensure that decisions can be made swiftly.

The architect must always chair all meetings which he or she attends. The fairly recent trend for employers to appoint project managers does not alter that principle unless the project manager is administering the building contract. Usually, even when a project manager is appointed, the architect will still be the contract administrator. The architect must chair all meetings because the architect is responsible for the administration of the contract and cannot administer it if someone else is deciding what should be discussed at a meeting.

It can be difficult to take notes at the same time as chairing a meeting. It is easier if you remember that all that should be minuted is the decisions. It is usually pointless to minute details of arguments between various people. It may be helpful to record the proceedings on a small recorder although this is likely simply to make the preparation of minutes a lengthier process. The real value of a recording is to save note taking during the proceedings and proof of what was actually said if there is a later dispute about that. However, it means that the architect must listen to the whole recording in order to prepare the minutes. I have heard of architects taking someone into a meeting solely to take notes but, unless the notetaker is very experienced, the notes taken may not be what the architects thinks are most relevant and it makes the meeting more expensive.

Minutes must be brief and to the point and issued within 24 hours of the meeting. Usually, it is only the decision that is important, not all the argument that went before. If there are errors in the minutes, they must be reported to the chairperson as soon as they are discovered and copied to everyone on the minutes circulation list.

The chairperson must keep control and silence the loquacious. How does one keep control? The short answer is by experience. It is essential to state the procedure at the beginning of the meeting and make quite clear that deviations will not be tolerated. Then if someone attempts to monopolise the meeting or a sub-meeting appears to start in one corner, the offending people must be courteously but immediately brought to attention. Needless to say, all oral contributions must be addressed to the chairperson. All this does not make the architect popular, but it may make him or her respected. Everyone eventually appreciates a short, focused meeting. Social chat has no place in a business meeting.

Agenda

The architect must have an agenda. The content of the agenda will depend upon the issue being considered. I have seen agendas which are so brief as to be useless for anything but the date and time of the meeting. On the other hand, some agendas include a short summary of each issue and allocate a fixed time for consideration. The important things to remember in any agenda are the following:

- It must be clear about the decisions to be made by the meeting. This is the case even if the meeting is simply to decide the important things to be decided by another meeting.
- It should list the people who must attend and make clear that no one else is welcome.
- It should give the date, time, and place of the meeting.
- The important issues must be at the beginning of the meeting because towards the end, people tend to agree anything just to get away. Of course, that tendency can be used to advantage on occasion.

Many meetings will involve providing the participants with documents to study beforehand. These documents should be sent out in time for everyone to read and digest them, but not so early that people put them on one side because they have plenty of time and finish up not reading them at all. It is infuriating when someone arrives at the meeting with a broad smile, saying that they have not had time to read the papers sent out. Having chaired several meetings where this has happened I can only say that, assuming that the papers have been sent out in reasonable time, such people are incompetent – there is no other adequate word. They waste the time of the other people at the meeting and may well cause the meeting to be postponed at significant cost in time and salaries or fees.

78

Clerks of Works

By Way of Introduction

Years ago, it was said, 'Make a friend of your clerk of works'. I believe those words originated in some early edition of Hamilton Turner's book on architectural practice and procedure. But why must the architect make a friend of the clerk of works? The theory is that the clerk of works will be a tower of strength, a fount of wisdom, and provide practical hints on a day-to-day basis. I suppose we all have had a mental vision of the ideal clerk of works. He is getting on a bit, steeped in building lore, and quite ruthless on site. Against all the trends, he keeps his teeth firmly clamped around an ancient pipe from which quantities of ash fall onto and are smeared across every drawing he sees and behind which he retreats whenever questioned. The contractor and even the architect proceed in awe of him.

Since those days, smoking is frowned upon (although still common in the construction industry depending on circumstances) and, of course, there are female clerks of works.

Categories of Clerks of Works

There are two kinds of clerks of works. Those who spend most time in the clerk of works cabin, snug and warm with an electric fire and a mug of contractor's tea in close attendance and always ready to answer the phone on the second ring. Then there are those who are out inspecting the work. The former should be relocated – perhaps on the office switchboard. But what about the ones who spend all their time inspecting the work? The clerk of works, more than anyone else, is a link person in the building process. A clerk of works should spend 90% of time checking the work and the materials. You will be lucky if that kind of clerk of works answers the phone on the 20th ring because he or she will be in the middle of noisy saws, hammers or machinery or will have difficulty answering the phone quickly while standing in a trench half full of water.

Professional Practice for Architects and Project Managers, First Edition. David Chappell.

Powers

In theory, in conformity with the principles of most building contracts, the clerk of works' powers are very limited. The main task of a clerk of works is to inspect work, goods, and materials used or intended to be used on the project. The clerk of works has no power to instruct the contractor or to vary the Works. That must be clearly understood; especially by the clerk of works. I vividly recall on one occasion having to countermand the instructions wrongly given by the clerk of works and wrongly accepted by the site agent to use quite unsuitable demolition debris as fill on one project. The contractor had to remove the fill and replace with what was specified at its own cost. I did not make a friend of that clerk of works.

It has been suggested, on more than one occasion, that the building contract should specifically state that the clerk of works has the power to give instructions on site, binding, presumably, on employer and contractor alike. What a vision of chaos this conjures up.

Liability

Architects often wonder whether they are responsible for a negligent clerk of works. Sometimes it is put another way: if the architect asks the clerk of works to do something, is the architect still responsible if it is done badly? Taking the second question first, the clerk of works' only contractual function is to inspect, therefore, if the contractor acts on any direction of the clerk of works, the contractor will be in breach of contract. If the architect delegates to the clerk of works some inspection functions which the architect should have carried out, then there is little doubt that the architect would be responsible for the clerk of works' failures. Architects' obligations generally to inspect means that they must make sure that they look at the important points. For example, if a large concrete floor is to be poured, the diligent architect will be present at the pouring of the first section to check that it is done properly and to explain to the clerk of works what is expected. Then, having set the standard, the clerk of works can be left to check the remaining pours. Responsibility for the clerk of works' negligent inspection will depend on whether the clerk of works is appointed and paid by the employer. If, as is usual, the clerk of works is engaged by the employer, the employer will be responsible for the clerk of works' actions. The relationship between architect and clerk of works in that instance has been said to be like that between the captain of a ship and the chief petty officer, and the architect's liability for inspection may be reduced by around 20%. That is not the case if the architect employs and pays the clerk of works.

A danger is that during the inspection process, clerks of works commonly deface unacceptable materials by marking them with wax crayon or scratched crosses. Obviously, unsatisfactory materials are not accepted, therefore, they are still the property of the contractor, who may wish to use them elsewhere on another project which requires a lesser standard. If the clerk of works defaces them, the employer may be charged with the costs of the materials anyway. The architect must be alive to this fairly common problem and must make clear to the clerk of works at the outset that unacceptable work or materials must be recorded and possibly photographed, but never defaced.

The Value of the Clerk of Works

What is to be made of all this? It is necessary to look behind the strict rules to find the value of the clerk of works. In practice, the clerk of works will continuously inform the site agent of defects, and the site agent will almost invariably take suitable action without the necessity for a written directive or the architect's confirmation. The clerk of works will also give much informal (though unauthorised) advice to the foreman in the interpretation of the drawings and bills of quantities, and assist the architect by making a preliminary inspection before the architect carries out the final inspection prior to issuing a certificate of practical completion. Clerks of works give assistance in numerous other small, but important, ways. The special value of clerks of works to architects is that they are essentially practical, experienced in the sludge and mortar of work on site and able to perform their nowhere-written-down-but-essential function of advising architects, quietly, and with due reverence of course, if their details are un-buildable.

Qualities

Good clerks of works are either naturals with an instinct or nose for quickly sniffing out and effectively getting around potential trouble, or they are well trained. In my experience, however good the training, there must be a natural talent. What are the ideal qualities of good clerks of works? They should be good leaders and able to make their presence felt. They should have integrity, shrewdness, intelligence, tact, firmness, a thorough knowledge of the building processes with a very clear idea of the boundaries of their responsibilities under the contract, and the implications of the contract as a whole. They should be in another job and they probably are.

Clerks of works are normally recruited from the ranks of time-served and skilled tradespeople. It used to be said that joiners made the best clerks of works since they were involved in a precision trade and had the opportunity to observe the activities of other trades. Experience teaches that, while this basically may be still true, there are very many former bricklayers, plumbers, plasterers, and so on who make excellent clerks of works. Increasingly nowadays, the clerk of works must be able to understand the highly technical matters involved in modern construction techniques.

Too often, however, the clerk of works falls short of what you in your wisdom, or ignorance, expects. It is interesting to speculate why this should be. One reason, I suppose, is that a person does not need to have any formal qualification to become a clerk of works. The Institute of Clerk of Works lays emphasis upon properly qualified clerks of works and it is disappointing that relatively few, proportionately, seem to be members of the Institute.

There are still too many indifferent tradespeople who do not want the responsibility of being a site agent, judged on results, and misguidedly choose the role of clerk of works as a soft option. Anyone who supposes that the job of a clerk of works is a haven of peace and quiet in a snug little cabin, with unending mugs of hot tea, is in for a rude awakening. They must tramp around the site in mud and rain, missing nothing. The idea of a soft option should vanish. Proper validation of the qualifications of clerks of works by the Institute should be an essential condition of employment. Failed tradespeople would then remain failed tradespeople rather than becoming failed clerks of works.

Practicalities

I suppose the job is unattractive to many people. Good clerks of works, by the very nature of their job, have to be lone wolves taking care not to be too friendly with the contractor, and on a badly organised contract they can become the object of intense dislike, often, it must be admitted, being unfairly criticised by the architect and contractor alike, the former because they are not getting a good standard of work, the latter because the clerk of works is too keen to root out defective work and inadequate standards.

It says much for the average clerk of works who manages to walk the daily tightrope with such success. The clerk of works may not always be the 'fount of wisdom' but he or she is often a fount of practical common sense.

79

Site Agent

What's in a Name?

'Site agent' is the name that is used in some standard form contracts to refer to what is also known as the 'site manager' or simply the 'person in charge'. 'Site manager' seems more accurate and a description of the task required than 'person in charge', which is awkward. Site agent is probably best, although it has tended to be used only in connection with major projects.

Attendance

Most contracts require the contractor to keep a competent site agent on the site either at all times, or sometimes, or at all reasonable times, or constantly, on site. Whatever the exact phrase used, it is safe to interpret it as meaning that the site agent must be on site whenever there is work in progress. If something else is required, the contract must spell it out very plainly. To expect the site agent to be literally on site constantly or at all times would be to impose a very onerous and, in most cases, unnecessary obligation. The key point is that, if the contractor wishes and receives permission to work outside normal working hours, the site agent must be on site and preferably wide awake and on top of the work.

If the Works are very small and simple, it may be enough that the site agent is a frequent visitor to the site. 'At all reasonable times' might bear this interpretation in that kind of situation. Frequent visits by the person in charge may suffice in the case of very small and simple projects. Many small projects have what used to be called a 'working foreman' but which now, on paper at least, must be termed 'working site agent', another awkward phrase. Perhaps 'working manager' might be simpler and better. Architects must be careful about allowing a working manager and it deserves thorough discussion before even a small project starts on site. The problem is that the identity of the working manager could change through the progress of the Works as different trades are needed on site. It may be convenient to the contractor to nominate a bricklayer, then a joiner, then a plumber, etc., but it does nothing for the project because the working manager ought to have a thorough understanding of the project and be able to act as a point of continuity as operatives change.

Clearly, it is impossible to insist on the site agent on any contract being the same person throughout if the person concerned moves employment. I am reminded of an

Professional Practice for Architects and Project Managers, First Edition. David Chappell.

incident when I worked for a contractor and we got word from site that the agent had vanished one Thursday lunchtime. On visiting the site, the agent's accommodation (we called it the site cabin) was missing the necessary agent but there was his pipe still warm to the touch in its ash tray and a pencil on a pile of drawings on which he had been working. No one saw him leave. There were shades of the Marie Celeste. Fortunately, it was discovered that he had suddenly decided that he did not want to be a site agent any more and he had simply gone home but forgotten his pipe.

Duties

Spare a thought for the site agent on any project. It is a very stressful job, requiring a high degree of skill and experience. On large projects, the site agent usually has assistants. The site agent is a the 'sharp end' of the contractor's organisation, often receiving criticism from the contractor and the architect – usually for entirely different reasons.

Many contracts include the word 'competent' to describe the site agent. Most people will understand what 'competent' means, but in case there is the slightest doubt, it means that the site manager must be able to skilfully carry out the work associated with the position.

The site agent is intended to be capable of receiving instructions from the architect as though those instructions had been given to the contractor at its office.

80

Site Inspections

Perfection?

Employers usually expect their finished buildings to be perfect. Not only should there be no defects but the standard of all goods, materials, and workmanship must be perfect. That is to say that there must not be the slightest scratch or blemish anywhere. That standard is virtually unobtainable of course, as every employer discovers. There are some, very expensive, buildings which come close to perfection, but the majority of buildings are somewhat less than perfect. An architect cannot ensure that buildings are free from defects, but the building must conform to the drawings and specification.

Duty to Inspect

So, what exactly are architects expected to do? Must they inspect every square millimetre of the building? No, unless there is something more specific in the architect's terms of engagement, the architect must use reasonable skill and care in inspecting the work. Just what that means depends upon the project and the specification. It follows that a project which requires a very high standard of workmanship and materials from the contractor will necessarily require a greater degree of inspection than a project which requires a poorer standard. Whatever the specified standard, the architect must obviously carefully check all the important points. Important points are all those things which, if not carefully constructed, would have a serious effect upon the integrity of the building and probably the client's purse. Items such as damp-proof membranes in the floor, damp course in the walls, roof coverings, tanking below ground levels, ground bearing, foundations, structural columns, beams, floors, and roof slabs immediately spring to mind. One can add all parts of underground drainage systems, concealed screeds, and insulation.

That does not mean that the architect can simply ignore everything else. Floors, doors, architraves, skirtings, plaster and other wall finishes, plumbing, heating, and electrics all require inspection, but possibly not on every visit to site and not all by the architect. Some would be inspected by the relevant consultant.

Three other factors must be taken into account:

- whether or not there is a clerk of works
- how often the clerk of works is required to be on site
- the experience and relative competence of the contractor and its workforce.

Professional Practice for Architects and Project Managers, First Edition. David Chappell.

A clerk of works should be able to deal with much of the routine inspection after the architect has made clear what standards are required by the particular specification, leaving the architect to make spot checks on those items. If the architect suspects that the contractor is lacking in competence or experience, or if there is evidence of poor workmanship, it is the architect's duty to inspect with greater rigour.

It is no excuse at all for an architect to say that a particular inspection could not be carried out because the item in question was covered. The inspection should be carried out when the item was visible. Nor is it any excuse to say that something, say on the roof, was difficult to access. If the contractor or sub-contractor can access the item, so can the architect. To make sure, there should always be something in the specification or bills of quantities preliminaries to stipulate that the contractor must not cover any work or materials until they have been inspected. There should also be a provision for the contractor to give all necessary assistance to enable the architect to safely inspect roofing and other potentially dangerously situated work.

Most contracts allow the architect to order the contractor to open up work that is covered and to carry out testing of materials such as concrete or bricks. If there is a clause in the contract or specification stating that the contractor must not cover any work until the architect has inspected it, the architect can instruct the contractor to uncover work without any cost to the employer. Otherwise, the basic principle is that if something is found to be defective, the contractor must stand the cost of uncovering or testing it. If it is not defective, the employer stands the cost.

'Inspection' and 'supervision' are often confused. Architects are commonly referred to as being responsible for 'design and supervision'. That, of course, is quite wrong. Inspection involves looking and noting, possibly even carrying out tests. Supervision, however, not only covers inspection, but also the issuing of detailed directions regarding the execution of the Works. Supervision is more onerous than inspection. It can only be carried out by someone with the requisite authority to ensure that the work is performed in a particular way. That is the prerogative of the contractor.

The Process

Before commencing an inspection of the Works, the architect must have a plan of campaign as follows:

- Never simply decide to go out and visit a site because it is rather a nice day. That happens far too often. Simply wandering onto the site without any preparation is worse than not going at all because it gives the contractor the wrong message.
- There must be a reason for every inspection. The reasons should be linked to particular stages in the Works.
- Make sure to have a detailed knowledge of what the contractor should be doing, when and where. To achieve this, it is necessary to be familiar with all the contract documents. This includes the contract itself, which will probably have something to say about standards, the specification, which will certainly have something to say about standards, all the drawings and details, and the contractor's programme.
- Remember that a defect is not a defect if it is due to the contractor carrying out exactly what is on the drawings and in the specification. It may be a design defect but

that is not the contractor's problem unless the contractor has design responsibility. However, if the contractor builds something exactly as detailed but it was obvious that the drawing was in error, it will usually have an obligation to notify you as soon as the error is found and before construction takes place. If the contractor is doing its job properly and planning the work in advance, most drawing and specification errors should be discovered before being constructed. I had a site agent on a project who took great delight in telephoning me several times to say that he had built my detail and it did not work. He was not a good site agent and the avoidable error had to be made good at the contractor's expense.

- Pre-planning is important. As soon as you receive the contractor's programme for carrying out the Works, an inspection programme should be prepared, based on the contractor's programme but able to be adjusted if the project is delayed (when was a project not delayed?). There will be certain key stages, some of which are noted above, when an inspection must be carried out. Before each inspection, you must draw up a list of what must be inspected on that particular visit. Additional items may be listed to be inspected if time allows. Comments should be made against the checklist as the inspection progresses. The checklist and comments should be put on file. They are not for distribution to the clerk of works and contractor. Clients commonly accuse the architect of failure to inspect whenever latent (hidden) defects appear after completion. Detailed contemporary records of inspections carried out can go a long way to answering allegations that inspections were negligent by showing that the inspections were planned, organised, and thorough.
- In carrying out the inspection, it is important to follow a logical system. One such system is illustrated by the flowchart in Figure 80.1.
- The contractor should not be made aware when an inspection is going to take place.
- Allow sufficient time to properly inspect the items on your list.
- It is essential that the site agent accompanies you on your inspection so that you can ask questions and make clear when something is not in accordance with the contract requirements. The site agent should note these comments as the inspection proceeds.
- The site agent may well try to divert you to look at other things as the inspection proceeds. Although it may simply be that the site agent is trying to make sure that you see certain things before they are forgotten, it is wisest to assume that the site agent is actually trying to stop you seeing some of the things on your list. I was once on my way up to the top floor of a four-storey project with the aim of checking whether four concrete columns had been properly cast. The site agent did everything possible to slow me down or divert me to look at other things. On reaching the top floor, I realised why the site agent was not anxious for me to see the columns. They had been cast without any steel inside and a labourer was up a ladder, unforgettably trying to hammer a length of steel into the top of one column. The concrete had not quite gone off, but the situation was not only quite unacceptable, it was impossible.
- You should always finish an inspection by carrying out a random inspection. In my experience, this is when the really serious problems are discovered.
- All comments regarding defective work should be put in writing to the contractor immediately on your return to the office.
- If a quantity surveyor is to carry out valuations, you must notify them of any defects in reasonable time so that they can be excluded from the valuation.

INSPECTION LOGIC

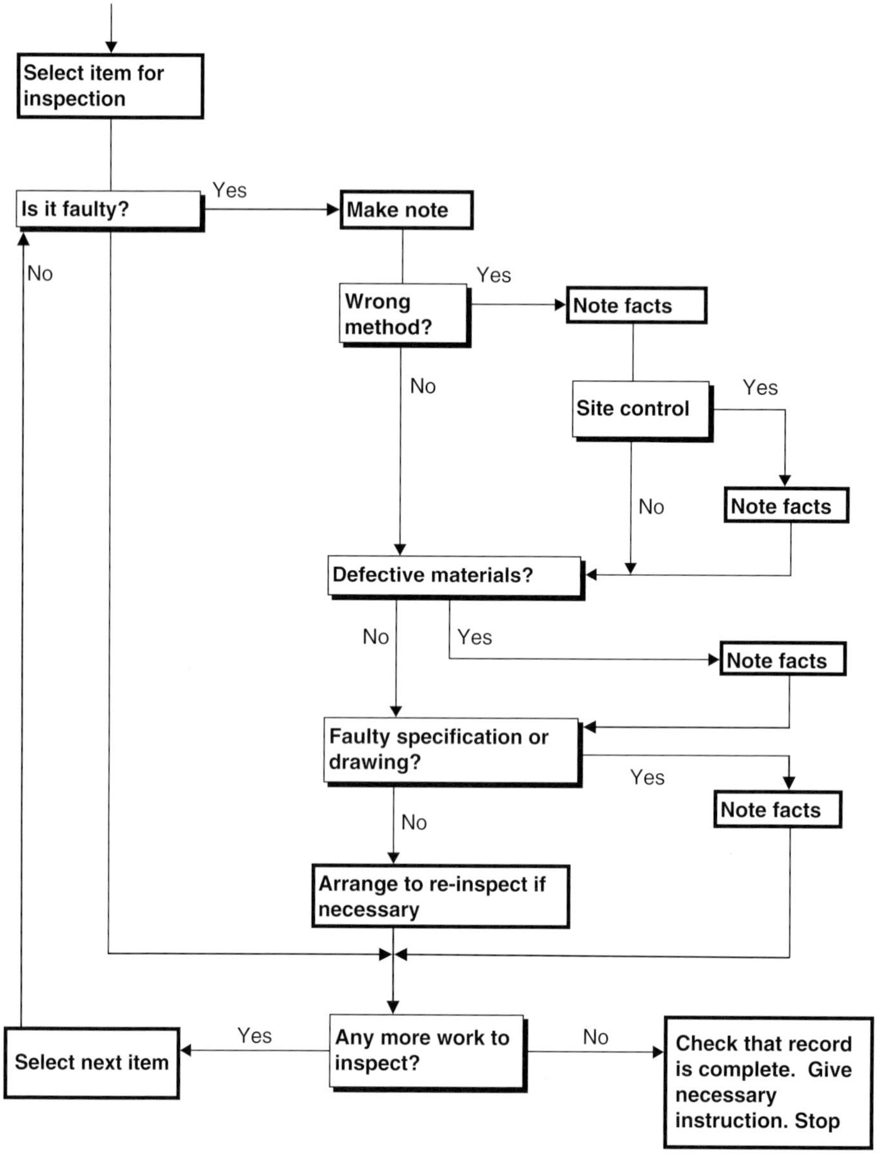

Figure 80.1 Inspection logic.

- During site inspections, the site agent is bound to ask questions. Many of the questions can be answered immediately but if the question requires a little thought, it is best to give answers on return to the office after careful consideration. There are few questions which cannot wait a day to be answered. Indeed, an architect is entitled to a reasonable time to answer questions and the contractor should make sure to have any questions ready in good time to allow consideration and perhaps research. I clearly remember once rushing to site at the request of a site agent needing urgent instructions. I arrived, made the decision, and issued instructions. The contractor did not attempt to do the work concerned until three months later.

- Finally, you should not assume that if you notify the contractor, the defects will be rectified. Always follow up each defect until you can tick it off your list. Your list should show the date or dates on which you notified the contractor of the defect. If the contract fails to correct any defects, you must be prepared to use the remedies available in the contract. Delay in doing so can be disastrous. The contractor must get the message at an early stage that you will not tolerate defective work.

Techniques

In my early days visiting site without a more experienced architect on hand I would inspect the work without really knowing either what I was actually looking for or the best way of finding it. My endeavours to look as though I knew what I was doing probably amused the site agent. How to really carry out a site inspection with all the techniques involved should be taught in every school of architecture.

An architect inspecting on site must have a thorough knowledge of construction and a thorough knowledge of the drawings and specification of the particular project. The best way to learn how to carry out a good site inspection is to visit a site with an experienced architect who will explain the inspection as it is being carried out. There is really no short cut to this.

Every architect will develop favourite techniques. That can be dangerous. When I worked for a contractor, the site agents would explain to me the things that a particular architect would always look for and what that same architect would never look at. For example, there was one architect who always looked very closely to check that the plaster was smooth and true, and the socket outlets were square but had never checked that the building was properly set out or that the damp-proof course was properly laid. Another architect would never set foot on the site itself until all the initial earth moving, excavation, and foundation work was complete. Not until the ground floor slab was in place did he set foot on site. That was because he chose to come to site wearing a light-coloured suit with suede shoes. If the site was at all muddy he would simply stand at the edge and look from there. Needless the say, the contractor ensured that the ground surrounding the building was always quite muddy even if he had to use a hose pipe in the summer to achieve that. One hopes that the architect has since changed his ways or his profession, or perhaps his shoes.

Some architects rely on the clerk of works to inspect. Some clerks of works are very good, some less so. They can be a source of useful tips but architects should never rely on them (see 78: Clerk of Works). There are one or two good books about inspecting work, but even the best books cannot replace experience on site.

81

Snagging

Contractors often use the terms 'snags' and 'snagging' when talking or writing about correcting defects. Perhaps that is because a 'snag' sounds somehow less serious than a 'defect'. Building contracts do not refer to snags at all. Let's be perfectly clear: a snag is a defect and a defect is a breach of contract. So, when a contractor says with a winning smile that there are only a few snags to deal with, what is actually being said is that there are still some breaches of contract to be rectified. Every building contract says that the contractor must construct the building in accordance with the contract documents. Therefore, the contractor must do it correctly. It is quite straightforward. Whether one calls the parts built incorrectly snags or defects or breaches of contracts, they are all breaches of contract and must be rectified.

When a project is nearing completion, the clerks of works usually spends a lot of time producing snagging lists. These lists are intended to remind the contractor of defects which must be rectified. The production of these lists, and snagging in general, by the clerk of works or the architect, pose dangers. The first point to get clear is that it is the contractor's job to check that the Works are properly constructed. In theory, the architect should be able to inspect only once, at practical completion, and all the Works should be perfect. Obviously, life is not like that, but the position on many building sites is that the contractor only feels compelled to rectify a defect (a breach of contract, remember?), if the clerk of works or the architect spots the defect.

One of the dangers of the architect producing a snagging list near the time of practical completion is that the contractor immediately assumes that it is a 'once and for all' list of what needs to be done, rather than simply a list of the defects that the architect has spotted on a routine inspection. The site agent may stop carrying out any real inspections of the Works and simply rely on the clerk of works or the architect. I have often had the experience of visiting site and going around to check whether the list given to the agent the previous week had been rectified. Typically, I found that most of the defects had been rectified, some had been missed, and I inevitably found further defects that I had not seen before. The agent's reaction was always to complain because of the 'new' defects I had found. My response was always the same as follows: 'Are you seriously suggesting that I carry a bag of defects ready to scatter around when I inspect?' The real reason for the site contractor's complaint is that I did not do its job and make a thorough inspection of every part of the Works so as to produce a definitive list of all the defects which actually exist. If the site agent was acting properly, no defects at all would be found when I inspected because the site agent would have made sure that the Works were constructed strictly in accordance with the contract.

Professional Practice for Architects and Project Managers, First Edition. David Chappell.

82

Defects

Definition

People in the construction industry think they know what a defect is, but the truth is that most architects, surveyors, and contractors have a very imprecise idea about defects. They have even been referred to as 'temporary disconformities', rather than breaches of contract, by people who should know better. In general terms every building defect is a breach of contract even if it is likely that the contractor will rectify it before practical completion is achieved. Because every defect is a breach of contract, the employer is entitled to seek and recover damages for each defect. The damages would be the reasonable cost of getting another contractor to rectify the defect.

It must be rare for that situation to arise in practice because most building work is carried out under a building contract and the contract makes specific provision about defects. But if there is no standard building contract in use and employer and contractor have simply exchanged emails and sometimes not even that, there may be nothing written down about defects. In that kind of situation, every defect is a breach of contract and the two parties will be governed simply by the common law as noted above. Remember that contracts may be oral as well as in writing (see 23: Contracts).

But What is a Defect?

This is quite a complicated topic. In terms of a building contract, a defect is when a contractor does not do something it is supposed to do or does something it is not supposed to do. In other words when the contractor fails to build what the contractor has agreed to build. If you are the architect, how do you know what the contractor has agreed to build? The only way you can know is by looking at the contract documents, that is, by looking at the printed contract form if there is one and any other bits of paper mentioned in the printed form or attached to it. Sometimes it is very difficult to decide just which bits of paper make up the contract, but let us assume for the moment that all the relevant paper is attached to the printed form. There are likely to be bills of quantities, the specification, the schedule of work, and drawings or some combination of those things.

The fewer and vaguer the documents are, the more difficult it is to decide that something is a defect. For example, if the specification or bills of quantities or drawings

Professional Practice for Architects and Project Managers, First Edition. David Chappell.

describe stone paving by specifying the type of stone and the thickness and the bed on which it is to be laid and the dimensions of the paving stones and exactly how much of it, where it must be laid and at what levels, it will be comparatively easy to check whether there are in defects in the stone or positioning or laying. But if all there is to show the contractor what to build is a rough drawing which says 'stone paving' and shows a general outline of the area, you will not find it easy to say that any part of it is defective unless it is seriously uneven or has parts missing.

Therefore, to say that the contract documents must be precise in specifying what the contractor must do is really just another way of saying that if you do not know what the contractor has to do, it will not be easy to say that it has not been done.

The fact that something is inadequately described or drawn does not give the contractor a free hand to effectively do whatever seems appropriate, unless of course that is what the contract actually says, which is unlikely except in very specific cases.

Is it a defect if the contractor constructs something which does not work because it has been badly designed? It is certainly defective in a general sense of looking at the building as a whole and it would be correct to say that what the contractor had constructed was defective, but it would not be something for which the contractor is responsible. Having said that, if a contractor discovers that a particular detail, if constructed, would lead to seriously defective work, it probably has a duty to point out the defect to the employer. The contractor has no duty to specifically look for defects, but common sense is expected. Long ago, a contractor's agent only decided to telephone me about errors in the levels of an underground sloping district heating duct when he had to stop building because the bottom of the underground duct was above ground and was about to require pillars to support it. Although the agent had no duty to look for the errors in my levels, I found it difficult to believe that no one noticed that the clearly labelled *underground* duct was actually considerably above ground.

So, who is responsible for a defect if the architect has not given enough information on the drawings and the contractor has used initiative to decide what was intended, but the result is not what was required? No doubt the contractor would argue that it would have wasted valuable time to wait for the architect to provide the necessary details and that it is most unlikely that the contractor would receive extra payment to cover the cost of operatives standing idle. Nevertheless, if the contractor proceeds to build something that is neither specified nor drawn, it takes the chance that it may have guessed wrongly. If there is not enough information to allow the contractor to construct something, the contractor must request the information within a timeframe that allows the architect time to provide it before the particular part of the Works is to be commenced.

Who is responsible if the architect does not notice a joint in the roof covering material that the contractor invented because there was no detail given and the joint leaks? By going ahead and constructing the joint, the contractor took design responsibility and will be liable to rectify it in accordance with what the architect belatedly decides. It may amount to a variation of course, but the contractor could not claim for dismantling the defective joint.

What if the contractor constructs part of the Works in a different way to what is specified but it works as well as what was specified? In that case, what the contractor has constructed is a defect because it is not what the contractor should have built. In theory, the architect can instruct the contractor to rectify the defect by taking down the item of work and replacing with what was specified and that is always the safest way forward. In practice, the architect may accept the change in construction if there are no aesthetic considerations.

If no architect is involved and the contractor is left much to its own devices because the contract information is very sketchy, there is still an implied obligation on the contractor to build in a good and workmanlike manner, using good and proper materials, so the contractor cannot get away with building rubbish.

Contractual Provisions

In the Preface I said that I was not going to refer to contract clauses and I do not intend to do so. But part of the principles which I am trying to get across is the simple fact that most of the standard forms of building contract say something about defects and it is useful to know the kind of things which they might say and what they mean in practice.

It is common for standard forms to make express provision for dealing with defects or defective work. Most contracts deal with defects in two ways:

- They specifically require the contractor to do the work properly in accordance with the contract documents (i.e. with no defects).
- They say what is to happen when there are defects.

Defects can be divided into defects which appear during the carrying out of the work and defects which do not appear until after practical completion, when the whole of the Works should be virtually finished. The architect is given power to require the contractor to make good any defects whether occurring before or after practical completion. The contractor is expected to deal with defects within a reasonable time of their appearance. Some contracts allow the architect to require the making good within a short space of time. If the contractor refuses to make them good or simply ignores them, the architect usually has power to get another contractor in to rectify the defect and to deduct the cost from money due to the original contractor.

Arguments

Sometimes, there is an argument about whether an item of work or materials is defective or not. The contractor may hire an expert to view the alleged defect and say that it is not defective at all. The architect may not know what to do. In this kind of situation, the architect should always remember that the decision whether or not something is defective is a matter for the architect in the first instance, not the contractor or its expert. The architect, with the consent of the employer, can commission an expert or take samples and carry out tests. Some contracts make provision for this and for apportionment of the costs. If the contractor is not happy with the architect's decision, it can always take the dispute to adjudication, arbitration, or litigation, whatever the contract allows. The contract may give the employer power to terminate the contractor's employment if it fails to rectify a defect after being required to do so. Generally, termination would only be justified if the defect was substantial and the contractor's failure affected the Works as a whole.

The Architect has No Duty to the Contractor

The final thing to be said is that the architect owes no duty to the contractor to discover defective work. Put another way: the contractor's duty to carry out the work properly is not in any way dependent on whether the architect notices defects. A contractor will sometimes say to the architect when a longstanding defect is pointed out 'You have been on site many times and said nothing and I thought you were happy with what we had done'. This ignores the simple fact that, if the contractor has built in accordance with the specification and drawings, it is right; if not, it is wrong. That is all there is to say.

83

Samples

Two Situations

There are two situations in which samples of materials may be required. These situations can be roughly divided into before and after the contract is signed.

Before

Before the specification and drawings are finalised, the architect will often seek samples of particular materials to make sure that they are specified precisely. Such things as bricks, stone, roofing tiles, floor and wall tiles, timber cladding, patent glazing, etc. may all require careful consideration and specification. There is no limit, other than practical considerations, to the numbers of samples that may be requested. Indeed, many architects' offices are crowded with the remnants of samples related to long-forgotten projects, still retained on the basis that they might one day be useful again.

Obviously, samples of materials that are supplied and then specified for use on a project must be retained. If practical, the sample should be signed and dated by the provider to show when and where it was obtained.

It is common to have to produce brickwork or stonework panels before submitting a planning application, particularly in a sensitive area. It also serves to show a client how a wall will look, which is often quite different from the individual materials, whether stone or brick is to be used.

After

A conservation planning officer will expect to see sample panels of various kinds for approval before that part of the work starts on site.

Once the contractor is on site, and particularly if a clerk of works is employed, the contractor is often asked to construct sample panels of brickwork, roofing tiles, and so on to serve as the standard below which the construction of those elements must not fall. I once had a clerk of works who boasted to me, quite sincerely, that he always kicked down the first sample panel of brickwork with suitable expressions of disgust whatever the standard. 'That shows them from the start that I have a very high standard',

Professional Practice for Architects and Project Managers, First Edition. David Chappell.

he said. On a subsequent project which I had the pleasure of administering, the site agent had previously been subjected to the clerk of work's treatment and he had the sample brick panel built the day before the inspection rather than on the same morning. Consequently, the panel was rock hard and the clerk of work's kick was accompanied by expressions of pain rather than disgust.

The specification should set out the size and location of the panel and whether it should be in a sunny position. Importantly, the timing of construction of the panel should be specified well in advance of the construction of the relevant part of the Works.

A contractor or a supplier may sometimes try to argue that, although the material supplied is not very good, it does comply to the sample which was the subject of the specification and, therefore, must be acceptable. That sounds like an unanswerable argument. However, it all depends on whether the full characteristics of the material were apparent to the architect when the sample was presented. Take the case of sample bricks examined by the architect and considered to be acceptable. When the bricks arrive on site and after a substantial amount of brickwork is constructed, it is discovered that the centres of most of the bricks are inadequately fired, causing patches of the brickwork to disintegrate. Assuming that the architect did not break a brick in half or if that was done the particular brick was found to be sound, the contractor or supplier will be obliged to rectify the problem. That is because the architect did not choose bricks with inadequately fired interiors, the architect chose bricks which were apparently sound. It is the apparent quality of the material which sets the standard, not some hidden defect.

Talking of 'quality', it is strange that the word is used as though it was synonymous with 'good quality' whereas it is meaningless without a qualifying adjective. So, we see references to 'quality food served here' or 'quality service' or 'we provide a quality experience'. All these, and many other, variations convey nothing about the quality. The reference could be to 'excellent quality', 'good quality', 'poor quality', etc. Everyone has seen this kind of thing. While it may be (just) acceptable when seeking a pub lunch, because we all assume that they do not mean 'poor-quality' food, it is certainly not acceptable in a specification. Even with a qualifying adjective, phrases such as 'good-quality rendering' are not sufficiently precise for a specification.

An important question is whether the clerk of works or the architect have the power to order the contractor to provide samples once the contractor is on site. The straight answer is no, they can't do that unless, of course, the specification specifically allows the clerk of works or architect to order samples. The contractor can simply say 'No'. In practice, the contractor probably agrees to provide samples, but after several requests the contractor might well decide that the requests are unreasonable and refuse. The architect and the clerk of works cannot oblige the contractor to comply, but of course the finished product must comply with the specification whether or not samples are provided.

This raises another point. If the specification states that samples are required, does that does give the architect and clerk of works free rein to choose whatever they wish? The purpose of viewing the sample is to make sure that it complies with the specification. If something better is chosen, the architect must issue a variation instruction.

In order to ensure that the contractor provides samples, the contract or the specification must say so, provided that the specification does not conflict with the contract. If it does, the contract must be amended (get an expert to make any contract amendments).

Generally worded statements such as 'samples of all goods and materials intended for use on the Works must be provided to the architect before ordering' or 'samples must be provided to the architect as required from time to time' are not sufficiently specific. From a simple common-sense point of view, the contractor will be unable to price for such vague provisions. That is what is important to the contractor and rightly so. Therefore, in writing a clause in the specification requiring the contractor to provide samples of materials, and possibly goods and workmanship as well, the architect must always think: 'If I was the contractor, could I price this?'

There are other things to consider:

- What samples must be provided?
- When must the samples be provided?
- Where must they be provided and stored and who is responsible for their safekeeping?
- What happens if the samples are disliked by the architect? The samples, after all, are not the actual material in its position in the building. The contractor is entitled to provide the required samples and then simply proceed with the Works unless approval of the sample is dealt with in the specification.
- Workmanship does not occur until two or more materials are put together, therefore is the sample required a sample of workmanship or materials or both? For example, the specification may state that 'the contractor must provide a sample of the floor finish one metre square, on the second floor laid on a sample of the floor construction in that area to show the standard of workmanship and the quality of materials'.

Design and Build

If the contractor is being employed on a design and build basis, the relevant building contract may include something about samples. It should not be assumed just because there is a clause mentioning samples that it gives the architect and clerk of works freedom to ask for whatever they want. It must be remembered that the idea behind design and build contracts is that the employer provides tenderers with what is effectively a performance specification. In responding, the contractors will be attempting to satisfy the specification at the least possible cost. It is likely that the proposals put forward by the successful contractor will be less detailed than if the specification was produced by the architect in a traditional contract situation. In this scenario, it is more than usually important that the employer or the employer's representative are able to inspect samples to see what the contractor is actually going to provide. The comments above are broadly relevant, but it must be remembered that the particular samples that will be required must be stated in the performance specification.

Finally, it must be remembered that if samples provided by the contractor comply with what has been specified or, in the case of a design and build contract, what the contractor has proposed, the contractor cannot be in breach of contract or be said to have built something defective. Therefore, if the employer or the architect is not happy with a sample which complies with the specification or contractor's proposals, any change will require an instruction and will amount to a variation.

84

Temporary Work

General

In the process of constructing a building a contractor often has to carry out a great deal of temporary work. That is work which, as the name suggests, is not usually intended to remain permanently on the site, but is constructed merely to allow the contractor to construct the permanent works which the architect has designed and specified. Examples of temporary works include roadways, trench supports, scaffolding, temporary shoring, formwork, etc.

Nowadays, there are masses of regulations which are intended to ensure that temporary works are constructed and used safely. There are severe penalties for infringing the regulations. That was not always the case or, to be accurate, the regulations were not as thorough and they were not enforced as stringently as they are today. Some contractors would risk taking what were inadequately termed 'short cuts'. Often it was the operatives themselves who tried to take short cuts. I well remember seeing a rather stupid (no other word I'm afraid) labourer at the bottom of a fairly narrow and deep but unsupported trench. When the labourer stood upright, he was not visible above ground. He was cavorting (no other word I'm afraid) along the trench aware that he was being observed and demonstrating how unconcerned he was as he continued to dig out the trench bottom. At my insistence, the site agent told him to leave the trench and half an hour later a large portion collapsed.

If bills of quantities are being used, temporary work is usually measured. If bills of quantities are not used, temporary work is not usually specified unless there is a particular reason for doing so. In the example above, the contractor should have allowed for adequate trench supports.

Another obvious instance is the use of formwork when *in situ* concrete is required. There are many other instances of temporary work which may be detailed in the specification. Although in most instances the contractor will have firm views about the location for siting spoil heaps and temporary storage of materials, the specification must state if any special restrictions apply.

Existing Buildings

Alterations to existing buildings will often require the erection of dust and noise screens to protects parts of the building, and possibly users. In such cases, temporary access may be necessary for the occupants.

Professional Practice for Architects and Project Managers, First Edition. David Chappell.

If alterations and extensions to domestic property are involved, temporary facilities such as relocating a washing machine and provision of a portaloo may be required.

Other common temporary work includes fencing around the site, temporary roof covering, lighting, and heating.

Although the contractor can be expected to provide the necessary scaffolding, ladders, and temporary supports without which it could not safely construct the building, it will readily be seen that other temporary work, not immediately necessary to enable the contractor to carry out its work, must be specified with particular clarity. Descriptions such as 'The contractor will take appropriate measures to protect existing furniture and fittings' are not really good enough.

85

Architect's Instructions

What is an Instruction?

Standard building contracts refer to instructions and whether they must be in writing or oral, how they may be confirmed and by whom. But strangely they rarely define an instruction. Perhaps they assume that everyone knows what is meant by the word 'instruction' and that is probably a reasonable assumption. Having said that, it is important that everyone does know what an instruction is because the contractor has to comply with instructions from the architect. Usually, for something to be described as an instruction there must be an unmistakable intention to order something and there must be some kind of proof that the instruction was given to the contractor.

Must an Instruction be in a Particular Form?

Although it may be possible to imply an instruction from what is written down, it is safer from the contractor's point of view to ensure that the words clearly instruct, for example a drawing sent to a contractor with a compliments slip is not necessarily an instruction to carry out the work shown. Most contractors no doubt assume that a drawing sent with nothing but a compliments slip is an instruction to do the work shown on the drawing. Many architects also believe that to be the case, but such an assumption may be misguided. The architect may be simply seeking comments from the contractor. It is always sensible for a contractor to seek clarification if there is nothing which means 'Do this'. A drawing should always be issued under cover of a letter which need simply say 'Please carry out the work shown on the enclosed drawing no…'. The same can be said about copy letters sent under cover of a compliments slip. Architects sometimes send a letter to the employer saying that they are going to instruct the contractor to do certain extra work in accordance with the employer's wishes. Those same architects wrongly believe that if they send a copy of that letter to the contractor, it amounts to an instruction to the contractor to get on with the work. That is wrong. At best it just tells the contractor to expect to receive an instruction at some time.

An instruction on a printed Architect's Instruction form is valid if authorised by the architect. It is not essential (as sometimes thought) that an instruction must be on a special coloured form, although it is useful to be able to pick out instructions easily by their appearance if they are filed along with other correspondence. An ordinary letter can be a valid instruction. An old architect I knew used to write instructions on site on pieces of

Professional Practice for Architects and Project Managers, First Edition. David Chappell.

old roof tile or on the side of a brick. Providing they are signed and dated and legible, they are all valid instructions, although not easy to photocopy. The minutes of a site meeting may be a valid instruction if the contents are expressed clearly and unequivocally and if the architect is responsible for the production of the minutes, but site meeting minutes are not a good way of issuing instructions because of the time problem.

Signing Instructions

Although all the standard forms of contract permit the architect to issue instructions under various circumstances, there is still a great deal of confusion. One architect even asked me whether he was obliged to sign an instruction. There appeared to be no ulterior motive for the question other than idle curiosity. The answer is straightforward. The architect is under no obligation to personally sign an instruction, but it must be clear from the instruction that it is authorised by the architect named in the contract. This is usually done by a signature.

Another connected question concerns whether an instruction will be invalid if not signed by the correct person. The simple answer to that question is that an instruction may be signed by any person who is authorised to do so by the architect named in the contract. Only the architect may issue certificates and instructions under the terms of the contract, but that includes anyone authorised by the architect. The architect should be careful to inform all interested parties of the names of persons authorised to act on behalf of the architect.

It is common for the name of the architect in the contract to be a firm, for example XYZ Architects. Therefore, the letter informing all parties of authorised persons must be signed by XYZ Architects. If the firm is a limited company, the signature of a director will do, if a partnership, it should be one of the partners. If a limited liability partnership, it ought to be one of the designated members on the letterhead.

If instructions are signed by an authorised person, that person should sign 'for and on behalf of'. This is certainly the best method. It is not sufficient that the letter or whatever is on headed paper. The important thing is that it must be plain that the signatory is not signing on his or her own behalf, but on behalf of the architect, be that company, partnership or sole principal. So it is probably sufficient if the name of the firm is typed where the signature would normally go and the authorised person signs immediately underneath. Sometimes people sign the actual name of the architect. For example, if the named architect is John Smith, one of the authorised persons, Betty Brown, may sign 'John Smith' provided she initials the signature.

Mechanical impressions of signatures, such as rubber stamp facsimiles, may not be valid unless initialled or signed by an authorised person.

Must an Instruction be in Writing?

Most contracts state that instructions must be in writing, but then go on to say what happens if the contract is not in writing, i.e. oral. Some contracts do not allow for oral instructions at all so what if the architect issues an oral instruction which the contractor carries out? Is the contractor entitled to payment? In most cases, if architects issue oral instructions, it is likely that they want them to be carried out. The problem comes if for some reason an architect will not authorise payment or denies giving the instructions in the first place (perhaps because it turned out not to be a good idea). Despite what it says in the contract, if the architect is in the habit of issuing oral instructions, and certifying payment for them, the law will not allow the architect to argue that the contractor is not entitled to payment on one occasion because the instruction was not written. If the contractor confirms the architect's oral instructions (even though there is no provision for this procedure in the contract) the contractor will not be allowed to argue later that the instruction was not properly issued because it was not in writing. But it is worth bearing in mind that, as a general principle, a contractor carrying out an oral instruction without written confirmation is in a tricky position and may not be paid.

Is the Architect Obliged to Confirm the Employer's Instructions?

Employers should never visit site unaccompanied by the architect, but they do. This is especially difficult to enforce when the project is an extension to the employer's house and the employer has not moved out. In those circumstances, nothing will stop the employer from visiting the Works in progress because they are in plain sight. Employers will visit the Works without telling the architect even when the project is a commercial building at some distance away. The problem is that they ask questions of the contractor and often get the wrong answers, which can and does lead to difficulties and wasted time. Employers may answer questions from contractors or give instructions even when no questions are asked. Unfortunately, employers sometimes visit site unaccompanied quite deliberately.

Many employers seem to think that they can get the facts about progress and other things from the contractor better than from the architect, who is still seen, occasionally it must be admitted with good reason, as not very practical. So, even though the architect will make very clear that the employer must not go on site without the architect, must not answer questions from the contractor or give instructions, and the contractor must not answer questions from the employer or ask for instructions, instructions are often given by the employer directly to the contractor. The contractor may carry out the instruction without reference to the architect. It may be that the instruction was given by the employer who told the contractor to check with the architect or it may be that the employer gave the instruction without really understanding what was being asked. Neither of these circumstances exonerates both employer and contractor from the charge of failing to act in accordance with the contract, but mistakes happen. People forget to do the correct things.

If the architect decides that the instruction, although given directly, is simply the kind of instruction which if the employer had asked the architect to issue it would have been issued without difficulty, the architect will presumably have no problems with ratifying the instruction. The position becomes difficult if the instruction is one which the architect would not have issued and which perhaps has a bad effect on the project. The employer and contractor are entitled to vary the terms of the contract as they wish. If the employer decides to give a direct instruction, even if the contract says only the architect may do that, and if the contractor accepts the instruction it is likely that either the law will imply that a fresh little contract has been formed for that item of work or, alternatively, it may rank as a variation to the original contract terms. Whichever it is, the architect cannot include the value of that kind of variation in a certificate unless it is the subject of an architect's instruction. If the architect does not confirm an instruction given by the employer, the cost of the variation must be paid for by the employer directly.

A contractor who accepts a direct instruction from the employer is unwise. If the contractor carries out the work, but the employer says that the instruction was never given, the contractor is in breach of its obligations under the contract and can be obliged to reinstate the work to conform to what it says in the contract documents.

Refusal to Carry out a Validly Issued Instruction

Most building contracts require the contractor to comply forthwith (i.e. as soon as it reasonably can do so) with architect's instructions. What if the contractor refuses to comply or ignores polite requests to carry out the instruction? Contracts vary in what they say the architect can do so it is always necessary to check carefully. If the contract says nothing, a sensible way forward is for the architect to write to the contractor giving it seven days in which to start complying with the instruction and warning that if at the end of the seven days no work on the instruction has commenced, the employer will engage others to carry out the work and the additional cost to the employer will be deducted from money payable to the contractor. The rationale behind that is simple. The contractor is in breach of contract by refusing to carry out the instruction. The employer is entitled to seek damages, but damages later might involve the cost of taking down part of the building to carry out the variation. Therefore, for all practical purposes and to mitigate losses, the variation must be carried out before that part of the Works is covered up or built upon. The employer is entitled to give due warning and then to act. The law says that the contractor cannot refuse access to the site by others to carry out the variation in that kind of situation.

Can the Employer Prevent the Issue of an Architect's Instruction?

If the employer attempts to prevent the architect from issuing any certificate (financial or practical completion, etc.) or prevents the architect from issuing an extension of time, the architect may be able to treat his or her appointment as at an end. That is because the building contract requires the issue of these certificates, extensions of time, and the like, and the employer and contractor, by signing the building contract, have agreed that the architect will comply with the terms of the contract in this and other ways.

The question of whether the employer can stop the architect issuing an instruction is rather different. Under most building contracts, the architect has the power, but is not usually obliged, to issue instructions. The architect's terms of engagement may well limit the issue of instructions and require the architect to seek authorisation before issuing any instruction which involves the expenditure of additional money. If the instruction which the architect proposes to issue has any monetary or design implications, there is little doubt that the client can instruct the architect not to issue it and the architect is obliged to comply. The position is less clear in the case of instructions which simply clarify something on a drawing or in a specification. Such instructions actually do not change the Works at all and it is unlikely that an employer will try to stop that kind of instruction. But, depending upon the precise terms of the conditions of engagement, the client can stop the architect issuing any instruction which results in a variation to the Works. It is unlikely that, short of termination, the client can prevent the architect issuing any other kind of instruction.

The contractor, of course, is not interested in the contents of the architect's engagement. Provided that an instruction issued by the architect is the kind of instruction which the contract says that the architect can issue, the contractor is secure in carrying it out because it will be paid for it. If the contractor is in any doubt whether the instruction is empowered by the contract it can always ask the architect to name the empowering clause.

86

Certificates

Kinds of Certificate

Most building contracts make provision for the architect or other contract administrator to issue various certificates. The first thing is to decide what we mean by a certificate. The following are the kinds of certificates which most building contracts include (although they may have slightly different names):

- payment certificate
- practical completion certificate
- certificate of failure to complete on time
- certificate of rectification of defects
- final certificate
- certifying a final account after termination has taken place.

To complicate matters, courts sometimes refer to the architect 'certifying' an extension of time.

What is a Certificate?

Fortunately, the courts have clarified what they and, therefore, the rest of us mean by a 'certificate'. It is the formal expression of the certifier's professional opinion for the purposes specified in the contract. In other words, it is something written down. Therefore, you cannot issue a certificate orally. You will be aware that in administering a building contract you are to some extent acting as agent for the employer, but that in certain circumstances you have to form an opinion, acting fairly between both parties. Those circumstances include when the contract states that you must certify, but there are other circumstances where a building contract probably does not say that you must certify, but where, nevertheless, you must form an opinion, acting fairly. Deciding an extension of time is one such situation, but there are others, such as when you decide whether or not workmanship or materials are in accordance with the contract requirements. This is a duty which is implied and affects all architects administering contracts. It is sensible to make this position clear to the client when appointed and to the contractor at the first meeting.

Professional Practice for Architects and Project Managers, First Edition. David Chappell.

So, in issuing a certificate, you must act fairly in stating your professional opinion, but there may be other situations where you have to act fairly and state your professional opinion, but where the contract does not specifically state that you are issuing a certificate, for example when you issue an extension of time.

What must a Certificate Contain?

Although there are standard forms issued by professional bodies for use with different forms of building contract, you do not have to use any of them. Having said that, the standard forms do assist by acting as a checklist of things to be filled in. If you want to issue your own certificate, you can easily do so. It can be on a special sheet of paper headed 'Certificate of …' or it can be in the form of a letter. It is important to start by saying 'I certify …'. The following important things must be included in every building contract certificate as well as the specific matter that is being certified:

- name and address of the employer
- name and address of the contractor
- date of the contract
- date of the certificate
- name and address of the certifier
- signature of the certifier or of someone authorised to sign on behalf of the certifier.

Timing

Certificates must be issued promptly in accordance with the time stipulated in the contract. It is very important to observe the time for issuing certificates set out in the contract. A certificate which is issued earlier than prescribed by the contract will usually be invalid. If the contract states a specific timeframe for issuing a certificate, the certificate may be invalid if issued later. That is likely to be the case if the lateness of a certificate is likely to disadvantage the contractor. If not, it may well be possible to issue a certificate later than stipulated in the contract provided the certifier acts reasonably and as quickly as possible. Obviously, the two parties to the contract can agree that the certifier issues a certificate later than stated in the contract.

Can a Certificate be Withdrawn?

Once issued, a certificate cannot be withdrawn. A certificate cannot be dated earlier than the date the certificate is prepared. A certificate cannot be post-dated. This is because the certificate records the professional opinion of the certifier on the date stated. That opinion may change and frequently does. Thus, an architect may issue a payment certificate in the sum of £20 000 and subsequently, in the next certificate, defects may become apparent and the architect's view may be that the value of the work previously certified may be only £15 000. Depending upon what work has been carried out since the previous certificate, the change in the architect's view may mean that the next certificate has a negative value. There is nothing wrong with issuing a negative certificate, although most contracts do not have any procedures to compel the contractor to reimburse the negative amount.

If the architect fails to issue a certificate, the contractor may have a claim against the employer if the contractor can show that the employer was aware of the architect's failure and failed to remedy the situation. If the employer attempts to influence the architect in issuing a certificate, it will usually be a breach of contract on the part of the employer.

87

The Architect's Conundrum

Is the Architect like an Arbitrator?

Many people ask if the architect is like an arbitrator. The short answer is no. Having said that, it is remarkable how many architects, some of them quite experienced, still wrongly believe that an architect issuing certificates under the building contract is immune from action for negligence on the basis of acting in an arbitral capacity. It is about 50 years since that view had even the glimmer of truth about it. Architects who over-certify payments to contractors are liable to be sued for negligence by their clients.

What Then?

An architect has a duty to act fairly between the employer and the contractor. This duty is owed principally to the employer. That means that the architect is most likely to be sued by the employer and unlikely (but not unknown) to be sued by the contractor. What sort of decisions are architects called upon to make under the contract, where they are supposedly weighing the evidence fairly between the two parties? There are more than you might think. They include deciding whether the standard of workmanship is in accordance with the specification, the issue of certificates (financial and otherwise), determining the reasons for and periods of extensions of time, ascertaining amounts of loss and expense, and any other matter which might arise as a dispute between the contractor and employer during the course of the work, for example the interpretation of the conditions and bills of quantities.

It tends to be thought that all that architects have to do to make sure that they are not liable in negligence is to make a fair decision, using normal reasonable professional skill and care. It sounds simple, but it is not. Just supposing, perish the thought, that you are the architect at fault and you are called upon to decide the issue. Perhaps you issued conflicting drawings or the specification was not as clear as it might have been. Perhaps you were late in issuing drawings or instructions. You are supposed to take up an independent position and decide the issue cold-bloodedly on the facts. Facts are seldom so clear in construction matters that they cannot be fudged (as if anyone would), but architects are usually in a position to know if they are at fault.

Let us take, as an example, the situation where a contractor asks you for an extension of time based upon your failure to deliver certain drawings on time, thus causing a delay. If you know that the drawings were late because the employer made some

Professional Practice for Architects and Project Managers, First Edition. David Chappell.

last-minute amendments or otherwise caused delay, you might feel confident in issuing the appropriate extension of time. But what if it was entirely your fault, perhaps due to pressure of work? If you then give an extension of time, it will do two things: it will, quite correctly, stop the employer being able to claim any liquidated damages for the period of the extension and it will show the contractor that you agree the delay, which may open the way for the contractor to take steps to claim loss and expense. The employer will not be pleased. The employer may sue you for the loss you have undoubtedly caused or might simply make a deduction from your fees. Many, perhaps most, architects try to carry out their duties without tailoring decisions to guard themselves from legal action. On the other hand, how many architects regularly give extensions of time for neutral events such as exceptional adverse weather rather than, more accurately, variations or late instructions which open the door to claims for loss and/or expense?

The concept of the architect being a quasi-arbitrator (like an arbitrator) was useful in this situation because, according to that idea, the architect was immune from actions for negligence when making these kinds of decisions. The current situation is that, while administering a building contract, you may be both judge and defendant. So, faced with the problem, what can you do? The fault lies in the system itself, which requires you to make decisions which are, in effect, a judgement on your own conduct. While the architect was considered to have immunity and clients were not so 'quick on the draw' anyway, it worked tolerably well, but now the concept of the architect as quasi-arbitrator is well out of date.

Is there a Solution?

Unfortunately, currently there is no good answer. Today, the architect is, realistically, only the agent of the employer. Architects should not, ever, be considered to be acting impartially and it is unfair to expect them to do so, although that is what the law expects.

Leaving aside the shortcomings of the contract itself, the simplest way would be to let the contract proceed on its normal course, the architect making the decisions required, but recognised as acting in the interest of the employer (albeit as honestly as possible).

Should the contractor wish to dispute any decisions, it would have recourse to a previously agreed adjudicator in an informal and inexpensive way.

To those architects who think I am trying to advocate a denigration of their professional status I would simply say that the members of no other profession (to my knowledge) have the duty of acting for a client and also deciding issues between clients and others to the extent of effectively admitting liability without being asked.

88

Sub-Contractors and Suppliers

Is Sub-contracting Wrong?

Once upon a time, a contractor was considered to be slightly dodgy if it did not carry out most of its work using its own operatives. The information that a contractor would be sub-contracting brickwork, for example, was greeted with horror. It was generally accepted that certain trades such as plasterers and roof tilers would be sub-contracted as needed, but every contractor worth its salt would have its own bricklayers, joiners, carpenters, and general labourers. I clearly remember one of my then colleagues breathlessly telling the rest of us that he had a contractor who only directly employed a couple of site agents and everything else was sub-contracted. We all forecast appalling workmanship, delays, and all manner of other difficulties – and so it turned out.

Things have dramatically changed and it is now common for all trades to be sub-contracted. Those sub-contractors which are selected by the contractor are usually called 'domestic sub-contractors' to differentiate them from sub-contractors which are imposed by the employer, such as 'named', specialist, or nominated sub-contractors. Some building contracts are actually based on the premise that the contractor merely exercises a managerial role (management contracts) in organising what amounts to a group of independent sub-contractors. In some contracts, they may be termed 'works contractors' or 'trade contractors', but essentially, they are all sub-contractors.

If the Contractor Allegedly Does Not Pay

Employers and, it seems, some architects and quantity surveyors do not fully understand the contractual relationships involved where sub-contractors are concerned. For example, it is relatively common for a sub-contractor who is in dispute with a contractor about payment to refuse to carry on working unless it is paid directly by the employer. The solution may appear very simple: the employer pays the sub-contractor and then deducts the same amount from payments to the contractor. The problem is that the employer has no means of knowing whether the sub-contractor is telling the truth. Moreover, the employer usually has no contractual relationship with the sub-contractor.

Put simply, the contractor has agreed to construct the Works for the employer and the employer has agreed to pay the contractor for constructing the Works. The contractor has, quite separately, agreed to pay the sub-contractor and the sub-contractor has agreed to construct part of the Works for the contactor. But even if the employer

Professional Practice for Architects and Project Managers, First Edition. David Chappell.

pays the sub-contractor for its part of the Works, the contractor is still entitled to claim the same money from the employer because that is what they have agreed. In short, the contractor is entitled to be paid for all of the Works constructed because the contractor does not have to prove that it has done the work, but simply that the work has been done. The employer will end by paying twice for the same work.

If the Contractor Goes Bust

What if the contractor goes bust? Can the employer then pay the sub-contractor directly any money owed by the contractor in order to get the sub-contractor to complete the sub-contract work, which might be highly complicated electrical installation? The straight answer to that is the same as before: the contractor, or in this case the liquidator, is entitled to claim from the employer for all the work carried out, including work by the sub-contractor. Moreover, the sub-contractor cannot be treated as a preferential creditor. It is owed money by the contractor just like all the other creditors even if the chances of getting the money are negligible.

It may be that the sub-contractor is not prepared to quote the employer for completing the complicated electrical work for the rate in the contract, and it may be that it is impossible or impracticable for the employer to get another electrical contractor to complete the electrical work without virtually starting again at high cost and long delay. Realistically, the employer may be obliged to accept a very steep quote from the original electrical sub-contractor. In those circumstances it is likely that the amount of the quote will closely approach the original contract rate for completing the work plus what the sub-contractor is owed by the contractor. But that is sheer co-incidence, if you get my drift.

Architect's Discussions with Specialist Sub-contractors

Another awkward situation that many architects get into arises because the architect insists on having direct discussions with the sub-contractor about aspects of the sub-contract work. This particularly concerns what tend to be known as specialist sub-contractors, who are chosen by the architect or employer rather than the contractor. Often these discussions take place before the main contract it agreed, but sometimes they continue afterwards also. The architect may have many meetings with the sub-contractor and feels confident that the sub-contractor knows exactly what is required. So why does that not translate to site? The architect appears not to understand that such discussions are very informal and neither the sub-contractor nor the contractor are bound by them. The sub-contractor cannot be bound by direct instructions from the architect because the architect has no status under the sub-contract and the contractor cannot be bound by discussions between architect and sub-contractor unless the architect gives direct instructions to the contractor under the building contract.

Many architects tell me that it is often vital that they have intensive discussions with proposed specialist sub-contractors in order to be sure that the sub-contractor knows exactly what is required. But the reality is that the only way to make sure that work is carried out as the architect or the employer wishes is to have it carefully described in the building contract documents. One can understand the architect's desire to ensure that the sub-contractor knows exactly what the architect wants, but the results of any of those discussions must be reflected in the contract documents. I am not sure how to explain this and make it clearer. I am anxious to do so because of the number of architects who regularly get in a mess as a result of thinking something was nicely sorted out with the sub-contractor and then finding that something else was done on site.

Another danger for architects who get involved in discussions with specialist sub-contractors is that, if there is a delay, the contractor will often telephone the architect to notify him that 'Your sub-contractor is delaying the job. Can you get them moving?' Actually, of course, it is the contractor's duty to 'get them moving', but it is surprising how often the architect is pushed into telephoning the sub-contractor and urging it to 'get moving'. That is a grave mistake and once that happens, the architect's life becomes even worse than usual and there will be future allegations that the architect interfered with the sub-contractor's work.

Shop Drawings

It is common for architects to receive so-called 'shop drawings' from contractors with a request that the architect checks or approves them. The architect has no duty to check those drawings. That is because both sub-contractor and contractor are actually saying to the architect, 'we think we have transferred the information from your drawings correctly, but we would like you to be responsible for confirming that'. No doubt, for peace of mind, the architect will check the drawings, but there is no obligation to confirm their accuracy. It is the contractor's duty to make sure they are correct and the architect should say so.

Employer Supply Problems

Employers often want to supply certain items themselves. It is a funny (i.e. strange) thing that an employer and contractor with the assistance of professional advisors can enter into a very sophisticated and comprehensive contractual document, complete with bills of quantities or specification, and yet deal with employer's supply items in a very off-hand kind of way. There are few standard building contracts that make provision for the employer to supply materials or goods yet, at best, there is often simply a brief comment in the bills or the specification to the effect that the employer will supply X.

The reasons why an employer wants to supply goods is either because the employer has not been able to decide on the type of goods required and believes (on no good evidence) that a decision will be easier if taken later or because the employer can save money that way. With very few exceptions, the best and cheapest way is to have all the work, goods, and materials specified for the contractor to price then supply and fix.

The items to be supplied by employer will become 'fix only' items as far as the contractor is concerned. By taking on the 'supply' duty, the employer must get the items to site exactly when the contractor requires them, neither too early nor too late. Too early and there may be nowhere to store them and too late and the contractor may be delayed. Late delivery of the goods will probably result in the contractor being able to secure an extension of time and possibly being able to make a financial claim for disruption or prolongation or both. It matters not that the employer has problems with the supplier. All that matters is that, by taking charge of supply, the employer has undertaken to supply the items in accordance with whatever programme the contractor prepares.

What if the employer supplies and the item is defective? If it is obviously defective, one can expect the contractor to reject it. But many defects in materials and goods may not be obvious until they are fixed in position and perhaps out of sight. In those circumstances, there is no doubt that the employer is responsible and if the item has to be replaced the employer will have to pay all the costs of replacement. On one project, the employer insisted on organising the supply of bricks. It was not until the building was virtually complete that it was discovered that the bricks, although apparently sound, contained a large number which had inadequately fired cores. Dealing with that problem cost the employer a great deal of money. Employers seldom understand that by taking on the supply of materials or goods, they are taking on responsibility which normally belongs to the contractor.

Even if the goods are not defective and the employer delivers them on time, it may cost more to fix the goods than anticipated and the extra cost would have to be borne by the employer unless the contractor had misquoted. In most cases, the contractor will be able to provide a fixed price for fixing employer's supply items provided the contractor knows exactly what is being provided. But employers sometimes have second thoughts and provide something substantially different from what the bills or specification described. In other cases, the contractor may not be given enough information to provide a fixed price and gives a provisional sum instead. The usual result of all these things is that the employer pays more than expected.

A much worse situation occurs if the employer decides to supply items after they are included in the contract sum. For the employer to take items out of the contract in order to get them elsewhere is a breach of contract, of course, because by signing the contract the employer agreed that the contractor would supply those items. Therefore, the contractor is entitled to claim damages for the breach. In practice that usually means that the contractor is entitled to loss of profit. It is not the slightest use the employer pointing to a contract clause permitting the architect to omit materials, goods, or work because that kind of clause only allows the omission, not the getting of the same goods or work elsewhere.

Architects must always advise clients of the pitfalls of undertaking to supply and the more so if the employer makes that decision after having agreed in the contract that the contractor will supply. Needless to say, much the same, although more complex, problems arise where the employer decides to take responsibility for supply and fixing, even though there is provision in some contracts for that to occur (see 89: Other Contractors on the Works).

89

Other Contractors on the Works

Why?

Sometimes the employer wants to be able to let other contractors access the site in order to carry out work. Building contracts often have clauses allowing this to happen. They used to be called, and sometimes still are called, ‘artists and tradesmen’ clauses. Employer’s operatives on site in these circumstances are termed ‘employer’s licensees’.

Sometimes the employer may wish to have this kind of access because, for example, they are the employer’s own employees in the case of a large organisation or local authority or the employer may have developed a special relationship with them in the case of sculptors or landscapers. The employer may simply want to have complete control over them, which would not be the case even if they were specialist or named sub-contractors. Often there is absolutely no good reason for bringing others onto site except that the employer mistakenly thinks that he or she can get the work done cheaper than leaving it to the contractor. The sentence ‘My brother has a company that can do the concreting quite cheaply’ is something that most architects, quite rightly, dread hearing. I exclude situations such as statutory undertakers carrying out their statutory duties because they will usually only respond to instructions from the employer (see 90: Statutory Undertakers).

How?

It is important to be clear that the law will say that a contractor who is given a project to construct is entitled to have exclusive possession of the site in order to construct it (see 67: Possession of the Site) unless the building contract specifically states otherwise. Not only is that the law, it also makes perfect sense (something to celebrate). In law it is termed a ‘licence’. Therefore, an employer cannot simply bring people onto the site without the contractor’s permission. Many building contracts do allow the employer to bring others onto site for particular purposes, but usually there are conditions laid down, often ignored or never read by the employer or even those giving advice. There are only two situations:

- The contract says that the employer may bring other contractors onto site.
- The contract says nothing, in which case, the employer may not bring others onto site and to do so would be a breach of contract.

Professional Practice for Architects and Project Managers, First Edition. David Chappell.

In the first situation, the contract would impose conditions such as requiring the contractor to have, at the time of tender, a very clear description of the work the employer's licensees would be doing. In the second situation, the employer's licensees would only be able to go onto the site if the contractor agreed.

Problems

There are no real advantages and a great many disadvantages for the employer who insists on bringing persons, other than the contractor, onto the site. One only has to consider for a moment the enormous complications facing the average-sized contractor organising and carrying out a contract of moderate size. Even if the contractor is in full possession and control of the site, the chances of an average contract reaching completion without any kind of delay are minimal. If one adds to that a number of independent contractors engaged by the employer and over which the contractor has no control, delays and disruption are inevitable.

Once on the site, or even before entering the site, the employer's licensees will inevitably cause delay and disruption. In the case of a small item such as a specially designed plaque to be fixed at the very end of the project in the entrance hall of a public building ready for unveiling, the disruption may be relatively small. However, very often the work to be carried out by the employer's licensees may be substantial and it may require carrying out early in the project. For example, the installation of expensive electronic devices may require conduits throughout the building which the employer's licensee insists on fixing itself. Whatever it is, if it is carried out late, so that the contractor is delayed, or sometimes even if it is on time, severe disruption, for which the contractor can claim additional costs, may result.

Having employer's licensees on site is very like giving the contractor a blank cheque. Although the contractor has possession of the site, it has no control over employer's licensees even if there is a clause in the contract to allow them on site. The contractor may notify them and the employer when they are required on site but the contractor cannot impose any sanctions if they are late because they are being paid by the employer. The employer would be able to impose financial sanctions if the employer's contract with the licensees gives the power to do that, assuming there is a contract in place between them. Whether or not there is a contract and whether or not, if there is a contract, there is a suitable clause, we all know that the employer is going to be in the position of having to choose whether to believe the contractor or the employer's licensee. It is obvious that problems will arise in proportion to the quantity and type of work they do and its position in the contract period.

So, the contractor will almost certainly be entitled to extensions of time, loss, and/or expense, and possibly be able to terminate its employment under the terms of the contract.

90

Statutory Undertakers

I always think that this is a slightly odd name for organisations such as water, gas, and electricity companies which are authorised by statute to construct and operate public utility undertakings. They derive their powers from statute. Their powers are extensive, but not absolute and in certain circumstances an action for damages can be brought in the courts.

Statutory undertakers are often involved in construction operations. They can occasionally be a source of frustration when part of the Works is delayed because the statutory undertaker concerned has not turned up on site to make a connection to the main service. It is important to understand that when they are performing their statutory obligations they cannot be liable for breach of contract because they will not have a contract with either employer or contractor. There is a fairly remote possibility that they may be liable in tort in some instances. What is not always appreciated is that statutory authorities will be liable for breach of contract if they enter into a contract with either the employer or the contractor. For example, the electricity companies may undertake electrical work like other electrical contractors and the water authorities may contract to carry out ordinary plumbing work.

If employers or contractors contract with statutory undertakers, they can include clauses in the contracts to deal with delays. This can be contrasted with the undertakers using their statutory powers to carry statutory obligations which may disrupt the contractor and cause delay but for which they cannot be held liable.

It is important to determine in which capacity the statutory undertakers are carrying out work. Statutory undertakers do not enter into contracts to carry out statutory obligations. Therefore, if they say that they will probably perform a specific statutory obligation on certain day and they do not arrive on that day, there is little that can be done except to wait until they do arrive. In practice, it is difficult to get a statutory undertaker to give any precise date. One just has to make the application for whatever is required in good time.

Professional Practice for Architects and Project Managers, First Edition. David Chappell.

91

Variations and Valuation

Definition

There is some confusion about what it means to say that the architect has issued a variation instruction. What is a 'variation'? There are two kinds of variation in connection with building contracts:

- a variation to the Works to be carried out by the contractor
- a variation to the terms of the contract.

All building contracts allow variation instructions to be given to the contractor by the architect varying the Works to be done. Building contracts do not usually allow the architect to vary the terms of the contract itself. To vary the terms of the contract requires an agreement between the employer (not the architect) and the contractor. For example, if the architect wants to issue an instruction requiring the contractor to increase the thickness of a specified bed of concrete, that is allowed, If the architect wants to vary the length of time before the final date for payment from 14 to 21 days, that is not allowed and only the employer and the contractor can do that, by agreement. Some building contracts include a clause to allow the employer to vary certain things, such as hours of work or access, but there will be a price to pay of course. This section only considers variations to the Works.

Does the Contract Allow Variations?

Don't expect to read here all about the variations clauses in forms of contract because they belong in a different kind of book. This simply contains a few reminders, suggestions, and things you might not know. For example, some construction professionals do not realise that an architect cannot issue an instruction for the contractor to carry out a variation to the Works unless there is a clause in the building contract allowing the architect to do so. Without that kind of clause, any variation would have to be agreed between the employer and the contractor as a variation to the contract itself. If the contractor did not agree, there could be no variation.

Professional Practice for Architects and Project Managers, First Edition. David Chappell.

Is There an Implied Term?

It is sometimes said that in every contract a term must be implied that allows the architect to instruct variations. That is wrong. A contract requiring the contractor to carry out the Works shown on specific drawings and described in the specification without a variation clause would require the contractor to construct the building exactly as drawn and described. The contractor could simply ignore any variation instructions. In practice, we all know that a contractor in that situation would carry out the instruction and apply for payment. We all know that it is very likely that appropriate payment would be made and that would be that. But what we are talking about in practice is architects and contractors doing things that the contract does not allow. What people do and what people should do are often quite different.

Change in Scope

Where there is a variation clause in the contract, if the extent of the variation or its nature is quite different from what was originally envisaged in the building contract the contractor can refuse to carry it out. A favourite expression of contractors trying to seek some financial advantage is that the variation caused a change to the whole scope and character of the Works.

In practice it is very rare for a variation to try and change the whole scope and character of the Works. In order to succeed in that argument, it seems that the contractor would have to show that there was a really significant difference. That kind of difference might be if the architect tried to instruct the contractor to construct a different kind of building, for example to change the Works from a large private house to a clinic, or where the instructed work was unrelated to the original contract Works.

Valuation

When additional work is properly instructed, its value should be calculated on the basis of the value of the work as stated in the contract. Therefore, if a particular amount of moulded concrete fascia was priced at £500 a metre run, an instruction to add a further 2 m would result in an additional cost of £1000. Many contracts add sensible provisions to the variation clause. A common one is that the valuation rate will vary with the amount of additional work of a particular kind. If that kind of provision was applied to the example above the valuation would probably not change, but if the run of fascia was increased by 50 m, the rate per metre would be adjusted downwards so as to be, perhaps, £400 or £450. But it is important to remember that adjustment to the rate can only take place if the contract says that it is to happen.

Reducing Variations is a Good Thing

Very often, the need for variations arises because the employer was in too much of a hurry to start on site and the architect was not able to convince the employer that an hour's thought before the contract is finalised is worth 100 hours later. This is particularly the case where a contract containing many provisional sums is signed (see 92: Provisional and Prime Cost Sums). The dangers of provisional sums are twofold. The obvious one is that the sum included in the contract may not be enough to pay for the work to be done or materials to be supplied. Less obvious is the fact that the contractor has no obligation to include provisional sum work in the programme unless it is very clearly defined so as to enable the contractor to know how long the work will take. Most provisional sums are very briefly described, for example 'sink unit', 'sanitary fittings' or 'garden paving'. When the architect instructs the contractor to expend the provisional sum in these cases, it is equivalent to instructing a variation to the Works. Only at that point does the contractor know how long the work is likely to take and it may well cause a delay to the project for which the architect must issue an extension of time. It may also cause the contractor loss and/or expense that can be claimed from the employer. Therefore, extra time taken pre-contract, to specify everything that can be specified and clearly defining any provisional sum work that cannot be defined for one reason or another, is time well spent.

A Final Thought

If a variation becomes necessary (or perhaps the employer thinks so) the employer always asks how much it is going to cost. Do not be tempted to give an off-the-cuff estimate because, as with all estimates, the employer will cling to that figure and be astounded if the final cost is a penny more. In those circumstances, the quantity surveyor must provide all estimates. It is useful to include something in the contract documents which imposes a time limit for the contractor to provide a quotation if so required.

92

Provisional and Prime Cost Sums

Not Difficult

I still vividly remember when I was a student of architecture hearing a lecturer explain provisional and prime cost, or as he called them 'PC', sums. It was memorable for all the wrong reasons. He began by saying how very difficult and confusing these terms were and that he would do his best to explain them but that few in the construction industry actually understood them. Having thus primed us and ensured that a good many of us simply switched off on the basis that it was pointless to listen if the subject was incomprehensible, he proceeded to confuse us for the rest of the lecture.

Actually, the terms are very simple and straightforward.

Provisional Sum

A provisional sum is a sum of money included in the contract by the employer, normally as an amount in the bills of quantities or list of prices. The idea is that it will cover the cost of something which is required as part of the building, but that has not been fully detailed or decided at the time tenders are invited. Provisional sums are commonly included for items such as sanitary fittings and kitchen fittings in houses, perhaps because the employer has not decided exactly what they want. It may be clear that a great deal of stone paving is needed, but no paving layout has been agreed and the employer, as usual, cannot wait and wants work to start. The architect in conjunction with the employer and the quantity surveyor, if appointed, will decide on a sum of money to include in the contract for the paving.

Let's say the sum is £12 000. During the progress of the Works on site the architect will prepare a paving layout and get the employer's agreement. The architect then instructs the contractor to omit the provisional sum and add the value of the paving as designed. The value is calculated in accordance with the way the contract states that variations are to be valued. If there is no price for any other paving in the contract, the contractor may be asked to submit a quotation or, more likely, the quantity surveyor will work out a fair price. The actual price may be £9750. Thus the £12 000 was 'provisional' until the design was prepared and the final sum for the paving is calculated as £9750, which would become a prime cost sum. One hopes that the provisional sum is sufficient to cover the actual cost, but whether it does or not, the provisional sum will be replaced by the actual calculated sum by the time the final account is prepared. Wherever there is a

Professional Practice for Architects and Project Managers, First Edition. David Chappell.

provisional sum, the architect must issue an instruction for the work it represents even if the instruction is simply to omit it.

Some contracts differentiate between provisional sums for defined or undefined work. In general terms, a provisional sum for defined work is where the contractor is notified of some basic facts about the work in the contract, such as the kind of work, its construction, its place in the building and the amount. Undefined work will give very simple information. In the example above, undefined work would simple state 'Paving'. Defined work might say '100 m^2 of natural stone paving to the front of the dwelling laid to falls and steps in paths'.

The significance is that if the work is defined, the contractor is deemed to have made due allowance for programming and pricing of preliminaries. Therefore, when the architect issues an instruction to omit the sum and add the paving as designed, the contractor is not entitled to notify a delay. The position with undefined provisional sums is quite different. In the example above, all the contractor knows is that it is for paving, without more information the contractor cannot hazard even a reasonable guess as to the length of time it may take to do the work or indeed when the work can be done within the context of the whole project. Therefore, an instruction from the architect to carry out work in a provisional sum for undefined work is treated as an instruction to carry out additional work and if it causes delay, the contractor will be entitled to an extension of time.

Sometimes a contractor asked to price a schedule of work or bill of quantities will insert provisional sums. I once saw a schedule of works in which the contractor had inserted provisional sums for almost every item. Remarkably a contract was entered into on that basis, but of course, after the architect had instructed each item, each provisional sum was replaced by the actual cost which, not surprisingly, was more than the provisional sum in each case. An architect who allows that to happen may well be sued for negligence. Obviously, provisional sums inserted instead of an accurate price by a contractor must be rejected.

Prime Cost Sums

A prime cost or PC sum is a sum of money included in the contract by the employer, normally as an amount in the bills of quantities or list of prices. That sounds exactly like a provisional sum. The difference is that a prime cost sum is a precise sum of money included in the contract to be expended on materials or goods from suppliers or on work to be carried out by sub-contractors nominated by the employer. It must be an exact figure because it should be the amount quoted to the employer or the architect by the supplier or sub-contractor. Even when a PC sum is included in the contract, it is often put down as a rounded-up figure. For example, if the employer obtains a quotation from a specialist firm of window manufacturers amounting to £5780, the figure will probably be put in the contract as £6000. The extra £280 is in fact a little contingency fund for unexpected extras. However, strictly speaking, in that case the sum is a provisional sum and not a PC sum because it does not represent the final value of the work.

Conclusion

That is the correct position, but in practice the phrases 'PC sums' and 'provisional sums' are used indiscriminately. That is possibly because many people in the construction industry are as confused as I used to be. Remember, a provisional sum is a notional figure which is hoped to cover the cost of the item while a PC sum is a precise figure based on a quotation. Contractor's profit is not added to provisional sums, but it is added to PC sums. It may be expended as the architect instructs, upon which a prime cost sum may arise.

93

Workmanship and Materials

Goods and Materials

There are four names often found in building contracts which can be confusing: goods, materials, workmanship, and workmanlike manner. Two of them are found in the phrase 'goods and materials'. Most building contracts draw a distinction between 'goods' and 'materials'. In building practice, the things used to construct the building, bricks, sand and cement, timber, nails, screws, etc., which are the raw elements of the building before any work has been done, are called 'materials'. Things such as door furniture, kitchen, and sanitary fittings are normally described as 'goods'. Certain acts of Parliament lump them together as 'goods'.

Inability to Obtain

Occasionally, in some forms of contract, the contractor is only to provide goods and materials 'so far as they are procurable', i.e. obtainable. This appears to be a perfectly innocuous statement until one day the contractor points to that particular clause in the contract to excuse the fact that something specified is not obtainable or, perhaps, not obtainable quickly or easily or at the price the contractor put in its tender. If you are faced with this in a contract you are administering, you must read the clause very carefully because slight changes in wording can make a great deal of difference.

The first thing to remember is that goods are still procurable even if they cost more than the contractor envisioned. So a higher price is no excuse. The fact that goods are on slow delivery or not easy to obtain does not usually mean they are not procurable. However, we all know that slow delivery or difficulty in being able to obtain goods can sometimes mean that for all practical purposes, they are not procurable. The question then is: when did it become known that there was a problem with either of these two situations? The answer seems to be that if the contractor could have discovered by reasonable enquiry before tendering that specified goods were simply unobtainable or extremely difficult to obtain or on an unreasonably long delivery period but still included them in its tender, the contractor will be liable for the inability to either obtain the goods at all or within a time period which enabled the project to be completed without delay. In those circumstances, the employer may not be able to insist on having those particular goods, but it will be a matter for the contractor to suggest suitable alternatives at no increase in cost.

Professional Practice for Architects and Project Managers, First Edition. David Chappell.

General point: occasionally the tenderer may raise a procurement problem with the architect during the tender period. On enquiry, the architect may be told by the supplier that there is no problem, at which point the architect may instruct the tenderer to proceed with the pricing for the supply of the material. If it subsequently transpires that the material is unobtainable, the architect will be obliged to instruct the use of an alternative material at a variation in cost.

On the other hand, if the contractor could not have discovered difficulties with goods by reasonable enquiry at tender stage, it will be the employer who must instruct the contractor, through the architect, to obtain and use different goods. The employer will then have to pay the difference in cost.

Workmanship and Workmanlike Manner

Workmanship refers to the skill in carrying out a task. Like the much-abused word 'quality', the word is severely limited in meaning unless provided with an adjective. Although you can say 'I am going to check the workmanship', just as you can say 'I am going to check the quality', it cannot be used alone to describe the standard of workmanship. You have to say 'good' workmanship or 'bad' workmanship or even 'acceptable' workmanship. So, what is the difference between 'workmanship' and the words 'workmanlike manner'? Of course, the first is a noun and the second is an adverb. For those who tend to glaze over at being told the names of parts of a sentence, like I used to do, what I am fumbling my way to saying is that 'workmanlike manner' is referring to the way in which an operative does the work rather than the finished product. It is closely linked to questions of health and safety.

The finished product should be of 'good workmanship', but in order to produce it, it is necessary for the operative to do the work in a workmanlike manner. It is to be assumed that 'workmanlike' refers to a good rather than a bad or indifferent workman. In the absence of an express term to the contrary, the contractor is under a general obligation at law to carry out its work in a good and workmanlike manner. Express terms of the contract sometimes impose a higher obligation. The two terms are obviously related because although a concrete floor in its finished state is a matter of workmanship, the process of preparing and fixing formwork and mixing and pouring the concrete may or may not be accomplished in a workmanlike manner. Having said that, if the floor is not laid in a workmanlike manner, it is unlikely to result in good workmanship.

94

Materials Off-Site

Different Situations

Some building contracts allow the architect to certify for payment for materials stored off the site. There was a time when it was left to the architect to decide whether or not to include in a certificate the value of materials or goods stored by the contractor off site. More recently, building contracts have, rightly, been tightened so that in many contracts payment for materials off site is hedged around by sets of rules. In most cases, the off-site storage takes place in the contractor's yard or storage facility, but occasionally a contractor will try to get payment for materials still on the supplier's premises. There are no circumstances where an architect should certify materials which are still at the suppliers where even the contractor has no control over them.

Why Certify?

Why certify payment for off-site material at all? Good question. The answer inevitably comes down to cash and, more particularly, cash flow. The contractor has to make sure that it has the materials on hand when required, but to do that means the tying up of large amounts of money. The contractor is always in the position of having to do work before being paid and, usually, by the time a payment is made the contractor has almost completed twice the value of work shown in the architect's certificate. In the normal way, materials on site, if not brought onto the site prematurely, are included in the certificate, but it would be premature to bring onto the site materials which may not be required for weeks, but must be obtained and stored to avoid delays. Moreover, there is no space available on most building sites for large quantities of materials. Hence the contractor's concern to be paid for materials for which the contractor has either already paid or, more likely, has a legal obligation to pay.

Problems

Inclusion of off-site materials in a certificate may raise serious practical problems. Often, contracts state that, once the employer has paid for them, the materials become the employer's property and the contractor is not permitted to remove the materials, nor to

Professional Practice for Architects and Project Managers, First Edition. David Chappell.

allow anyone else to do so, except for use on the Works. All the while, the contractor is to remain responsible to the employer for any loss or damage. But how can the architect be sure that the materials or goods are being held safely in the contractor's yard or storeroom? The short answer is that the architect cannot be sure. Different contracts set out different regulations before off-site materials can be certified.

A common stipulation is that the materials or goods should be set on one side and clearly labelled as being for the employer's project. Architects or quantity surveyors will be sure to visit the contractor's premises to make sure that the rules are complied with before certification. The director of a contracting company once explained to me how he had, in his view, neatly got around this problem. He said that, at a time when the company was very short of cash, he had secured the contracts for two fairly substantial housing schemes for different employers. It was his great good fortune, he said, that all the sink units and sanitary fittings were exactly the same specification for both contracts and in similar although not identical quantities. He ordered and had delivered to his large storeroom all the sink units and sanitary fittings for the larger of the two projects and lined them up on the left side of the door as one entered the room. They were all labelled clearly as being destined for the largest project. The quantity surveyor duly arrived, inspected and approved the goods and left, saying that they would be included in the next valuation. Once he had left, the correct number of goods were moved to the right-hand side of the door and relabelled for the other project in time for the arrival of the other quantity surveyor the following day. The excess goods were covered with sheets. The other quantity surveyor duly arrived and confirmed that the goods would be included in the next valuation.

The director saw no ethical problems with what he had done. So far as he was concerned the ruse simply gave him some cash in hand and both employers eventually got their goods. I did not task him over the ethical aspect but wondered why he went to the trouble of moving the goods from one side of the door to the other. He was obviously expecting this and said: 'I know that quantity surveyors often talk to each other, perhaps over a pint at the pub. They might realise that they could both have been looking at the same goods. Then one might say, "Whereabouts were they?" and the other would say, "On the right-hand side as you walk into his warehouse". Then the other would say "That's alright then because the ones I saw were on the left."' He laughed long and hard about that. Obviously, if the contractor had gone bust after being paid by both employers, some serious questions would have been aimed at the quantity surveyors concerned, who would certainly not have been laughing. It is always difficult to be sure that the materials inspected at the contractor's yard are not really intended for some other project.

How can the Employer be Protected?

The contract may stipulate what steps must be taken to protect the employer if it is thought prudent to certificate off-site materials. If the contract says nothing, but the employer is happy for the materials off-site to be certified for payment, here are a few things to bear in mind:

- Whether the materials to be certified are on or off the site, it should go without saying that they must be exactly as specified. There are no circumstances under which it is acceptable to certify visibly defective materials.

- The contractor must have provided reasonable proof of ownership of the materials. This is not an easy thing to do. Probably the best that you can do is to be as sure as possible that there is nothing which suggests that the contractor does not own the items, for example the contractor should provide proof that it has paid for the materials. One of the problems is that there may be what is known as a 'retention of title' clause in the supply contract. That is a clause which states that the supplier retains ownership of the materials until they are paid for. If you do not get proof that the contractor has paid for them, the supplier will still own the materials even after you have certified them and the employer has paid the contractor. Even if the contract states that ownership passes to the employer as soon as the contractor has been paid, it does not affect the situation because the supplier is not bound by the contract between the employer and the contractor. The contractor cannot give ownership to the employer if the contractor does not own the materials in the first place. Therefore, it is essential that the contractor provides proof of payment.
- The contractor must provide proof that the materials are insured for their full value under a policy which protects employer and contractor. The policy must cover the whole period from the commencement of the contractor's ownership to delivery to the Works.
- The materials must be set apart from other goods or materials and they must be clearly marked to identify the project and the employer.
- To be certain that the employer is fully protected, the contractor must have provided a bond (see 21: Bonds and Parent Company Guarantees).

95

Payment

What Kind of Payments are We Talking About?

In the building construction world, payments are usually made by the employer to the contractor in return for the construction of a building. Payments are rarely made as a single payment unless the project is very small. Normally payment is made to the contractor as the work progresses and in arrears so that, at any given time, the contractor has done a greater value of work than that for which it has been paid. That is good for the employer but not good for the contractor if the employer suddenly stops paying. The contractor makes payment to its own workforce and to suppliers of goods and materials and to sub-contractors. Suppliers and sub-contractors pay their suppliers and so on down the chain. This system can cause severe cash flow problems, particularly for small companies at supplier level and below, because, although the law now stops contractors from formally operating the dreaded 'pay-when-paid' (commonly known as the 'pay-if-paid') system, the reality is that small suppliers and sub-contractors often have to wait for their money. The practice of making payments to the contractor at intervals throughout the contract period is to ease cashflow. Most building contracts now make the payment of the contractor dependent on the architect issuing a certificate showing the amount to be paid. The exception to that is of course a design and build contract, where it is the contractor that applies for the amount it believes is due.

Something to Forget

Not very long ago, it was the custom for architects to issue payment certificates (often called 'interim certificates') roughly every four weeks. I say 'roughly' because in my experience some architects could be quite cavalier about the timing. Occasionally the four weeks could in practice stretch to six weeks, but in any event it was rare for certificates to be issued at exactly four-week (or whatever the agreed period) intervals. Generally, the variation was only a few days early or late and serious complaints from the contractor were not common. Everyone understood that payment had to be paid no later than 14 days (some local authorities changed that to 21 days on the unconvincing premise that their computer which generated cheques required three weeks to process anything) from the date of the architect's certificate. As an aside: when I worked for local authorities in the past, I found that if one sat next to the desk of the Chief Finance Offer and refused to budge until he produced the required cheque, he or she would eventually

Professional Practice for Architects and Project Managers, First Edition. David Chappell.

discover, with many a sigh, that the council did have a chequebook and he did have a pen and a cheque could actually be produced in a few minutes of reasonable effort.

The point is that in the case of any contract other than one concerning a residential property for a resident owner, the date of the architect's certificate is no longer the important date. The days when the architect could issue certificates on a date the architect found convenient are over, so just forget that.

Something to Remember

Since the Housing Grants, Construction and Regeneration Act 1996, the key date is something which is usually referred to as the 'due date'. I have promised not to delve into long explanations of Acts of Parliament or building contracts because these things are updated or amended frequently and what I say about them today may be out of date in a few months' time, so let's stick to basics. The only thing of value that I will say about the issue of certificates is that you must read what it says in the contract about when you are to issue certificates and how you are to issue them. Forget the past and remember that if you fail to issue the payment certificate within the window of time allowed by the contract, your certificate will be invalid and the contractor will be able to issue something called a payment notice. Unless the employer then issues a 'pay less notice' (see below) within the prescribed time period, the contractor will be entitled to what it demands.

Pay Less Notice

Put simply, if the employer wishes to pay less than the amount certified by the architect or included in a payment notice from the contactor, the employer's only way is to give the contractor a pay less notice. This is simply a letter from the employer to the contractor specifying the amount that the employer considers to be due to the contractor on the date the letter is given to the contractor. Included in the letter must be the basis on which the employer has calculated the amount. It must also be sent before the deadline stated in the contract.

Before any architect rings the RIBA to ask the question, I should make clear that there is no such thing as a 'pay more notice'.

Over-certification by the Architect

When you certify the amount due to the contractor, it is not essential that you get the figure precisely right. The purpose of certifying payments, as noted earlier, is to provide the contractor with adequate cashflow. From that point of view, it does not matter if the amount certified is rather more or less than the exact sum which would represent the value of the work properly carried out and the materials reasonably on site. That is because the certifying process is cumulative and the gross amount obviously changes (hopefully increases) in subsequent certificates so that with each certificate the valuation is done again for the whole of the executed Works. Therefore, deviations from the exact sum are corrected in later certificates. Moreover, by the time the employer has to pay the amount certified, the contractor will hopefully have carried out more work on site.

The problem arises when the architect seriously over-certifies and the contractor either walks off site for some reason or, worse, becomes insolvent. That can happen quite suddenly. If the contractor simply walks off site, the employer may still recover any losses by using the dispute resolution mechanism in the contract. If the contractor becomes insolvent, the employer has virtually no hope of recovering any amount over-certified and paid. In that situation, the employer may well be able to recover the over-payment from the architect on the basis of the architect's negligent certification.

Some architects believe that they are insulated from that danger if they simply certify what the quantity surveyor gives them as a valuation. This is the point at which you should ask yourself when was the last time you heard of a quantity surveyor being sued for negligence? The hard fact is that under most building contracts, it is the architect who is responsible for certifying payment. The architect can certify a different amount from the valuation figure provided by the quantity surveyor and must do so unless satisfied that the quantity surveyor's valuation is correct. That is one reason why the project quantity surveyor must not issue copies of the valuation to the contractor. The valuation is carried out for the benefit of the architect. The architect is not expected to revalue the work done with the same degree of accuracy expected from a quantity surveyor, but the architect must always be provided with a breakdown of the valuation from the quantity surveyor so that it can be roughly checked during a walk around the site. For example, it is important that the quantity surveyor is notified of all defects in the Works and that no defective work is valued. Architects are well advised to err slightly on the low side in certifying payment.

Banks

It is quite common for employers to be funded by banks or mortgage companies. In those cases, the payments to the employer are usually preceded by a site visit from a surveyor appointed by the bank or mortgage company. The surveyor's job is to make sure that the work done on site is worth at least the amount being advanced at each stage.

It is important to understand that the activities and opinion of the surveyor have no relevance to the amount the architect certifies. In other words, you must not simply certify what the bank or mortgage company is prepared to advance. That is a matter for the employer to sort out. You must always form your own view of the amount you certify, otherwise the certificate does not represent your professional opinion, you will certainly not be acting in a professional manner, and the certificate may well be invalid.

96

Delays and Extensions of Time

Back to Basics

It is really important to understand why building contracts have clauses to allow the architect to extend the time for completion of the Works.

Let's suppose that Ms Smith wants Mr Brown the builder to build her a brick wall round her rear garden because she wants to stop her dog straying into other gardens nearby. They agree the length, thickness, and height of the wall, its cost and that Mr Brown will start on Monday and finish on the following Friday. By Wednesday, he is making good progress and Ms Smith is so pleased that she asks him if he can incorporate a small enclosure attached to the wall and with a simple roof on for her lawn mower. He agrees and they agree an extra £500 for the work. Friday arrives and it is clear that Mr Brown will not be complete until about the following Tuesday due to the extra work. Ms Smith is upset by this. Can she insist that he finishes the Works by the end of Friday as agreed or pay her damages for the delay, or can she give him an extension of time to a date she thinks is fair and reasonable, or is Mr Brown entitled to finish within a reasonable but unknown time?

The answer is that Ms Smith cannot insist on the original date for completion because, by asking him to do more work, she has prevented Mr Brown from finishing on Friday so she cannot recover damages from him. She cannot give him an extension of time that she thinks is fair and reasonable because they never agreed that she should be able to do that. The law says that in those circumstances, Mr Brown is entitled to complete within a reasonable time. What is a reasonable time? It is a period of time which is reasonable after taking all the relevant circumstances into account (see 26: Reasonable Time). Neither Ms Smith nor Mr Brown can say what that is. Therefore, provided that Mr Brown continues working at the same pace, Ms Smith will have nothing to complain about, although no doubt she will. When a contractor's obligation to finish a project by a certain date is changed to an obligation to finish within a reasonable time, it is commonly referred to as time becoming 'at large', i.e. no fixed time any more. In practice, it rarely happens.

Building Contracts

I have not known any project yet which finished on the date for completion agreed in the contract (please don't write in). Almost every contract has variations or delays for one reason or another. It would be unacceptable if every slight delay or variation resulted in time becoming at large and the contractor being able to finish, if not whenever it chose, something very like that. Therefore, building contracts always have a clause which allows the architect to give a reasonable extension of time for various reasons.

Most contracts list the reasons. They usually fall into two categories which we can call 'employer's actions or inactions' and 'neutral causes'.

Employer's actions or inactions include anything that the employer or the architect may do which causes a delay to the date for completion. So, instructions requiring variations or postponing part of the Works or the employer, having agreed to supply various goods or materials, failing to do so, all fall into that category; in short, all those things which are the responsibility of the employer and which may cause the completion date to be missed.

Neutral causes are all those things which may cause the completion date to be missed but which are not the fault of either the employer or the contractor. These include such things as adverse weather conditions, strikes, and statutory services. Although it is essential to have an extension of time clause dealing with employer's actions or inactions, to prevent time becoming at large, it is not necessary to include neutral events. They would not render time at large if they were excluded. The contractor would be expected to deal with them. The fact that some neutral causes are often included as events for which the contractor is entitled to an extension of time is a concession to the contractor.

But note that, if the architect failed to use the power in the contract to extend time when it is clear that the architect should have done so, time would still become at large. Therefore, every architect called upon to decide whether a contractor is entitled to an extension of time must take great care to arrive at a fair and reasonable period and comply exactly with the contract clause. Nowadays, it is extremely unusual for time to be declared at large because it does not really help the parties. A court or arbitrator is more likely to decide on the amount of extension of time that should have been given.

Dealing with Extensions of Time

You can find lots of books demonstrating how to make claims and how to respond to them, some of them mine. This is not the place for a detailed treatise, but it is the place where I can share some of what I hope are useful tips to bear in mind. It is quite common for contractors, seeking an extension of time, to bombard the architect with reams of paper purporting to show the effect of various delays on the progress of the Works by means of computer-generated programmes. This, together with accompanying long lists of delays, should be treated with a certain amount of scepticism. Although at first sight it may seem impressive, if it is difficult to follow the reasoning, it is worse than useless.

Use of Programmes

The most important programme in this scenario is the contractor's original programme submitted at the start of the project, showing the length of each activity, the logic links between activities, the lead and lag times, and the labour and plant resources (see 71: Contractor's Programme). It should be accompanied by a network analysis in electronic form. The invitation to tender and the contract documents should make clear that the contractor is required to produce a programme in this form. It is the most important programme because later programmes issued by the contractor can be massaged. Linking activities from the end of one activity to the start of another will produce an entirely different result from what would happen if activities were linked start to start. Although the initial network programme is rarely made a contract document, it is valuable because it shows the contractor's intentions at the commencement of the Works. It can easily be turned into a Gantt (bar) chart for plotting progress, but it is much better than a Gantt chart.

Using a Computer

All kinds of computer techniques have been suggested in order to assess delays. I once employed a programme planning consultant to work on the contractor's programme to assist the contractor in making a case for an extension of time. The simplest and, in my view, the overall most useful, although unsophisticated, method for dealing with numerous delays is as follows:

- The architect makes a list of all the delays alleged by the contractor.
- The cause of the delay must be established. If it falls into the category of delays which the contract states would entitle the contractor to an extension of time, it should stay on the list. Any other kind of delay should be removed from the list.
- The architect considers what effect each separate delay had by looking at clerks of work's reports, site meeting minutes, and other indicators of progress. So, if concrete in the foundations is delayed, the architect might conclude that the time taken for pouring the concrete was extended by the delay from the originally programmed four weeks to five weeks and three days.
- All the additional periods of time are inputted into relevant activities in the original programme. The knock-on effects of the delay to one activity should not be calculated for successive activities – the computer program will do that. The computer program will calculate the effect on the date for completion of the whole project. The result will show what would have happened if the contractor has progressed the Works exactly as shown on its programme without taking any steps to mitigate the delay. Therefore, that will be the maximum time to which the contractor could conceivably be entitled. Once measures for mitigating the delay are taken into account, that time should be reduced. As can be seen, this is a very rough guide to the amount of extension of time to which the contractor is entitled, but it is a useful baseline. If, before inputting the delays, the architect jots down his or her gut feeling about the length of the extension of time and compares it with the eventual result, it is interesting to see how often the two correlate.

Without a Computer

Everyone knows that a computer performs thousands of calculations in the same it would take an ordinary human to perform one and a computer can be programmed to carry out these calculations in a specific way. That is the key benefit of using a computer to deal with extensions of time. But that does not mean that it is always necessary to use a computer. Computers are not a magic answer to all the architect's or the contractor's problems. Any significant error in the data being fed into the computer program can invalidate the whole analysis. One has only to consider the cases where expert programmers for each side produce widely differing results from what seem to be identical data.

It is quite possible to decide on the critical path by applying reason and common sense to deduce the effect of delays. This is particularly the case where the number of delays is limited. I have often seen the eyes of an adjudicator glaze over when presented with sheet after sheet of computer-generated programme charts while, in other circumstances, the adjudicator can become very involved in considering a claim for, or a decision about, an extension of time presented in simple graphics with clear explanatory text linked to evidence of the facts.

A Final Two Points

- It is worth remembering that the architect is not required to decide a precisely accurate extension of time, but merely one that is fair and reasonable. Therefore, the architect has a certain amount of latitude, but not a great amount.
- Anecdotal evidence suggests that if the question of extension of time is referred to adjudication and the architect has given no extension of time at all, the chances are that the adjudicator will award some extension. If the architect has already awarded some extension, but the contractor wants more, it is less likely that the adjudicator will award more.
- The third of the two points is that many contractors, quantity surveyors, and architects believe that if the contractor is given an extension of time, it will be entitled to some money. With the possible exception of the NEC contracts, that belief is quite wrong. All that an extension of time does is to allow the contractor more time to complete the Works, so that no liquidated damages are payable for that period. If the contractor is looking for additional money, it must comply with the procedure in the contract for claiming loss and/or expense, or make a claim at common law through the courts (see 99: Financial Claims).

97

Liquidated Damages

Damages

Before looking at liquidated damages it is important to understand what is meant by damages. Damages are the sum of money which is claimed by a person or organisation. They are claimed to compensate the claimant for some wrong they have suffered. For example, if you purchase a holiday abroad from a travel agent and the holiday turns out to be nothing like what was advertised, you might claim damages (i.e. compensation) for the ruined holiday. The claim may be against the travel agent or the holiday company or both depending on circumstances. You will say that there has been a breach of contract. If a surgeon carries out an operation on you which leaves you severely handicapped and the reason is that the surgeon was negligent, you may claim damages which a court will award. The idea of damages is to put the person who is claiming in the same position, as far as money will do that, as if the holiday had been as described or the operation had been properly carried out.

Liquidated or Unliquidated Damages

Liquidated damages are given that name to differentiate them from the kind of damages claimed in the example above, which are unliquidated or general damages. To claim unliquidated damages, it is necessary to prove that there has been some wrongful act (such as breach of contract or negligence) committed by the person from whom the damages are claimed. Then it must be shown that the act caused some kind of damage to the claimant and the amount of that damage must be calculated and proved. If the person does not pay up, the claimant will have to take the matter to a court or, if a construction contract is involved, to arbitration or adjudication. As can be imagined, all this is usually quite expensive.

Liquidated Damages

In order to avoid all this expense, in suitable situations liquidated damages are used. Obviously, there is no scope for liquidated damages in negligence cases, but where an employer suffers loss because a building contractor does not finish the construction work (let's not use that awful slovenly term 'the build') by the dated fixed for

Professional Practice for Architects and Project Managers, First Edition. David Chappell.

completion, liquidated damages is tailor-made. Most construction contracts include a clause providing for liquidated damages in the case of delay caused by the contractor. The idea is simple: employer and contractor agree on a fixed sum to be paid by the contractor to the employer for every day or week that the contractor fails to complete by the fixed date. This sum is then written into the contract so that there cannot be any argument about it later. (That is not strictly true, of course, because there can always be arguments and if you want to read the arguments that can arise, please turn to 98: Penalties, but not before you have finished reading this please.) For example, the liquidated damages for a small house might be £500 per week. When I say that the 'employer and the contractor agree on a fixed sum' I do not mean that they should sit down and hammer out the figure between them. No, they 'agree' in the sense that the employer puts a figure in the contract which the contractor signs, thus signifying agreement.

Rules and Myths

You will not be surprised to learn that there are things you can and can't do with regard to liquidated damages and that there are myths which concern those things. When I was an architect in a large city architect's department, I thought the council should take advantage of the liquidated damages clause in a long overdue contract. What would now be called my 'line manager', but then was simply called the 'principal architect' of our little group informed me that, as it was a 'contract matter', it must be referred to the principal quantity surveyor, who knew about such things. When consulted, the principal quantity surveyor sucked on his pipe (those were the days) and told me gravely that liquidated damages was a very complex matter and that they should never be imposed unless the employer could prove the loss. That was complete nonsense, even I knew it was nonsense. That encounter was a huge contributory factor in my decision to focus on construction law for the rest of my career.

Once the figure is in the contract and the contract is signed, the amount stated can be deducted or claimed by the employer after a delay even if the employer has not suffered any loss at all or even if the employer has actually made a profit by the delay. On the other hand, the employer cannot claim more than the amount stated even if it happens that the loss is twice as much as the figure in the contract.

Calculating a Figure

So, can the employer simply insert any figure which comes to mind? Although it might seem like a good idea to insert £15 000 per week for a small house, if that amount was deducted for delay, it is likely that the contractor could use whatever dispute resolution procedure was in the contract to have the amount declared a penalty (see 98: Penalties, but not yet) and unenforceable. The figure inserted must be an attempt to represent what the employer honestly believes to be the loss that will be suffered for every week of delay. It is useful to know that in cases where the employer has very little information to use to calculate the likely loss, a best guess is acceptable. Essentially, it should not be exorbitant when compared to the importance to the employer of getting the building completed on time.

It is always the employer's job to state the liquidated damages rate to put in the contract, but the employer is entitled to expect the architect to give some advice. The following is a list of some of the costs that may be included in liquidated damages, but all projects are different and it is important that the employer includes every cost which will result from a delay to the completion date:

- architect's and other consultants' additional fees
- clerk of works additional salary
- rent for alternative accommodation
- storage of equipment or furniture
- movement of staff
- insurance
- interest on capital outlay
- inflation.

When the employer has finished adding all the likely costs together, it may be a substantial sum per week. At that point, it is important to look at the liquidated damages amount in relation to the likely total cost of the project and consider the extent to which contractors may increase their tender prices. The managing director of the contractor where I used to work always called a meeting to decide on his price. He would ask the estimator for the total cost and then ask the contracts manager how long it would take to build. Then he would ask the length of the contract period and if it was less than the time the contract manager quoted, the managing director would ask for the rate of liquidated damages, multiply the rate with the projected overrun, and then add the result to his tender figure. If the liquidated damages was a substantial sum per week, he would add a little something extra. I am certain that other contractors did much the same thing. With this in mind, the employer has to decide whether it is worthwhile including the whole of the expected delay costs as liquidated damages or whether to include a lesser rate.

If you put a figure 'per week' only whole weeks can be counted. Some architects write 'per week or part thereof' thinking that means that for three days of delay the employer may deduct three sevenths of the weekly figure. What it actually means is that the employer can deduct the whole figure for a week or any part of a week. That may be a penalty and unenforceable. What was intended was £XXX per week or pro rata for periods of less than a week. Alternatively, you could specify the liquidated damages per day. But would that mean that if the three days were Saturday, Sunday and Monday, it would be a penalty for Saturday and Sunday if there was no work done on those days? Probably not, but one cannot be sure. It is permissible to set out the liquidated damages in stages so that for, say, the first two weeks one figure is deductible but the figure increases by a set amount for every other week of delay. This may reflect an increasing rate of loss to the employer.

If the employer wishes to recover unliquidated damages, the liquidated damages provision in the contract must be deleted in its entirety. Then the ordinary principle of damage recovery, explained earlier, will apply. Do not make the mistake of writing £Nil as the figure for liquidated damages because that will not change the damages to unliquidated, it will simply mean that every week of delay will incur £Nil damages and 10 weeks of delay will still amount to £Nil.

Process

Most contracts stipulate, and in any event it is good practice, that the contractor must be warned by a notice (in other words a letter) before the damages are deducted. The notice should state the length of the overrun and the rate of damages multiplied together to give the total amount to be deducted. The employer may deduct less than that but not more.

Sometimes, an employer will tell the contractor that liquidated damages will not be deducted. This may be done with the intention of keeping the contractor sweet. But if the employer subsequently has a change of mind and wants to deduct damages after all, it is probable that a court would keep the employer to the promise so that damages could not be deducted even if the Works were considerably delayed. A key factor is whether, following the employer's promise not to deduct, the contractor acted in a way that it would not have done without the promise. For example, if after the promise the contractor paid off all its sub-contractors in full instead of waiting to see the extent of liquidated damages and deducting some of it from the sub-contractors, the employer's change of mind would be a serious problem.

Within these principles, contracts which include a liquidated damages clause have slightly different procedures for claiming the damages and the relevant provisions must be carefully studied.

98

Penalties

If you are reading this before you have read 97: Liquidated Damages, I suggest that you stop, go back, and read 'Liquidated Damages' first.

If you have already read, or if you have gone back and read, 'Liquidated Damages' after my warning, proceed.

Some contractors and even some architects, who should know better, still refer to penalties or the penalty clause when they actually mean liquidated damages. Fortunately, the courts, arbitrators, and adjudicators do not take much account of the name used, but consider the facts in order to decide whether a clause is a penalty or liquidated damages. This is important because penalties are unenforceable. That is to say that if an employer claims them from a contractor the court will reject the claim. If the employer has deducted them, the court will order repayment.

What are penalties? In simple terms, a liquidated damages sum in a contract becomes a penalty if, at the time the contract is entered into, it is a great deal more than the actual likely loss which will be suffered or incurred by the employer if the project is delayed beyond the contract completion date. To be precise, you have to ask yourself the question: when the employer's concern to have the building constructed is taken into account, is the sum in the contract exorbitant or unacceptable? Having said that, it is rare for liquidated damages to be held to be a penalty on that basis alone. However, it is possible for the sum to be considered a penalty in certain circumstances. For example, if a contract is divided into sections and if each section has the same sum as liquidated damages per week but the sections are different sizes and values, it may be held to be a penalty because, the argument goes, if the sum is appropriate for the largest and highest value section, it is clearly too high for the other sections.

Some employers look upon the liquidated damages clause as a means of compelling the contractor to finish on time. On that basis, the sky would be the limit for the sum. That idea is exactly what the penalty rule is intended to stop. Liquidated damages are intended to be a compensation to the employer for the losses incurred if the contractor delays the completion date. It becomes a penalty, invalid and unenforceable, when it is a punishment for being late.

Professional Practice for Architects and Project Managers, First Edition. David Chappell.

99

Financial Claims

Introduction

Although this topic is the lengthiest, it is really just a general survey with some basic advice included. Anyone dealing with financial claims, whether contractor or architect, must become knowledgeable about this complex subject.

Prolongation

Many forms of building contract (but not all) have a clause to allow the contractor to make claims for what may be termed loss and/or expense or expenses or compensation. In other words, the additional loss or expense suffered by the contractor for various reasons over and above the simple additional costs involved in, say, an instruction to carry out extra work. One of the most common forms of claim is for prolongation of the contract period (in other words: delay) due to carrying out the additional work or due to some other reason such as late provision of information by the architect. Although there may be different reasons, the basic cause must be some action or default on the part of the employer or someone for whom the employer is responsible, such as the architect. The contractor may argue that it is entitled to be reimbursed for the extra cost of keeping plant and accommodation on site for the extra period. Although prolongation is the most common cause of financial claims, probably because it seems to be the easiest to put together and understand, there can be other causes, such as disruption. That is where the Works are not necessarily delayed as a whole but where something for which the employer is responsible causes the contractor to have to spend extra money.

Disruption

The best way to understand disruption is to compare it with prolongation. Prolongation occurs because one of the activities on the critical path of the contractor's programme is delayed. Disruption usually occurs when an activity which is not on the critical path is delayed. An activity will not be critical if the time needed to perform it is less than the time available in the programme. For example, if underground drainage will take three weeks to carry out, but there are 10 weeks available to do the work, that activity

Professional Practice for Architects and Project Managers, First Edition. David Chappell.

will not become critical unless it is delayed by longer than the difference between the two periods, i.e. seven weeks. This 'spare' time is usually referred to as the 'float'. The completion date of the whole project is not delayed but the contractor nevertheless suffers loss because one of the operations which should have taken, say, three weeks, now takes six weeks (see 71: Contractor's Programme).

Types of Claim

There are also two principal categories of financial claim:

- a claim based on what is allowed by the claims clause in the building contract
- a claim for damages for breach of contract under common law.

Claims clauses in building contracts usually set out exactly what may be claimed and exactly what must be done by both parties when a claim is made. A contractor who is making a claim under the claims clause in the contract must be careful to do everything in accordance with the clause. The claims clause will usually state the kind of things for which the contractor can submit a claim. It is important to understand that these are the only kinds of claims that can be submitted by the contractor under the contract. For example, the claims clause may include architect's instructions requiring a variation. It may include late instructions and failure to give access to the site.

It is always open to the contractor to make a claim for damages for breach of contract instead of or as well as claiming using the contract procedures. A claim for breach of contract can only be made, of course, if the employer is in breach of contract, either directly or through the actions of the architect or other consultants. So, if the contract allows a financial claim for the result of an architect's instruction requiring a variation, the contractor cannot choose to make that claim as a breach of contract. That is because it cannot be a breach of contract for the architect to issue instructions if the contract allows instructions to be given.

An advantage of claiming a breach of contract is that the contractor does not have to comply with the contract procedure. Therefore, if the contract states that a contractor must claim within a specific time period after the event and the time period has elapsed, the contractor can still claim at common law if the event was a breach of contract. A disadvantage is that the architect is not usually empowered to decide claims for breach of contract and if the employer is not prepared to negotiate, the claim would have to go to one of the dispute resolution procedures as set out in the contract.

The following are some of the common heads of claim.

On-Site Establishment Costs

The contractor will often call this 'preliminaries' or 'site overheads'. There is a practice which has grown up in which the contractor's application for loss and/or expense will be based on a number of weeks of delay which the contractor then multiplies by the weekly figure it has inserted in the bill of quantities or the specification for preliminaries costs to arrive at the total claimed under this heading. This is entirely the wrong way to calculate the amount of loss and/or expense. At best, it will only produce a rough approximation. At worse, it will be very far from reality.

The reason is simple. What the contractor is entitled to recover as loss and/or expense is to be calculated in the same way as damages at common law. In other words, it is for the contractor to prove that it has suffered the kind of loss it claims. The contractor must prove the length of time it has been kept on site longer than the contract stated. Then the actual (not assumed) costs and expenses must be calculated properly. Many of these costs will not be related to time. They may be related to usage. The contractor should have all the necessary information to substantiate its claim. The preliminaries inserted in the contract document pricing by the contractor is simply the contractor's estimate of what it will cost every week. It may be an underestimate or an overestimate, but it will not represent the actual preliminaries costs spent.

Head-office Overheads

This claim is not for actual head-office overheads but for the loss of opportunity to contribute to head-office overheads during a period of overrun. Every contract is assumed to contribute to the head-office overheads of the contractor. To put it simply, if the contractor was carrying out five similar sized contracts a year, each contract would be contributing 20% of the head-office overheads. The idea is that if the contract period is prolonged or extended beyond the contract completion date, the contractor will be prevented from earning a contribution to head-office overheads during that period and, therefore, it should be paid that amount of contribution by the employer as part of the loss and/or expense.

The theory is fine, but in order to make the claim stick the contractor must show that it had to turn away work during the overrun period because if it had no other work to do, it could not be said to be losing the opportunity to do it. It is not enough for the contractor to show that it did not bother to tender for any work during the period, there must be solid evidence that the work was available to do. In fact, it is very difficult for a contractor to show that it was prevented from working elsewhere because it was held up on a project.

Not only has the contractor to prove that there was other work available, it also has to show that it could not have done that work. That is virtually impossible for a largish contractor to demonstrate and the only type of contractor who could be reasonably certain of making a good claim would be a contractor that only carried out one project at a time. Other considerations which point away from a successful claim are that the site agent and operatives working on the completion of one project are unlikely to be the same people who would be required at the beginning of another project. Contractors often put agents on site who have particular experience in starting a project and replace them with different agents after the superstructure has commenced. When the project is nearing the end, finishing site agents are often put in to bring the job to a conclusion. Virtually all contractors use sub-contractors and that seems to negate the argument that operatives are tied up on site.

If the contractor is successful in making out a case for recovery of head-office overheads, the next question is how must money can be recovered? Calculating the amount has caused much difficulty. Ideally, the contractor should be able to provide detailed evidence about its head-office costs. Realistically, that is not always possible and it has become usual to rely on the use of a formula. There are several formulae available.

The contractor will have to submit certified accounts for at least three years to show details of turnover and total overhead cost and profit.

Uneconomic Working

It may be necessary for the contractor to employ additional labour and plant or the existing labour and plant may stand idle or be under-employed in either a delay or disruption situation. A situation involving idle plant and labour is also called 'loss of productivity'. Although the contractor is entitled to claim for this, it can be difficult to establish the amount of the actual additional expenditure involved.

Contractors sometimes try to deal with this problem by presenting the claim on the basis that they are entitled to be paid for all the work they have done and for all the resources they have used. This type of claim can only be sustained if the contractor can show that the labour forecast in the tender was entirely accurate, that the contractor was blameless, and that none of the labour and plant time was occupied other than by carrying out the work. Contractors attempt to show loss of productivity by reference to original tender figures to establish anticipated percentage productivity and actual labour figures to show the fall in productivity. The tender breakdown is irrelevant. The contractor's intended use of labour and plant by reference to the original programme of work is unlikely to be an accurate forecast, a new percentage being calculated to form the basis of the claim. As already noted, the contractor's pricing in the contract documents is simply its estimate. Therefore, in comparing the estimated costs in the contract documents with the actual costs is not comparing like with like. To do that, it would be necessary to establish what would have been the actual costs incurred, but it will clearly be impossible to prove as a matter of fact what the costs would have been had the delay or disruption not occurred. The problem is that the intended use may be inadequate. Some of the additional labour and plant time may be the difference between the contractor's wrongly estimated proposed resources and what it would have had to use even if the contract had proceeded without delay or disruption.

Another common method used by contractors claiming uneconomic working is to say that over the period in question the labour was only working at 80% or 70% or some other spurious percentage. The contractor will often say that is its estimate of the percentage or even that is the 'recognised' percentage. There will be no answer to the obvious question: who recognised it? The contractor knows that labour has been working uneconomically but has no idea how uneconomically and cannot see how to calculate it. I cannot see either.

It is sometimes possible to demonstrate the true loss by ignoring the tender breakdown showing intention and simply comparing a period of normal working with a period when disruption is present. Assuming that the building work is of a fairly repetitive nature, this method can be acceptable.

Architects must remember that, if the contractor submits whatever evidence there is, it is a matter for the architect and quantity surveyor to determine the amount due. It is reasonable to assume that some loss will have been suffered as a result of uneconomic working wherever delay or disruption has occurred. Although the contractor will be unable to prove in every, or sometimes any, detail the loss it has suffered, the architect and the quantity surveyor cannot refuse to ascertain for that reason even if realistically it amounts to a best guess.

Winter Working

This is a claim which is effectively one for loss of productivity due to the carrying out of work in less favourable circumstances, e.g. excavation work carried out in winter rather than in summer. It is often referred to as the 'knock-on effect' because it often occurs if there is a delay on the part of the employer which then causes the contractor to work in weather conditions which are worse than the contractor could have reasonably expected when it priced the Works. In such circumstances there is potentially a claim in respect of the additional costs caused by working in winter when, but for the delay, the work would have been completed during the summer period. Obviously, there will be little to no chance of a claim on this basis where work scheduled to be carried out in winter is pushed into spring or summer.

Site Supervision Costs

The contractor's site supervision may vary from the site operative who also carries out supervisory duties to the site agent or manager with several staff, with most situations falling somewhere in between. Site supervision is normally part of on-site establishment costs, but sometimes a contractor tries to claim that there was a need for additional supervision. In order to claim it must be shown that extra supervision would not have been required on site at the time in question had it not been for the thing which caused the claim.

I doubt that it will surprise anyone to hear that it is not unknown for a contractor to put an extra supervisor on site simply because another project has just finished and the contractor has no other project suitable for the supervisor at that particular time. The contractor must show that there is a purpose in the supervisor's presence on site. I have known contractors to say that the need for additional staff is that the architect has been issuing too many instructions for the existing supervisory staff to deal with. Before accepting this kind of argument, you could ask yourself these questions:

- Before appearing on your site, was the additional supervisor previously employed on another project being constructed by the same contractor which it has just completed or is in the closing stages?
- Are the grounds for requiring extra staff credible?
- Before the need for an additional supervisor was raised, was the contractor generally organising work on site efficiently?
- Is the contractor's problem due to it raising more and more needless requests for information?
- Are there many defects in the Works?

On the other hand, it sometimes happens that some disrupting event for which the employer is responsible does not result in any prolongation of the contract period, but it may require additional supervision for that particular activity. It is essential that you establish, in every instance, that the attendance on site of an additional supervisor is a necessary result of the disrupting event.

Where small projects are concerned, it is common for the supervision to be in the hands of a working person-in-charge. That is the contractor's decision when preparing its tender. If the assumption that a working supervisor would be sufficient turns out to be wrong, that is the contractor's problem, not yours. The same principle applies to larger projects of course. A contractor cannot claim the cost of additional supervision just because the tender was wrongly priced.

Plant Hire

If the contractor claims the cost of hired plant and equipment during a period of delay caused by the employer, it must be established whether the plant and equipment is hired from external sources or whether it is the contractor's own plant. If hired from an external source, the contractor would usually be entitled to charge the hire cost as part of the loss and/or expense claim, unless of course it could be used elsewhere on the site rather than standing idle.

If it is the contractor's own plant, the most that can normally be claimed is depreciation. A contractor cannot, as is sometimes argued, claim what it would have had to pay hire charges if it did not have its own plant. If the contractor, with enforced idle plant, can show that it could realistically have used the plant profitably elsewhere, it may be able to claim for loss of opportunity.

If a contractor uses its own plant but it also runs a plant hire business as part of the same company, it may argue that it is entitled to charge the hiring costs. It can only do that if it can show that if the plant was not being used by the contractor, it would have been able to hire it out. Sometimes a contractor will say that it has hired it from another branch of its company. In that case, it would have to show that it suffered a loss because it would effectively simply be paying itself. Where there was a completely separate sister company devoted to hiring out plant, it would have to be demonstrated that it did not get a discount and that there was no method by which the contractor could reclaim the hire charge from the sister company in some other way.

Increased Costs

As we all know, in the construction industry prices go up, but never down. Additional expenditure on labour, materials or plant due to increases in cost is an allowable claim as a result of a delay for which the employer is responsible. A claim may be sustainable in situations where disruption has resulted in labour-intensive work being delayed and carried out during a period after an increased wage award. The calculation is the difference between what the contractor would have spent on labour, materials and plant and what it has actually had to spend over the whole period of the work as a direct result of the delay and disruption concerned. I must stress that detailed proof is necessary and allowance must be made for any recovery of increased costs under any fluctuations clauses there may be in the contract.

Contractors often try to make the calculations easier by using a formula or a notional percentage applied to all items in the contract to produce the result. That kind of rough approximation is not acceptable in a claim. The proper calculation can be quite complicated in the case of goods or materials because the contractor must first show that the increase is not due to late ordering but entirely to the delay. Not all work and all materials after the period of delay or during a prolongation period after the contract completion date will automatically suffer a price increase.

If it is to have any chance of success, this kind of claim must be made item by item, whether for increases in labour, goods or materials costs. In each case, it must be proved that it was a direct result of the delay and that it could not reasonably have been ordered early enough to avoid the increase in cost. Evidence must be produced to support the precise increase. It is very laborious to prepare, which is probably why the use of formulae or notional figures is so attractive if the contractor can get away with it.

Costs of Preparing the Claim

Contractors often try to claim the costs of employing a claims consultant to prepare a claim. Whether this kind of claim will be successful depends upon the terms of the particular building contract being used. In general, a contractor will not be able to include this cost unless it was paid with the prospect of legal proceedings in mind. At best, the contractor would have to prove that it was necessary to employ the consultant in order to make the claim. This kind of claim seldom succeeds.

Finance Charges

This can be looked at in various ways. It can be considered to be the financing charges levied by the contractor's bank when the contractor has to borrow money because it has been kept out of the money to which it was due as a result of the claim. It can be considered as the contractor's failure to earn interest by investing the claim money. A claim for financing charges is not a claim for interest on a debt, it is a claim for a constituent part of the loss and/or expense.

Global Claims

This is a complicated topic. The extent to which a global claim can be made depends upon the terms of the building contract being used. The basic principle is that where there are several events, each of which is a contributory cause of delay or disruption but the interaction of the events is very complicated so that it is impracticable to analyse cause and effect for each event and apportion the total extra cost between each event, the contractor is entitled to make a claim on a global cost basis. That is to say that the contractor can simply include all the events causing the delay and then show the total cost resulting from that delay. If it is possible to separate any of the events from the main body of events and show by cause and effect the financial result of a particular event, that should be done. Even where a global cost is being claimed, the contractor must provide all the evidence available. The contractor must show that:

- events occurred which entitle it to loss and/or expense and
- the events caused delay and disruption and
- that delay or disruption caused the contractor to incur loss and/or expense.

A favourite so-called 'total cost claim' is when (in simple terms) a contractor sets out the total cost of all the labour, plant, and materials involved in the project and then deducts the contract sum, saying that what remains is obviously the extra cost of completing the project which forms the claim. This approach assumes that the contractor has been entirely accurate when preparing its original price and that, during the progress of the Works, all the hitches and delays have been the fault of the employer. Needless to say, that approach has no chance of success.

The contractor is entitled to set out its claim in any way that it wishes, but global claims are difficult to prove. An 'all or nothing' claim will fail in its entirety if some of the events included are found not to be contributory causes. Put simply, if the contractor cites five causes of a delay and shows that the effect of the delay is to cost the contractor £50 000, what effect will there be if it can be shown that one of the causes is not the responsibility of the employer? One cannot simply say that the claim is now four-fifths of the £50 000, i.e. £40 000.

Conclusion

Many claims fail because contractors and subcontractors do not know how to substantiate a claim and they do not appreciate the effort required. It is not a case of simply throwing a few programmes and rough estimates of losses together. I once explained this to the director of a contracting firm who appeared to have excellent grounds for a claim. He said, with masterly exaggeration, that it would cost him more to prepare the claim than the claim was worth. He was seeking to recover £250 000 and all he offered by way of substantiation was three sheets of dubious calculations, a lever arch file of letters (this was before emails), and a coloured bar chart. But these are the key things required when the contractor makes a claim:

- The facts giving rise to the entitlement must be set out. Unless obvious, the facts must be evidenced.
- The contract term (or breach of contract) must be quoted which gives the entitlement and the financial basis for the claim must be shown in detail and properly evidenced.
- Any preconditions stated in the contract must be satisfied.

100

Termination

Common Misconceptions

Contractors and employers tend to talk about ending the contract or terminating the contract or walking away from it. All of these statements are strictly incorrect, but we all know what they actually mean. They are actually saying that they are not prepared to continue carrying out their obligations under the contract. It is still widely believed that if you have had enough of a particular contract you can simply tell the other party and that will be that. Nothing could be further from the truth. The basic position is that once a person or company has entered into a contract with another person or company, neither of them can end the contract unless there is an exceptionally good reason. Even then, very great care must be used or the person attempting to finish its obligations may face serious consequences.

Most building contracts, and architects' and consultants' terms of engagement have extensive and often hard-to-understand provisions to deal with termination. More of those later.

It is important to appreciate that if there were no termination clauses in the contract, the only way to bring the employment of the contractor to an end would be in accordance with one of the ways under the general law of contract. Even where there are specific termination clauses in a contract, it is usually still possible to end obligations under a contract using the general law and it is sometimes a matter of tactics, rather than law, which is the deciding factor. Under the general or common law, the parties' obligations, and in some cases the contract itself, can be brought to an end in one of six ways:

- performance
- agreement
- frustration
- breach
- novation
- operation of law.

Performance

This is the best and most usual way of bringing obligations and the contract itself to an end because it means that both parties have carried out their obligations under the contract and there is nothing else for either of them to do. The contract was entered into by both parties for a purpose, for example to get a building constructed or designed. That purpose has been fulfilled and the contract comes to its natural and intended end.

Agreement

The second-best way to bring obligations and the contract itself to an end is by agreement. Ironically, the best way to do that is to enter into another contract, the sole purpose of which is to end the first contract. If I had an emoji handy, I would be tempted to insert the one with tears of laughter here. If it is not done formally, there is a danger that one of the parties will subsequently try to argue that the contract is still in place and that the other party has committed a breach of contract by simply walking out on it. An exchange of letters or even emails may suffice, but if the original contract is of any value, a formal agreement to bring it to an end is important.

Frustration

The frustration here is not quite the commonly referred to frustration when one says 'I am really frustrated by this' or 'you are really frustrating', but it is related to it. Frustration in the legal sense occurs when, without fault on either side, a contract cannot be performed because something changes which significantly alters the performance so as to be something quite different to what was agreed. More difficulty or more cost in carrying out the Works is not frustration. If the contract allows for something, that something cannot be said to frustrate the contract. If there was a contract to build a small extension to an existing large property and before the work could be started the existing property burned down so that there was nothing to extend, that would be frustration.

Where a contract is ended by frustration, both parties are excused from further obligations and any money already paid is recoverable. In practice, it is very rare for a contract to be frustrated.

Breach

Sometimes one of the parties commits a breach of contract which is so serious it entitles the other party to accept it and end all further obligations under the contract. That kind of breach is sometimes called 'fundamental' because it goes to the basis of the contract and indicates that the party in breach is not prepared to be bound by the contract. Under a building contract that could occur if the contractor simply walks off site in the middle of the project, which happens more often than might be imagined. The contractor's action in that instance is a 'repudiation of the contract', but effective only if it is accepted by the employer.

The innocent party can either accept a repudiation and sue at once for damages or it can continue to perform its obligations under the contract and hold the other party liable for all the money due under the contract. Of course, that can only apply if the innocent party is capable of performing its own obligations under the contract. In the example above, the employer has no option but to accept the repudiation because if the contractor refuses to build, the employer cannot continue the contract alone. Acts of repudiation are not often so clear.

It must be remembered that not every breach of contract by one party will entitle the other to refuse to perform its own obligations; the breach must be sufficient to make clear an intention to repudiate the whole of the contractual obligations.

Novation

It may be surprising to find that novation is a termination of the contract. Most architects and contractors probably think of it as simply a replacement of one party to a contract by a different party. Novation is the ending of one contract and replacement by another contract, with a change in the identity of one of the parties. The terms of the second contract are often very similar to the terms of the first. This method of bringing a contract to an end must be by agreement of all parties.

Operation of Law

I include this for completeness, but it is very unlikely that an architect will encounter this situation. It may possibly occur if one of the parties becomes bankrupt or sufficient time passes to stop the contract remaining effective. How much time? As you might expect, it will depend on all the circumstances.

Contractual Termination Clauses

Building contracts and consultants' terms of engagement will contain ways of ending the employment of the contractor or of the consultant. Note, there are seldom provisions for bringing the contract itself to an end. In each case, there will be certain conditions which must be satisfied and it is really important that they are satisfied. If not, there is a possibility that the contractor, the employer or the consultant, as appropriate, may be considered to have repudiated the contract. One thing is certain: if the conditions are not satisfied, the termination of employment will not be effective.

Typical conditions are:

- time periods: the need to give a certain number of days' notice
- service of the notice: if the contract says special delivery, ordinary post will not do
- number of notices: some contracts require two notices to be effective
- reasonable notice (that irritating word again: if the contract is not specific, it is better to give longer notice than you think
- the reason for termination must be one of the acceptable reasons set out in the contract
- the person to be notified: contractors often make the mistake of notifying the architect instead of the employer.

Some contracts specify insolvency or criminal activity as not requiring a notice.

Something that certain clients like to include is what is usually called 'termination at will'. That means that one or both parties are entitled to terminate without any reason, simply because they wish to do so. One often finds this kind of termination clause in appointment documents that developers want consultants to sign. That kind of appointment document usually only allows the developer to terminate; there is no equivalent provision for the consultant. I have often found cunningly worded sub-clauses in the termination provisions which effectively deprive the consultant of common law termination options.

The golden rule when thinking of termination is to read the relevant clause very carefully. If it refers to the giving of a notice (basically a letter), just check to see whether there is a separate clause which says something about how to give a notice. It can make the difference between successful termination and failure.

So, if the contractor simply walks off site, never to return, or says that's what it is going to do, you need to carefully analyse if the particular contract allows the contractor to do that (unlikely). If not, is the contractor in breach of the contract and in breach of the general law? In any event, it is a serious problem and you and/or the employer must immediately seek specialist advice.

101

Practical Completion

Definition

'Practical completion' is a term used in certain building contracts. If the contract you are using actually says what practical completion means, that is what it means in connection with that contract and you are bound by it. If there is no definition in the contract, which is the situation considered here, it means that when you are satisfied that the Works are in accordance with the contract with no obvious defects, even though there are some trifling things left to be done, you can issue a certificate. The trifling things left to be done are at your discretion, but in exercising that discretion, a useful rule of thumb is that you must consider as 'trifling' only those items which can be subsequently carried out by the contractor without seriously interfering with the client's use of the building. However, be careful. The test is not whether the employer can use the building for the purpose intended, but whether the defects are trifling in nature.

Although practical completion is something which most contracts leave to the opinion of the architect, in reality you have very little discretion. Practical completion is very largely a question of fact in each case. The Works are either practically complete or they are not.

Some architects refuse to issue certificates of practical completion unless the Works are finished in every particular. That is wrong for two very good reasons:

- In a practical sense, no building is ever totally finished. Show me a building which you say is complete in every particular and I will always be able to find something slightly wrong or not done, whether it is something small like a missing screw or some unwanted scratches or something more substantial such as a piece of flashing missing. If you refuse to certify until every possible thing is complete, you will never certify. What actually happens in the case of those architects is that eventually they certify when there are still outstanding things. Therefore, they have not certified total completion as they maintain. What they have done is to wait an unreasonably long time and insisted on an unreasonable level of completion, contrary to what they should have done.
- If practical completion meant completion down to the very smallest detail, however trivial, it is probable that the liquidated damages clause would amount to a penalty and would be unenforceable.

Professional Practice for Architects and Project Managers, First Edition. David Chappell.

Qualifying the Certificate

It seems to be common practice for architects to issue certificates of practical completion with a long list of outstanding work and defects still to be completed. Often, the certificate is made 'subject to the list'. That is just nonsense of course. I once asked an architect who had issued a 'qualified' certificate of practical completion why he had not issued his practical completion certificate at the start of the job and just made it subject to doing everything. He did not seem to get the point.

Premature issuing of certificates of practical completion is often done because the employer wishes to move into and use the building before it is finished (more of this below). Even if the list is short and, on any sensible view, consists of the kind of minor items of work which ought not to preclude practical completion, it is obviously wrong to refer to them on the certificate: a qualified certificate is not acceptable. If the list contains items that would preclude the issue of the certificate, the certificate is invalid. It is not a certificate of practical completion because the reference to substantial defects and other work unfinished is a contradiction to the certificate stating that it is the opinion of the architect that practical completion has occurred. If the architect has attached a list, it is crystal clear that he or she is not of the opinion that practical completion has occurred. It is always open to the employer to use the dispute resolution procedures available to challenge any certificate of the architect, including the certificate of practical completion, even when there is no list attached. By attaching a list, the architect is providing the employer with evidence that the certificate is invalid. For obvious reasons, the contractor is unlikely to challenge the certificate except on the ground that it is too late.

Although having made clear that a qualified certificate is invalid I could stop there, for the sake of completeness it is worthwhile looking at another, but connected, practice, that is quite pointless. I refer to the fact that, having qualified the certificate, many architects proceed to attach a schedule for the completion of the listed work, giving dates by which each item must be finished. Sometimes architects will include a covering letter making clear that failure to finish the items by the dates indicated will invalidate the certificate. Often, the contractor does not finish as directed and the architect is unsure what to do.

The first point is that the certificate, being qualified, is invalid and, therefore, the whole structure of the process envisioned by the architect falls to the floor: practical completion is not yet certified, but of course the contractor will argue that the certificate has been issued.

The second point is that even if the certificate was valid, it cannot be invalidated by the subsequent action or inaction of the contractor. If a perfectly valid certificate of practical completion was issued on 8 May 2019 and on 9 May 2019 a serious defect was discovered which entailed demolishing part of the building, the certificate would still be a valid certificate because it was a formal representation of the architect's professional opinion on the day it was issued.

Therefore, after practical completion has been certified, the contract moves into the period when the contractor must rectify any defects in the Works which the architect notifies. The dates given by the architect for the contractor to complete the listed work are irrelevant because the contract does not recognise them and the contractor is entitled to finish the unfinished work and any minor defects during the defects rectification period within a reasonable time, whatever that may be (see 26: Reasonable Time).

Inspection Before Certification

It is usual, although not obligatory, for contractors to inform the architect when they believe that the project is ready for a certificate of practical completion. Contractors will be anxious to achieve practical completion because, depending on the contract, it usually signifies the start of the defects rectification period, the end of the accumulation of liquidated damages, brings to an end the contractor's obligation to insure the Works, and releases usually half the retention amount. For those reasons, the contractor's notice to the architect may be premature.

It is for the architect to decide whether to inspect. In general, it is advisable for the architect to inspect fairly promptly after receiving the contractor's notice or the contractor may later argue that practical completion had been achieved long before the architect deigned to inspect the building. Of course, if the architect inspects and finds that practical completion has not been achieved, the contractor will no doubt request details of the things which are preventing the certificate from being issued. It is at that point that the architect has to consider whether it is prudent or not to provide the contractor with a list of defects and unfinished work (see 81: Snagging).

Many architects will provide a list but must be aware that the contractor will assume that, when the work in the list is finished, the certificate will be issued. The architect on further inspection at that stage may decide that there are other, previously unnoticed defects still unremedied. The architect may have to respond to several unnecessary calls to site and, indeed, may have to write a strongly worded letter to the contractor noting that the architect's time was being wasted.

However, it is only fair to note that some architects may delay issuing a certificate because the employer is content to receive liquidated damages, particularly if for some reason the employer is not ready to retake possession. Such conduct is reprehensible and it should go without saying that no architect should agree to delay a practical completion certificate on those grounds.

There is nothing wrong and much to be said for architects who point out defects to the contractor. But architects should not be persuaded to carry out detailed inspections of every part of the building and prepare long lists for the contractor, i.e. so-called 'snagging lists'.

Certification

You must not certify practical completion before you are of the opinion that practical completion has taken place. Nor should you delay the certification if satisfied that practical completion has taken place. The certificate is a formal expression of the architect's opinion and, therefore, not something to be taken lightly. You are not entitled to certify practical completion merely because the client has instructed you to do so. Some architects believe that they must certify practical completion if the client's solicitor instructs them to do so. No, remember that the client's solicitor is not advising you. The client's solicitor is acting in the interests of the client. You must ignore instructions and certify only when you are satisfied that the Works are at that stage.

Moreover, the Works have not reached practical completion simply because the employer occupies them. Many architects think that because after practical completion is certified the employer can move into the building, if the employer moves into the building the architect must certify practical completion. That really is the tail wagging the dog. Sometimes, an employer will retake possession before the building is certified practically complete simply because the delay is longer than expected. You should carefully explain to the employer before the contract is signed that the purpose of the liquidated damages clause is to compensate the employer adequately if the project overruns through the contractor's fault. An employer who retakes possession of the whole building before practical completion is certified has only himself or herself to blame if the contractor then says that it is impossible to complete properly. I am tempted at this point to branch off into a discussion of the many clients I have encountered who sign a contract with a contractor and then think that they can ignore it whenever it suits them, but I will resist the temptation.

Where there is provision for sections, a section completion certificate must be issued at practical completion of each section. On practical completion of the last section, the architect should issue a section completion certificate for that section and also a practical completion certificate for the whole of the Works. This removes any doubt that there may be some small part of the Works which has not (technically) reached practical completion.

Many architects believe that practical completion cannot be issued unless the Building Control officer has issued a certificate of completion. Although buildings must comply with the Building Regulations (see 49: Building Control), the architect cannot delay the issue of a certificate of practical completion until a Building Control completion certificate has been issued unless the contract expressly says so. That is because the certificate of practical completion is issued in accordance with the building contract and is depending solely on the architect's opinion (obviously exercised in accordance with the law).

Handover

Some projects have a formal so-called 'handover procedure' which often the contractor knows nothing about until it is time to certify practical completion. For example, some local authorities insist that when the architect believes that practical completion has been achieved, there is a meeting on site including the chief clerk of works, any specialist clerks of works, and various council officers from the department of the council which commissioned the building. It is not unknown for the architect to be in a minority in believing that practical completion has been achieved and to be instructed not to issue the certificate until certain things have been done.

The views of the council officers may equate practical completion to full and entire completion, which is not correct of course. I have witnessed many of these handover meetings which are nothing less than an elaborate charade: a collection of worthy people standing around and poking at bits of the building with stern expressions. All the while, it is the architect and not the employer or the employer's employees, however exalted they may be, who is contractually authorised to decide when practical completion has occurred. The contractor is entitled to, and should, argue that the employer is interfering with the issue of a certificate, which is a serious matter under most building contracts. Architects should also make the position clear to the employer whenever there is the slightest suggestion that a gang of folk from the employer's office instead of the architect will decide practical completion. That kind of decision has no validity and another example of the employer thinking that the contract only binds the contractor.

Partial Possession and Section Completion

Many people confuse partial possession with sectional completion. Where section completion applies, the project is divided into sections and each section has its own dates for possession and completion, and its own amount of liquidated damages. The contractor cannot take possession before the stated dates for each section and must complete each section by its stated date.

Where partial possession applies, there is only one date for possession and completion for the whole contract. Some contracts allow an employer (if the contractor agrees) to take partial possession of part of the Works. For example, a commercial client may want to put the factory into operation as soon as possible even if the offices attached are not ready or a family may want to move into their new house even though the external works are far from ready. I came across a case where the external painting had hardly begun and the employer took partial possession of the whole of the interior of the building, excluding the whole of the exterior. All these situations are perfectly fine. The architect's task is simply to write a note to the employer and contractor confirming what was taken into partial possession by the employer and when. It is helpful to attach a marked-up drawing to clearly indicate the part taken into possession. Partial possession is usually deemed to be practical completion of the part. 'Deemed' is a curious word. If something is deemed to be X, it means that everyone knows that it is not actually X but that everyone is going to act as if it was X.

When the employer raises the possibility of partial possession and if the contract allows it (but not otherwise), you should carefully consider whether the proposal will hinder the contractor in completing the remaining work. If so, it is best to reconsider the extent of the partial possession.

However, if the client takes partial possession of the whole of the Works, it is deemed to be practical completion of the whole Works. Then, the architect should not issue a formal certificate of practical completion, but merely a written notice confirming that the employer has taken possession as noted above. The architect may issue a certificate of practical completion only when, in the architect's opinion, practical completion, in the true sense, has taken place.

So in a nutshell, the difference between section completion and partial possession is that the contractor is obliged to comply with the section completion dates, but it is not obliged to agree to partial possession.

Things can get very complicated if the employer wishes to take partial possession of part of a section or even parts of different sections. The start dates of the defects rectification periods at different times and noting when they finish requires a steely concentration on the part of the architect.

Phased Completion

Some architects and quantity surveyors think it is enough to put a list of so-called 'phase' dates in the specification or bills of quantities to ensure that the contractor completes the various phases by the dates stated. Oh, if it was so easy! If there is only one completion date in the contract, that is the only date which will be applicable. The 'phase' dates in the specification or bills of quantities cannot usually override what the main contract document states as the completion date.

102

Rectification Period

What is the Recitification Period?

Most building contracts include a period after the contractor has completed the Works (usually referred to as 'practical completion') which is variously called the 'defects liability period' or even, more misleadingly, the 'maintenance period'. The idea is that any defects (i.e. work not in accordance with the contract) which appear during the period are reported to the contractor and the contractor is allowed to come back onto the property to rectify the defects at its own cost.

Let me say immediately what is wrong with referring to the 'maintenance period'. The term should not be used because it suggests an obligation to keep the Works in the same condition as when practical completion occurred rather than a duty to make good defects. The only kind of defects which most forms of contract require the contractor to make good are those which are due to the work not being in accordance with the contract. If the contractor was required to maintain the building for the rectification period, it would impose a duty to deal with fair wear and tear, which would be unworkable because the cause of the wear and tear is out of the hands of the contractor. I know of no contract which actually imposes that kind of duty on the contractor.

Why is the Rectification Period in Building Contracts?

The reason for the period is often misunderstood by both clients and contractors. It is inserted primarily for the benefit of contractors. If there was no rectification period, the employer, after notifying the contractor of any defects, could arrange to have them corrected by another contractor and charge the original contractor with the cost. Even without a rectification period, it would be sensible to give the contractor an opportunity to come back and rectify any defects because in most instances it will be the simplest way forward and avoid the employer having to show that the other contractor's charges were reasonable in order to recover the costs from the original contractor.

What About Defects After the End of the Period?

Another very common misconception, particularly among contractors, is that at the end of the rectification period the contractor has no further liability for defects. It cannot be

Professional Practice for Architects and Project Managers, First Edition. David Chappell.

stressed too much that a defect is a breach of the contract on the part of the contractor and the contractor is liable for all defects. There is no time limit to the contractor's liability, but the law imposes a 6 year period (12 years if the contract was a deed) after which the contractor could argue that it was beyond the limitation period and the claim could not proceed. The start of the limitation period for contractors is the date of practical completion. So, if there was a serious defect in the foundations which was not discovered during the progress of the Works or during the rectification period, the employer could still make a claim against the contractor provided it was done before the limitation period expired. After it expired, the contractor need only point out that the limitation period had expired and a court would dismiss the claim. If the employer made the claim in time, it could include all the reasonable costs incurred by the employer in getting the defect rectified and any other foreseeable costs associated with the breach of contract (see 24: Limitation Period).

Length of the Period

Because the rectification period is not properly understood, employers tend to think that the longer the period, the better. That is far from the truth. As we have seen above, the contractor is still responsible for defects after the end of whatever length of rectification period is prescribed. Twelve months is often specified so that the mechanical services system can be exposed to the full 12-month cycle. That is not wrong, but neither is it wrong to specify three months. The length of the period must be balanced against the cost. Most contractors will no doubt accept a three- or even six-month period without quibble, but longer than that and the contractor will increase its original tender to allow for the fact that, under most contracts, half the retention is retained by the employer until the rectification period has ended and the defects have all been made good. In recent years, any kind of retention has been criticised and other safeguards suggested.

It is wrong to try to insert different rectification periods, e.g. for heating and mechanical and for general building. Different periods can only be inserted if the contract specifically allows it, for example by dividing the project into sections.

How Does the Rectification Period Work?

The general principle is that the architect, or sometimes the employer, must notify the contractor during or at the end of the rectification period listing all the defects which have been found by inspection. The contractor should make good the defects within a reasonable time following notification. It is worth saying that where there are defects, it is essential to notify the contractor and to allow it to inspect the defect even if, ultimately, the employer intends to have the defect corrected by others. Failure to notify will prevent the employer from recovering any costs from the original contractor.

It is difficult to be precise about the meaning of a 'reasonable time' (see 26: Reasonable Time). The slick answer given by the courts is that it is the time taking into account all the relevant circumstances. Some of the factors to be taken into account will include the number and type of defects and the difficulty of access to them. In my earlier example of a defect in the foundations, it might well show itself in cracking of some of the structural parts of the building, but to rectify it would involve excavation and probably underpinning. On the other hand, if the defects notified are just the usual suspects of shrinkage cracks, ironmongery problems, some spalling brickwork and careless finishing, it will simply require a team of appropriate operatives to descend on the property and get on with the work. In the first example, the contractor may easily be engaged for several weeks or even months, and in a run of the mill situation, the contractor may be finished in a couple of weeks.

A useful rule of thumb is that if the contractor is notified about an urgent defect, it could be expected that it will receive attention within 24 hours at latest. If the notification is at the end of the rectification period it could be expected that the contractor, who would obviously know that the list was due, would start attending to the defects within two to three weeks. That is a reasonable time to allow the contractor to consider the list and to assemble the relevant operatives to do the work. If the architect believes that the contractor is not acting quickly enough, the architect should give the contractor seven days' notice to make a start and, if there is no positive response, the architect should discuss the matter with the employer with a view to giving notice, on behalf of the client, that if the making good is not started within a further seven days, the employer will engage others to do the work and the costs involved will be charged to the contractor. That would usually be achieved by a deduction from the final account.

One thing the architect must not do is to simply sit and give it another week and see what happens. It is also counterproductive to make threats that are not carried out. Most contractors get to know the characteristics of local architects and they know how to play them. It is good to have a reputation of being firm but reasonable (the old 'firm but fair' description has no place here because fairness is not a specific factor when dealing with the essentials of most building contracts). The architect must be ready to act as soon as any time period has expired.

The Employer's Role if there is a Rectification Period

It is clearly a good idea to get the contractor to provide a method statement and programme for undertaking the rectification work unless the project is small domestic work. The problem is that few, if any, building contracts require the contractor to produce method statements and programmes for remedial work. Architects who believe that they can simply demand these things from a contractor before allowing it to start the work are seriously mistaken. It is arguable that an architect might issue an instruction for these things, but the contractor could make a charge for carrying them out. I would not advise an architect in these circumstances to go down the road of arguing that any contractor who was competent would prepare a method statement and programme. The argument might well be correct, but any particular contractor's idea of an adequate method statement and programme for its own use is unlikely to be what the architect had in mind. 'It is a method statement, but not as we know it Jim', as someone once almost said. Far better to get the contract amended to include that provision or include it in the specification if that does not conflict with a particular contract; expert help is indicated.

It is important that the employer understands that if the contractor is effectively prevented from carrying out the making good of defects, the contractor will not be liable for its failure to make good. Some employers can be extremely difficult at this stage in the job. I encountered one employer who believed she was entitled to stipulate that the contractor could only have access on Monday afternoons and Thursday mornings. She refused to understand that she must be reasonable and the whole thing ended in a messy, but totally avoidable, dispute. In another example, the employer insisted on producing his own list of defects which was based on his own ridiculously high standards, none of which had been in the specification. Again, a dispute ensued which the employer lost. Being a solicitor, one might have thought that he would have been alive to these dangers; but apparently not.

Some contracts empower the architect, with the employer's agreement, to instruct the contractor not to make good the defects and to deduct an appropriate amount from the contract sum. Even if the contract does not expressly say that, it is likely that the architect and certainly the employer has that power. Where this power exists, it must be exercised with great care.

The question is: what is an appropriate amount? The answer is that if the contractor refuses to carry out the rectification work or if it simply does not do it after proper warnings, the employer is entitled to employ others and recover from the original contractor the total cost of getting the rectification work done. Obviously, the cost must be reasonable and the employer may have to show that competitive tenders were invited if the work is extensive. It sometimes happens that although the contractor is apparently willing to rectify the defects, the effect of the supposed rectification is that the defects just get worse. Some contractors may visit the site on numerous occasions, trying to rectify defects and each time the defect is left as bad or worse than before. It is likely that in those cases, the employer also has the power to recover the whole cost of getting another contractor to do the work. But if an employer refuses to allow the original contractor to return to site to make good the defects for no other reason than the employer's convenience, then the appropriate amount is not the cost of engaging another contractor, but what it would have cost the original contractor to do the work. If it is sub-contract work, it may cost the contractor nothing at all to rectify the defects and the employer would likewise be entitled to recover nothing if other contractors were engaged.

Potential Problems

Some problems have already been discussed but there are two kinds of problems which worry people. The first is whether the employment of another contractor to carry out the work may invalidate any product or equipment warranties which the original contractor is to provide under the contract. If the warranties have been provided, as they should have been, at practical completion or its equivalent stage, there should be no problem. If there are outstanding defects which affect the equipment or products concerned, practical completion should not be certified until the defects have been corrected – no excuses. If for some reason a warranty has not been obtained and another contractor has to be employed to rectify defects, it is worth contacting the supplier of the missing warranty to check whether rectification by another contractor, e.g. another heating engineer, will void the required warranty. If there is no satisfactory response but the replacement contractor is able to provide a similar warranty or an insurer is prepared to provide a similar warranty, albeit at a greatly increased cost, the total cost should be recoverable from the original contractor as part of the cost of rectification.

The second kind of problem concerns defects. Concern is often expressed that the employment of other contractors to rectify defects which the original contractor refuses to make good may confuse the situation if further defects occur where the defects were rectified. Who is responsible? In most cases, it should be relatively easy to see whether the defect is essentially the same defect as before or a result of the remedial work carried out. If the latter, the liability clearly falls on the contractor who rectified the defect. That contractor will have undertaken to correct the defect in a workmanlike manner and causing a further defect is a clear breach of that undertaking. If the new defect is not related to the remedial work, it is the responsibility of the original contractor. Although the diagnostic part may be difficult, most further defects will fall into one or other of these two categories and then the responsible party is plain to see.

There will be some cases where it is impossible to allocate responsibility to one or other in that straightforward way. In such cases, it seems likely that the original contractor will be held liable on the basis that, if it had carried out its duty to rectify the original defect, the problem of identifying the party responsible for the subsequent defect would not have arisen because it would have been the responsibility of the original contractor who carried out the Works.

103

As-Built Records

As-built records are drawings and other information that, as the name implies, show the construction and installation of all the work as it has actually been carried out on site, including construction, materials, and, possibly most importantly, all services. These drawings are necessary because the Works as actually constructed will almost certainly be different in various ways from what was designed and included in the production information, bills of quantities or specification. The differences may be slight or substantial, but need to be properly recorded. Possible causes of the differences could be instructed variations or dictated by site conditions. I have never yet been on a project where the clerk of works has not made some change, often substantial but uninstructed, to the underground drainage: 'I thought it would be cheaper'.

The person best placed to produce the as-built drawings is the contractor because only the contractor, or more accurately the operatives on site, really knows what has actually been built. Sometimes, the architect is given the responsibility of producing the as-built drawings and more than once an architect has asked me if it is acceptable simply to provide the original drawings supplied to the contractor. The question reveals a total lack of understanding of what is required. The clue is in the name of course: 'as-built'. Effectively, in order to produce a good set of as-built drawings, the architect must survey the finished building. Even then, hidden work will not be discovered and systematic inspections of the site for the purpose of noting changes to the contracted Works during progress is necessary.

As-built drawings are usually provided by the contractor for the purposes of the health and safety file but some contracts stipulate that the drawings must be provided before practical completion can be certified.

Ideally, the contract documents should specify exactly what is required in the as-built drawings, for example precisely specifying the location and the scale and type together with the information to be put on the drawings.

Professional Practice for Architects and Project Managers, First Edition. David Chappell.

104

Final Certificate

Final

Most building contracts say that the architect must issue a final certificate. I once had an architect tell me that he had issued a final certificate and then, because the contractor seemed unhappy about the possibility of substantial liquidated damages being deducted by the employer, he issued a further extension of time. It seemed that the employer was unhappy. One can see why. What is not to understand about 'final'. 'Final' really does mean FINAL. It is the last thing that a contract administrator can do under the terms of the building contract. Once you have issued the final certificate, your powers under the contract are at an end. It must never be forgotten that you can only do what the contract says you can do. There is no such thing as a divine right of architects to do anything that seems appropriate, although some architects but not contractors wish, and sometimes act, as if it was so.

Conclusive or Not

There seems to be a general impression that the issue of a final certificate by the architect indicates that the architect is satisfied that the Works have been carried out in accordance with the contract and there are no defects of any kind in the building. That is rubbish of course. The basic purpose of the final certificate is to mark the end of the contract and to state how much one of the parties owes the other. The final certificate is only conclusive about anything, even the amount, if the contract says that it is.

If the contract says nothing about the final certificate except that it must be issued, it is not conclusive about anything at all. Even the amount stated in the final certificate can be challenged either immediately or within six years after it has been paid. If the contract says that the final certificate is conclusive about something, it is important to carefully read and understand exactly what the contract is saying.

Should the Final Certificate be Issued?

When arguments about the effect of final certificates were at their height, many architects got into the habit of not issuing a final certificate because they feared that it might

Professional Practice for Architects and Project Managers, First Edition. David Chappell.

be held to be an irrevocable guarantee to the employer that everything about the building was as it should be. At one point, the RIBA issued what turned out to be useless stickers which architects could stick to the front of the final certificate. Some of the stickers, when translated from the strange wording used, seemed to say: 'Although this might look like a final certificate, it isn't really one and, therefore, it does not have the effect that the certificate might be thought to have had'. The effect was that the piece of paper was not a final certificate, which rather negated the point of the sticker.

Instead of issuing a final certificate, some architects certify, as the last interim certificate, virtually all the money due to the contractor except for a minimal amount, say £5. Then the employer pays the full amount certified plus the extra £5. Usually, the contractor does not press for a piece of paper stating that it is the final certificate and, therefore, everyone appears to be happy.

However, in the case of most contracts, the architect does not have any choice about issuing the final certificate. Not only must it be issued, there is usually a specific time frame within which it must be issued. The effect of not issuing it depends on how the contract is worded. It may provide that the architect's power to issue the certificate ceases and that the contractor is entitled to, effectively, state how much money it wants. Alternatively, it may simply mean that the contract has not actually come to a formal conclusion, which is always an unsatisfactory state of affairs. If the contract does not say that the final certificate is conclusive about the contractor's compliance with the contract, what is there to lose by issuing the final certificate? If, rarely, the contract does say that the final certificate is conclusive about the contractor's compliance with the contract, should the architect not be checking compliance as part of the job?

The plain fact is that if the contract states that you must issue a final certificate and you do not do so, you are in breach of your duty under the contract and, therefore, in breach of your duty to the employer. Moreover, if and when the employer knows that you have failed to issue a final certificate, the employer will be in breach of a duty to the contractor to make sure that you comply with your contractual obligations.

Whose Opinion?

It should not need to be said, but I will say it anyway, that when you issue a final certificate it is the formal expression of your professional opinion. Therefore, it should not be what the employer tells you to certify.

Very often, at the end of a project, the employer and the contractor negotiate the amount of the final payment and do a deal. In those circumstances, the employer will often ask the architect to issue a final certificate based on that amount and, all too often, the architect will do just that. What happened to the architect's power and duty to do that and only that which the contract permits to be done, to say nothing of the architect's certificate being the formal expression etc. etc.?

Some architects rightly point out that the employer and the contractor, being the two parties, can agree anything they wish. That is absolutely correct, which is why there is nothing to stop them doing a deal. But their deal is very unlikely to be the same figure as the architect's professional opinion exercised in accordance with the building contract terms. Yes, they could employ a solicitor to amend the contract at that late stage, but even if the solicitor amended the contract to say that the architect must issue a final certificate in the amount agreed in the deal, the architect could not issue that certificate because it would not be the architect's professional opinion. Therefore, it would not be a certificate.

The Process

Although it seems that contractors are the most likely to challenge the final certificate, it may be the employer who is unhappy. One employer, believing the final certificate to be over-certified, challenged it. The employer successfully argued that the architect had not followed the correct administration procedures under the contract prior to the issue of the final certificate and therefore, as the final certificate had not been correctly issued, the certificate itself was not valid. Nowadays, contractual provisions for the issue of the final certificate are becoming ever more complicated. Not only must you issue the final certificate on time, you must be sure that you have done all the things that the particular contract lays down must be done before the final certificate is issued. For example, I cannot think of any contract that would not require a certificate of practical completion (or its equivalent) to be issued before the final certificate. Although that may seem obvious, I have encountered an architect who wished, with his client's lawyer's approval, to do just that!

105

Review

When the project is completed and the building contract comes to is natural end, the RIBA Plan of Work (both the 2007 and the 2013 versions) assumes that the architect will write to the client and other consultants inviting feedback. The 2013 version puts it in what I think is a rather awkward way referring to 'Project Performance', 'Project Outcomes', 'Project Objectives', etc. Why do people think that creating new names for perfectly ordinary activities will make them easier to understand when they are easy to understand without trying to coin a new name for them? Putting what the RIBA Plan of Work says about the review into plain English, what it seems to be saying is that it might be a good idea when the project is completed and had some use to check and see whether it works as well as it should do and everyone might gain from sharing the experiences and errors made.

That is an excellent idea in theory and it has the advantage that all the people involved will learn something and that something can be put into practice in the future. My problem with this is that it assumes that all the people involved in the review will take part in a dispassionate way, looking at all the little glitches with a view to how they can be overcome on future projects.

In reality, the client is likely to have some very juicy remarks to throw at the architect and anyone else if the project is not working as well as it should be. In my experience, it is a very brave architect who is prepared to ask the client, in effect, whether the client is happy with the finished building in every detail. Even a client who has not really given the topic much thought will immediately find numerous problems. A client may not think of complaining until you ask if there are any complaints. I put it that way because however the Plan of Work dresses up the situation, what it is advocating is that everyone puts their cards on the table, admitting errors and other mistakes in the design, construction, and administration of the project.

Is it really suggested that, stripped of all the jargon, some months after the final certificate has been issued, there should be a big meeting with everyone there and that all parties should bare their contractual or constructional souls? Can you imagine for a moment the reaction from the client if the architect was to say that the internally exposed brick wall was not instructed to give a better sense of dialogue between solids and voids to operate contextually within the stripped-down grey sky experience, but to cover up a ghastly architectural error? No, neither can I, because no architect in his or her right mind would venture such a statement (I don't mean the bit about the grey sky experience – some architects do talk like that). Is the contractor going to reveal all

Professional Practice for Architects and Project Managers, First Edition. David Chappell.

the times that it got away with using an inferior material because neither architect nor clerk of works were on site that day?

Although the idea of a coming together of all concerned in the project to learn lessons sounds sensible and obviously has a great deal to commend it, it does open up some of the participants to legal action from the client. Even if the client is excluded from the gathering (good idea), it may not be a good strategy for the rest of the team to bear their souls to each other.

106

Dispute Resolution

Some Basics

All building contracts contain details of the way in which disputes can be sorted out on a formal basis. There are three formal processes:

- adjudication
- arbitration
- litigation.

There are also what are usually termed 'alternative dispute procedures', which include:

- mediation
- negotiation
- conciliation
- mini trial.

Theoretically, adjudication can be used by parties to a construction contract without the assistance of solicitors or counsel. It is 'theoretically' the case because in practice so many aspects of adjudication have now been considered by courts that anyone deciding to use adjudication to settle a dispute will be well advised to engage experts in adjudication to assist them.

So far as arbitration and litigation are concerned, neither the contractor, nor the employer, nor any of the construction professionals actually need to know very much about the detail because if any of those procedures are employed, the employer or the contractor will almost certainly engage specialists in arbitration or solicitors for litigation. Architects and surveyors dealing with building contracts should steer well clear of arbitration and litigation and not risk giving advice about these procedures to clients other than to refer them to experts.

It cannot be emphasised too strongly that the parties need to be properly represented by specialists in adjudication, arbitration, or litigation. The easy way may seem to be to advise the employer or client to telephone their solicitor as soon as the contractor or its representative notifies that one of the dispute resolution processes is to be invoked. However, it must be understood that solicitors, like other professions, specialise. Many solicitors deal with litigation (legal proceedings), but there are different sorts of litigation and the client needs a solicitor who is well versed in construction law. Also, some solicitors, more used to litigation, may be uncomfortable with adjudication and arbitration, and a party may get better representation from an architect or quantity surveyor

Professional Practice for Architects and Project Managers, First Edition. David Chappell.

who has specialist knowledge and experience in the field. There are many independent consultants practising in these areas.

Having said that, all constructional professionals should have a very basic knowledge of what is involved. The topic is too large to be dealt with here. In any event, there are many other sources of information. All you will find here is a simple description and a few comments which may be useful.

When to use What?

Most building contracts contain references to adjudication, arbitration, and litigation, so can either of the parties to the contract deal with a dispute by any of the three processes? Not quite. Either party can start adjudication proceedings (the correct phrase is 'refer the dispute to adjudication') at any time even if arbitration or litigation is already in progress. It is relatively easy to do. Adjudication is intended to be a quick process. The decision is binding, but only until the dispute is dealt with by one of the other two systems. If the dispute is never referred to one of the other systems, the adjudication decision is effectively permanently binding.

The parties must choose which of either arbitration or litigation they wish to have as their main dispute resolution process before signing the contract. They can refer a dispute straight to their chosen process without going through adjudication if they wish. Therefore, a party with a dispute may refer it for a decision by adjudication and, if either party is dissatisfied it may then refer the same dispute to either arbitration or legal proceedings (whichever is the chosen process in the contract). Alternatively, the party with a dispute may ignore adjudication altogether and immediately start either arbitration or litigation proceedings (whichever is in the contract).

Adjudication

A simple explanation of the adjudication process is contained in 107: Adjudication. Adjudication was required to be included in all construction contracts by statute in 1996 (in 1997 in Northern Ireland). Excluded are contracts relating to work on dwellings occupied or intended to be occupied by one of the parties to the contract. But there is nothing to stop dwellings owners using adjudication if it is included in the building contract. Originally, and before it became too complicated, the idea was to allow either of the parties to the contract to use the adjudication procedure without assistance if they wished. The statute discouraged the parties from engaging expensive legal assistance by providing that both parties had to stand their own costs even if they were successful in the adjudication. That is in contrast to arbitration and litigation, where the unsuccessful party usually pays most of the legal costs of the successful party. It must always be borne in mind that adjudication is only binding until one of the parties decides to take the dispute to either arbitration or litigation. Anecdotal evidence suggests that disputes dealt with in adjudication are not usually referred again to arbitration or litigation, probably because both sides doubt they would get a different result by using a more expensive and lengthy process. Adjudication is attractive because it is intended to be short (no more than 35 days from the notice of intention to refer to the adjudicator's decision) and relatively cheap.

Arbitration

Arbitration is probably still the most satisfactory procedure for the finally binding resolution of construction disputes and employers would be well advised to complete the contract particulars accordingly. Arbitration is commenced by one of the parties notifying the other that it wishes to refer a dispute to arbitration. It is usual to suggest three possible arbitrators, who are usually members of the construction industry who have specialised in arbitration. If none of these are acceptable, the contract will state the name of the organisation that will appoint the arbitrator. There is no particular time limit to arbitration and, unless otherwise stated, the powers of the arbitrator are very wide under the Arbitration Act 1996.

A common misconception is that the arbitration process is an informal get together to enable the parties and the arbitrator to have a chat about the dispute before the arbitrator draws all the views together in order to arrive at a consensus decision about who should be successful. The reality is that the majority of arbitrations are conducted quite formally, like private legal proceedings, which is what they are. Representation is essential from the outset.

Most arbitrations seem to be conducted like private versions of a civil trial before a judge with exchanges of claim documents (termed 'pleadings') culminating in a hearing where oral evidence is heard from expert and other witnesses and formal submissions are made. Often solicitors and counsel are employed by the parties. Occasionally, it may be useful for the arbitrator to conduct the process in a similar way to a full arbitration but to have a very short (perhaps just a day) oral hearing. If everything is contained in the written documents, it may be possible to dispense with an oral hearing altogether.

If arbitration is the chosen method of binding dispute resolution and a party tries to deal with a dispute by litigation, the other party can ask the court to grant a stay (postponement) of legal proceedings until the dispute is settled by arbitration. The court has no discretion about the matter. The result is not only that the party intent on legal proceedings will have to revert to arbitration, but it will have to pay the other party's legal costs incurred in opposing the legal proceedings. Some perceived advantages and disadvantages of arbitration are set out below.

Advantages of Arbitration

- *Speed.* A good arbitrator can dispose of most cases in months rather than years.
- *Privacy.* Only the parties and the arbitrator know the details of the dispute and the award.
- *The parties decide.* The parties can decide the timescales, the procedure, and the location of any hearing.
- *Expense.* It should be more expensive than litigation because usually the losing party has to pay for the arbitrator and the hire of a room, but in practice the speed and technical expertise of the arbitrator usually keeps costs down.
- *Technical expertise of the arbitrator.* The fact that the arbitrator understands construction should shorten the time schedule and possibly avoid the need for expert witnesses if the parties agree.
- *Appeal.* The award is normally final because the courts are loath to consider any appeal unless it is a matter of law of general importance.

Disadvantages of Arbitration

- In theory, it is more expensive because the parties (usually the losing party) pay the cost of the arbitrator and the hire of a room for the hearing.
- If the arbitrator is not very good, the process may be slow.
- If the dispute mainly concerns points of law and the arbitrator is not an expert on the law, expert witnesses in law may be required.
- It is only possible to join other parties into the dispute by agreement of all parties.
- Parties who are in dispute may find it difficult to agree about anything. Therefore, the arbitrator may be appointed by the appointing body and the procedure, the timing, and the location of the hearing room may be decided by the arbitrator, with the result that neither party is satisfied.

Litigation

It is assumed that most people are aware of the basics of litigation. Although in theory a party may choose to represent themselves throughout the process, there are so many technicalities involved, some of which may be the difference between success and failure, that in practice it is essential to be represented by solicitors and, if appropriate, by counsel. The perceived advantages and disadvantages of litigation are set out below.

Advantages of Litigation

- The judge should be an expert on the law.
- Judges are required to manage their caseloads and encourage the parties to settle the dispute before it comes before the court.
- Cases can reach trial quickly.
- The claimant can join several defendants into the proceedings to allow interlocking matters to be decided.
- Costs of judge and courtroom are minimal.
- A dissatisfied party can appeal to a higher court.

Disadvantages of Litigation

- Even specialist judges know relatively little about the details of construction work.
- Parties cannot choose the judge, who may not be experienced in construction cases.
- Costs will be added because expert witnesses or a court-appointed expert witness may be needed to assist the judge.
- Lengthy timescale and complex processes may result in high costs.
- The possibility of appeals may result in an unacceptable level of costs.

One of the perceived advantages of litigation over arbitration is that claimants can take action against several defendants at the same time and any defendant can seek to join into the proceedings another party who may have liability. This facility is not readily available in arbitration, which usually takes place only between the parties to the contract unless all parties agree something else.

Therefore, if there are two or more sets of proceedings about the same topic, but under different contracts and arbitration agreements, anyone who is to appoint an arbitrator should consider whether the same arbitrator should be appointed for both sets of proceedings. This situation often occurs when there is an arbitration under the main contract and also between the contractor and a sub-contractor about the same issue.

Negotiation, Conciliation, and Mediation

It is always open to parties in dispute to settle the dispute without resorting to formal procedures. Compared to arbitration or litigation, the cost of negotiation, conciliation, or mediation is minimal.

Negotiation is the cheapest because it is just the cost of the parties' time. I suspect that most small disputes and many larger ones are settled by negotiation.

Conciliation depends upon a respected third party being called upon to consider the position of both parties and to give a view as to how the dispute should be concluded. The conciliator's view is not binding on the parties, but it does serve as an indication of the way in which an arbitrator or court might see the matter. A party that has been blinded by its own heavily biased view may be persuaded that its success in court is more problematic than it thought.

In practice, mediation seems to be effective if the mediator is competent and if the parties really do want to compromise. Mediation can take whatever form the parties agree. The principle of mediation is usually that the mediator meets with the parties individually and frankly discusses their cases, pointing out any drawbacks but not revealing the drawbacks of one party to the other. When the mediator believes that the parties have reached a realistic understanding of their respective cases, the parties meet together under the guidance of the mediator. If an agreement can be reached, it is immediately put on paper and signed by the parties. Mediation can proceed in any way that suits the parties and the mediator.

107

Adjudication

Is Adjudication the Same as Arbitration?

No, adjudication is not the same as arbitration. Arbitration is rather like a claim in front of a court except that everything is done in private. It can take many months to move from starting an arbitration to the giving of an award (the arbitrator's decision) by the arbitrator. Arbitration is normally used when complex or high-value disputes are involved. The arbitrator has the power to award costs. In contrast, adjudication is intended to be a very speedy process. It is rather rough justice. It should only be used for relatively low-value or simple disputes. Unfortunately, that is not how adjudication is used and I once had to decide a dispute in adjudication where one party was claiming almost £2 million from the other in a very complicated contract. An adjudicator can refuse to take on the dispute, but most adjudicators simply do their best with them and ask for longer time.

Some General Things

I receive many questions from architects regarding adjudication. It seems to me that what most people in the construction industry want is a simple explanation. Architects, in particular, need to be able to explain adjudication to their clients.

Adjudication is now very common and it will be useful to set out in simple terms some basics which every architect should know. Initially, the idea was that any party to a construction contract could refer a dispute to adjudication. However, because the courts have made a great many decisions concerning adjudication, the handling of adjudications has become largely the province of solicitors and others who specialise in that kind of service. As an adjudicator, I sometimes still do get referrals from architects and contractors who do not use legal services but opt to do it themselves.

Strictly, there are two kinds of adjudication: statutory and contractual. Statutory adjudication is imposed by Parliament, like it or not, on every construction contract (a statute is an Act of Parliament). A 'construction contract' has a particular meaning in statute law. It includes architectural services but excludes a contract concerning a dwelling which one of the parties intends to occupy as a residence. If a construction contract does not have proper provision for adjudication, the way in which the adjudication must be conducted is set out in another government document (called the 'Scheme').

Professional Practice for Architects and Project Managers, First Edition. David Chappell.

Contractual adjudication is when the adjudication process is stated in the contract as being one of the dispute resolution procedures. It is important to realise that if there is provision for adjudication in a contract involving a private residence, it still applies to the employer even though, if it was not in the contract, the statute would not require it. In building contracts concerning work to a dwelling owned and occupied, or to be occupied, by the employer, any provision for adjudication can be deleted if that is what the employer wishes. In most cases, adjudication is included in the building contract but, with the exception of a dwelling, would be required by the statute in any event.

Costs

Unless the parties agree otherwise, the adjudicator generally has no power to order one party to pay the costs of the other. The adjudicator does have power to decide who pays the adjudicator's fees and expenses, and will normally order the losing party to pay or sometimes orders each to pay 50% of the fee. Sometimes, it is not very clear who has won and sometimes one of the parties has made so much unnecessary extra work for the adjudicator that although winning, the adjudicator makes that party pay a part of the adjudicator's fees and expenses. Therefore, if parties are assisted by consultants or solicitors in presenting their cases to adjudication, it can be an expensive business for the loser. The idea of parties paying their own costs is that where the dispute is of relatively modest value, it dissuades a party from hiring a QC and a team of expensive lawyers because the costs are not recoverable.

Some parties opt for the DIY approach. The one thing that can be said about that is that it saves paying the costs for assistance which ordinarily cannot be reclaimed. The downside is that if the other side is assisted by a company which is well-versed in adjudication, the unassisted party may be at a disadvantage. It is not the adjudicator's job to make out a case for those who cannot do it for themselves. That said, I have received some poor submissions by solicitors, but at least they know the procedure and tend to do all the right things at the right time.

Deciding to Refer a Dispute to Adjudication

The correct term for asking an adjudicator to decide a dispute is to 'refer' the dispute to adjudication. Before an adjudicator can be asked to decide a dispute, there must be a contract between the two parties. The contract may be in writing or oral. If oral, there must be some evidence to show what the terms of the contract are. The adjudication clause must be in writing. If not, the adjudication provisions in the Scheme apply.

The next thing is that there must be a dispute, otherwise there is nothing to refer. In order for there to be a dispute, in simple terms, it must be clear that both parties disagree about something. For example, if the contractor submits a claim and the employer or architect rejects it, there is an obvious dispute. If the claim is not rejected, but the employer or architect do not respond for several weeks even when the contractor reminds them, that is a dispute. However, if the contractor was to submit a claim and after waiting, say, two weeks, referred the claim to adjudication, the employer might quite reasonably say that there was no dispute because the employer or the architect had not had enough time to consider it.

The Process

Some contracts state that the procedure is to be in accordance with the Scheme. Other contracts may specify other procedures. What follows assumes that the Scheme applies, although all the procedures follow similar basic rules.

Unless both parties agree otherwise, it is only possible to refer one dispute at a time to adjudication. Therefore, if a contractor believes that an interim certificate has been undervalued and also that not enough extension of time has been given, each dispute requires a separate adjudication. The procedure is started by one party giving to the other a Notice of Adjudication. The Notice must state details of the contract, the names and addresses of the two parties, the dispute, where the dispute arose, and the redress required. It is essential that the parties to the adjudication are the same as the parties to the contract. For example, if one of the parties to the contract is John Smith Limited, the Notice must refer to and be addressed to John Smith Limited, not simply to John Smith or John D Smith Limited or John Smith & Sons Limited. It is surprising how often this kind of mistake occurs – even by consultants holding themselves out as being capable of dealing with adjudications. I was once asked to decide a dispute and it transpired that the limited company named as the Referring Party had been dissolved some years earlier. Not all of the examples shown may be fatal to the adjudication starting, but it is not worth the risk.

The adjudicator only has the power to decide the dispute which has been notified, therefore it is extremely important to describe the dispute correctly. For example, if the contractor says the dispute is that it disagrees with the valuation in the interim certificate, the adjudicator may decide that the contractor is correct but be unable to order the money to be paid because the contractor has not asked for it in the Notice.

On the other hand, if the contractor says that it wants the adjudicator to order payment of £30 000 and the adjudicator decides that the amount to be paid is only £28 000, the adjudicator cannot order the £28 000 but only say that the £30 000 is not due. The way to surmount this regular difficulty is for the contractor to ask for £30 000 'or such sum as the adjudicator decides'. That gives the adjudicator the power to decide something different. Although the adjudicator can, usually, only decide one dispute, other things can be decided if it is necessary in order to decide the dispute. For example, if the contractor says that the employer has wrongly deducted too much liquidated damages, the adjudicator can, indeed must, decide whether any or more extension of time should be allowed because that has a fundamental bearing on the answer to the principal question. By this time you may be thinking that adjudication is not that simple – and you would be correct. That is why each party should get expert help.

Timing

The party serving the Notice of Adjudication (the Referring Party) must serve it on the other party (the Responding Party) and the claim itself (the Referral) must be given to the adjudicator with a copy to the other party within seven days of the date of the Notice of Adjudication. This is quite a tricky seven days because the Referring Party must first serve the Notice on the other party and then apply to the Nominating Body in the contract to nominate an adjudicator. Obviously, if the contract actually specifies an adjudicator by name (not usually a good idea), an enquiry must first be made to see if he or she is willing to act. The usual situation is that the contract lists a number of different Nominating Bodies from which a choice can be made. The Scheme has a complex nomination procedure which requires careful reading.

If the adjudicator does not receive the Referral within the seven days, the Referring Party must start the process all over again.

The adjudicator must reach a decision within 28 days of the date of the Referral. This has been interpreted in some instances as the date the adjudicator receives the Referral. Nowadays, when the Referral is often sent by email, its date and the date of receipt is usually the same day. The adjudicator may ask the Referring Party for an extension of up to 14 days for the decision and, if both parties agree, the date can be extended beyond the 14 days. Having reached a decision, the adjudicator must make sure that it reaches the parties as soon as reasonably practicable. In these days of electronic communication, there is seldom a good reason why the Decision cannot be sent to the parties within a very short time of it being made.

During the process, the adjudicator will usually allow the other party (the Responding Party) about seven days to respond to the Referral. If the matter is fairly complicated, the adjudicator will probably be persuaded to allow more time provided that the Referring Party agrees to extend the time for the Decision by a similar amount. Usually there is no difficulty about this because neither side wants the adjudicator to think of them as being unreasonable. On receipt of the Response, the adjudicator will usually allow a few days for the Referring Party to reply to anything in the Response which is new (the Reply). That is often the end of the exchanges, but the Responding Party may ask to submit a further reply (the Rejoinder) if the Referring Party has introduced new evidence. The Referring Party has been known to insist on submitting what is known as a Surrejoinder after that. At some point, the adjudicator will call a halt to the submissions. Just to get this clear, the order of submissions is:

- The Referral by the Referring Party.
- The Response by the Responding Party.
- The Reply by the Referring Party.
- The Rejoinder by the Responding Party.
- The Surrejoinder by the Referring Party.

Sometimes less but often more. It is a brave or foolish adjudicator who would refuse to consider a later submission unless the time available positively prevents it. Although the adjudicator must ensure that each party has the opportunity to submit its case, there is a need to move things along quickly. During the process, the adjudicator may ask specific questions of the parties and state how long they have to answer. Usually the period is very short, often just hours.

Meeting

The adjudicator must have an eye on costs and avoid incurring unnecessary expense, therefore in most cases the Decision is reached without a meeting. The main reasons for a meeting are if it is essential that the adjudicator visits the site of the Works or if there are witness statements and the adjudicator cannot decide on the truthfulness of the statements without seeing the witnesses or if there are a great many questions or complexities and the adjudicator believes that the cheapest solution is to have a meeting to go through the dispute and the evidence.

The Referral

The Referral is the claim being sent by the Referring Party. I have received many Referrals when acting as adjudicator and I have both prepared Referrals and seen others when acting for one of the parties in an adjudication. The biggest problem is that many parties preparing Referrals forget that all the adjudicator knows about the dispute is what the parties say. Many Referrals in particular fail to put the adjudicator fully in the picture. By that, I do not suggest that adjudicators should be submerged in paper, but simply that all the relevant information must be stated clearly.

From time to time, I receive Referrals and Responses which allege entirely opposite views without either producing a shred of relevant evidence. It is not clear what they expect the adjudicator to do. The adjudicator's task is to establish the facts so far as possible, then to apply the law to the facts in order to reach the Decision. It is little assistance to the adjudicator if the parties make statements which they cannot back up by evidence. They are just bare statements, neither better than the other. Wherever possible, the statements must be supported by evidence of some kind.

Most parties gather their evidence into a section following the Referral or the Response and entitled 'Appendices' or 'Exhibits'. The important thing is to put a page number on every single page of the evidence submitted. Then, when referring to the evidence, it should be by the page number. This enables the adjudicator to go straight to the relevant page and saves much time and frustration. Many is the time that I have been confronted by appendices, not in chronological order, not paginated and reference in the Referral simply to the date of an email so that I have to look through virtually the whole of the appendices for each reference. In despair, I once had to reorder the appendices in chronological order just to give myself the chance to find the relevant evidence before I forgot what I was looking for.

It is standard practice in court pleadings and in arbitration to number each paragraph. That makes it easier to respond and easier to refer to specific paragraphs. That practice should be adopted in adjudication.

If each party puts itself in the position of the adjudicator and says, 'What would I want to read and see in order to make my Decision'?, the situation could be made much clearer and reduce the adjudicator's fees.

The Response

Most of what I said about the Referral applies also to the Response. There is this extra consideration. When the adjudicator is reading the Referral, that is all the adjudicator has to concentrate upon. However, when reading the Response, the adjudicator is reading what the Responding Party has to say about the Referral and also reading what the Referring Party said in the Referral and the accompanying evidence and comparing them.

It is always entirely a matter for each party to present its evidence in any way it chooses. All I can do is to look at it from the adjudicator's point of view. Many Responding Parties say at the beginning of the Response that they are not going to provide a paragraph by paragraph response to everything in the Referral but, instead, they propose to put forward their own view. That is all well and good, but if the Responding Party believes that it can avoid answering a point put by the Referring Party that way, that is a bad policy. Indeed, that style of Response tends to provoke a suspicion that points are being avoided.

Most adjudicators look at the Response, trying to find the answers to what the Referring Party is saying. If the answers are not referenced to the paragraphs in the Referral, it makes it more difficult to find them. But the adjudicator will still look carefully through the Referral and through the Response to see if each relevant point has been addressed. Where there is a Reply, a Rejoinder, and a Surrejoinder together with answers to the adjudicator's questions, each stage of the adjudication Decision will necessitate a careful scrutiny of the relevant part of each document.

Final Thoughts

It is often said that the Referring Party has the advantage because it has longer time to prepare and it can choose the time for submission of the Referral. Both points are certainly true, but that is the way that adjudication is structured. Every adjudicator knows the score and understands that the Response is being produced under pressure of time whereas the Referring Party usually can prepare the Referral at leisure. So far as timing of the Referral is concerned, adjudicators are alive to the problems inherent in submissions on Christmas Eve and usually allow a generous period for the Response in such cases.

The adjudicator will sometimes know of a legal case which seems to provide the answer to the dispute. Where that happens, the adjudicator must notify both parties of the case and point to what appears to be relevant while asking each party to submit its views on the case within a special time period. This is the time when, if one of the parties is not represented by an expert in law, an expert view should be sought immediately for submission to the adjudicator.

Although every adjudicator will make certain allowances for an unassisted party, an adjudicator will not give legal advice to either party.

The final, final thought is that the adjudicator is choosing between two views. The party producing the simplest, clearest, and most persuasive view is apt to win.

Index

Professional Practice for Architects and Project Managers, First Edition. David Chappell.

d